Other Books and Series by Jeff Bowen

Applications for Enrollment of Chickasaw Newborn Act of 1905
Volumes I thru VII

Cherokee Intermarried White 1906 Volume I thru X

Applications for Enrollment of Creek Newborn Act of 1905
Volumes I thru XIV

Applications for Enrollment of Choctaw Newborn Act of 1905
Volume I, II, III, IV, V, VI, VII, VIII, IX, X, XI, XII, XIII, XIV, XV, XVI, XVII, XVIII,

Visit our website at **www.nativestudy.com** to learn more about these and other books and series by Jeff Bowen

APPLICATIONS FOR ENROLLMENT OF CHOCTAW NEWBORN ACT OF 1905

VOLUME XIX

TRANSCRIBED BY
JEFF BOWEN

NATIVE STUDY
Gallipolis, Ohio
USA

Other Books and Series by Jeff Bowen

1901-1907 Native American Census Seneca, Eastern Shawnee, Miami, Modoc, Ottawa, Peoria, Quapaw, and Wyandotte Indians (Under Seneca School, Indian Territory)

1932 Census of The Standing Rock Sioux Reservation with Births And Deaths 1924-1932

Census of The Blackfeet, Montana, 1897- 1901 Expanded Edition

Eastern Cherokee by Blood, 1906-1910, Volumes I thru XIII

Choctaw of Mississippi Indian Census 1929-1932 with Births and Deaths 1924-1931 Volume I
Choctaw of Mississippi Indian Census 1933, 1934 & 1937, Supplemental Rolls to 1934 & 1935 with Births and Deaths 1932-1938, and Marriages 1936-1938 Volume II

Eastern Cherokee Census Cherokee, North Carolina 1930-1939 Census 1930-1931 with Births And Deaths 1924-1931 Taken By Agent L. W. Page Volume I
Eastern Cherokee Census Cherokee, North Carolina 1930-1939 Census 1932-1933 with Births And Deaths 1930-1932 Taken By Agent R. L. Spalsbury Volume II
Eastern Cherokee Census Cherokee, North Carolina 1930-1939 Census 1934-1937 with Births and Deaths 1925-1938 and Marriages 1936 & 1938 Taken by Agents R. L. Spalsbury And Harold W. Foght Volume III

Seminole of Florida Indian Census, 1930-1940 with Birth and Death Records, 1930-1938

Texas Cherokees 1820-1839 A Document For Litigation 1921

Choctaw By Blood Enrollment Cards 1898-1914 Volumes I thru XVII

Starr Roll 1894 (Cherokee Payment Rolls) Districts: Canadian, Cooweescoowee, and Delaware Volume One
Starr Roll 1894 (Cherokee Payment Rolls) Districts: Flint, Going Snake, and Illinois Volume Two
Starr Roll 1894 (Cherokee Payment Rolls) Districts: Saline, Sequoyah, and Tahlequah; Including Orphan Roll Volume Three

Cherokee Intruder Cases Dockets of Hearings 1901-1909 Volumes I & II

Indian Wills, 1911-1921 Records of the Bureau of Indian Affairs Books One thru Seven;
Native American Wills & Probate Records 1911-1921

Other Books and Series by Jeff Bowen

Turtle Mountain Reservation Chippewa Indians 1932 Census with Births & Deaths, 1924-1932

Chickasaw By Blood Enrollment Cards 1898-1914 Volume I thru V

Cherokee Descendants East An Index to the Guion Miller Applications Volume I
Cherokee Descendants West An Index to the Guion Miller Applications Volume II (A-M)
Cherokee Descendants West An Index to the Guion Miller Applications Volume III (N-Z)

Applications for Enrollment of Seminole Newborn Freedmen, Act of 1905

Eastern Cherokee Census, Cherokee, North Carolina, 1915-1922, Taken by Agent James E. Henderson
    Volume I (1915-1916)
    Volume II (1917-1918)
    Volume III (1919-1920)
    Volume IV (1921-1922)

Complete Delaware Roll of 1898

Eastern Cherokee Census, Cherokee, North Carolina, 1923-1929, Taken by Agent James E. Henderson
    Volume I (1923-1924)
    Volume II (1925-1926)
    Volume III (1927-1929)

Applications for Enrollment of Seminole Newborn Act of 1905 Volumes I & II

North Carolina Eastern Cherokee Indian Census 1898-1899, 1904, 1906, 1909-1912, 1914 Revised and Expanded Edition

1932 Hopi and Navajo Native American Census with Birth & Death Rolls (1925-1931) Volume 1 - Hopi
1932 Hopi and Navajo Native American Census with Birth & Death Rolls (1930-1932) Volume 2 - Navajo

Western Navajo Reservation Navajo, Hopi and Paiute 1933 Census with Birth & Death Rolls 1925-1933

Cherokee Citizenship Commission Dockets 1880-1884 and 1887-1889 Volumes I thru V

Copyright © 2013
by Jeff Bowen

ALL RIGHTS RESERVED
No part of this publication may be reproduced
or used in any form or manner whatsoever
without previous written permission from the
copyright holder or publisher.

Originally published:
Baltimore, Maryland
2013

Reprinted by:

Native Study LLC
Gallipolis, OH
www.nativestudy.com
2020

Library of Congress Control Number: 2020918113

ISBN: 978-1-64968-113-3

Made in the United States of America.

This series is dedicated to the descendants of the Choctaw newborn listed in these applications.

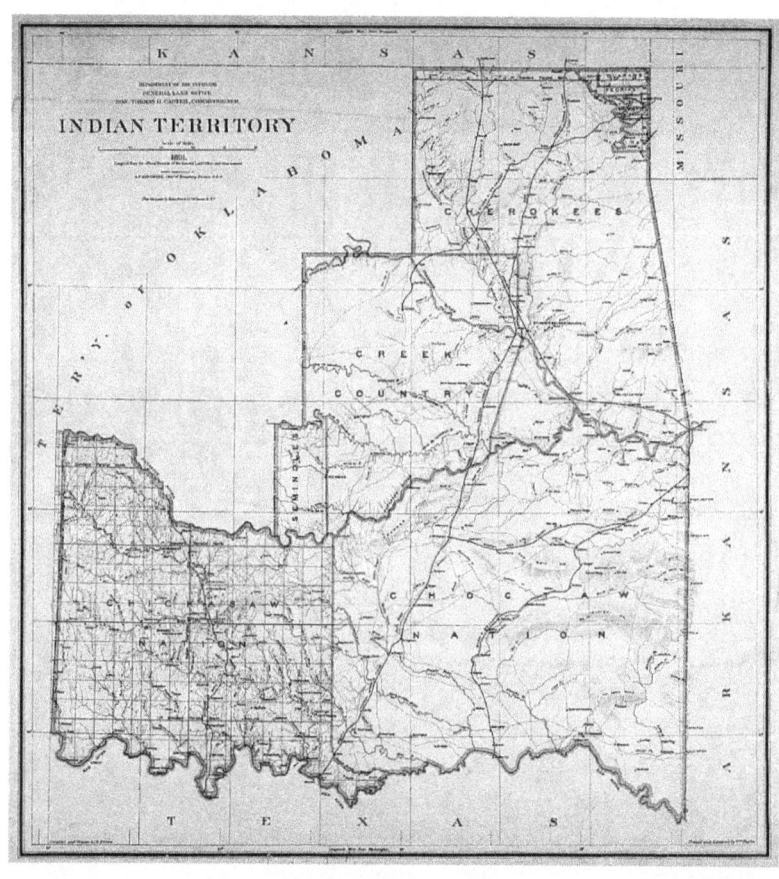

This map of Indian Territory shows how large the Choctaw and Chickasaw Nations' land base was that contained huge deposits of asphalt and coal. Just the size and territory involved was flooded with the "Grafters".

DEPARTMENT OF THE INTERIOR.
Commissioner to the Five Civilized Tribes.

NOTICE.

Opening of Land Office at Wewoka,
IN THE SEMINOLE NATION, INDIAN TERRITORY.

Notice is hereby given that on Monday, September 4, 1905, the Commissioner to the Five Civilized Tribes will establish a land office at Wewoka, in the Seminole Nation, Indian Territory, for the purpose of allowing citizens and freedmen of the Seminole Nation to select allotments of land for their minor children enrolled under the Act of Congress approved March 3, 1905 (33 Stat. L 1060), and for the further purpose of allowing citizens and freedmen of the Seminole Nation, whose allotments are incomplete, to select additional land in order to bring the value of their allotments up to the standard of $309.09, as nearly as may be practicable.

Each child whose enrollment in accordance with the Act of March 3, 1905, has been duly approved by the Secretary of the Interior, is entitled to receive an alllotment of forty acres without regard to the character or value of the land selected.

Selection of allotments for minor children must be made by their citizen or freedmen parents or by a duly appointed guardian, or curator, or by a duly appointed administrator.

                        TAMS BIXBY,
                                 Commissioner.
Muskogee, Indian Territory,
    July 29, 1905.

This particular notice for the Seminole and Creek Newborn makes mention of the Act of 1905. It is likely that a similar notice was posted in the Choctaw and Chickasaw Nations for the registration of newborn children.

DEPARTMENT OF THE INTERIOR,
Commission to the Five Civilized Tribes.

Rules and Regulations Governing the Selection of Allotments and the Designation of Homesteads in the Choctaw and Chickasaw Nations.

1. Selections of allotments and designations of homesteads for adult citizens and selections of allotments for adult freedmen must be made in person except as herein otherwise provided.

2. Applications to have land set apart and homesteads designated for duly identified Mississippi Choctaws must be made personally before the Commission to the Five Civilized Tribes. Fathers may apply for their minor children and if the father be dead the mother may apply. Husbands may apply for wives. Applications for orphans, insane persons and persons of unsound mind may be made by duly appointed guardian or curator, and for aged and infirm persons and prisoners by agents duly authorized thereunto by power of attorney, in the discretion of said Commission.

3. At the time of the selection of allotment each citizen and duly identified Mississippi Choctaw shall designate as a homestead out of said selection land equal in value to one hundred and sixty acres of the average allottable land of the Choctaw and Chickasaw Nations, as nearly as may be.

4. Each Choctaw and Chickasaw freedman, at the time of selection shall designate as his or her allotment of the lands of the Choctaw and Chickasaw Nations, land equal in value to forty acres of the average allottable land of the Choctaw and Chickasaw Nations.

5. Citizens, freedmen and identified Mississippi Choctaws who are married, whether they have attained their majority or not, will be regarded as of age for the purpose of making selections.

6. Selections may be made by citizen and freedman parents for unmarried male children under twenty-one years of age and for unmarried female children under eighteen years of age, and a male citizen or freedman may make selection for his wife, if she is entitled to make selection, unless she shall, at the time or previously thereto, protest in writing.

7. Where the father of an unmarried minor citizen, freedman or identified Mississippi Choctaw is a non-citizen, the citizen, freedman or identified Mississippi Choctaw mother of such children must make selection in person in behalf of said children.

8. Selections of allotments and designations of homesteads for minor citizens and selections of allotments for minor freedmen may be made by the citizen father or mother or freedman father or mother, as the case may be, or by a guardian, curator, or an administrator having charge of their estate, in the order named.

9. Selections of allotments and designations of homesteads for citizen, and selections of allotment for freedmen, prisoners, convicts, aged and infirm persons and soldiers and sailors of the United States on duty outside of Indian Territory, may be made by duly appointed agents under power of attorney, and for incompetents by guardians, curators, or other suitable person akin to them.

10. Selections may be made and homesteads designated by duly identified Mississippi Choctaws, who have, within one year after the date of their identification as such, made satisfactory proof of bona fide settlement within the Choctaw-Chickasaw country, at any time within six months after the date of their said identification.

11. Persons authorized to make selections by power of attorney, as provided in rules 2 and 9 hereof, must be the husband or wife, or a relative not further removed than a cousin of the first degree of the person for whom such selection is made.

12. It shall be the duty of the Commission to the Five Civilized Tribes to see that selections of allotments and designations of homesteads for the classes of persons mentioned in rules 2, 6, 7, 8 and 9 hereof, are made for the best interests of such persons.

13. Selections of allotments for citizens, freedmen and identified Mississippi Choctaws who have died subsequent to September 25, 1902, and before making a selection of allotment, shall be made by a duly appointed administrator or executor. If, however, such administrator or executor be not duly and expeditiously appointed, or fails to act promptly when appointed, or for any other cause such selections be not so made within a reasonable and practicable time, the Commission to the Five Civilized Tribes shall designate the lands thus to be allotted.

14. In determining the value of a selection the appraised value of the land selected shall be increased by the appraised value of such pine timber on such land as has heretofore been estimated by the Commission to the Five Civilized Tribes.

15. Selections of allotments may be made only by citizens and freedmen whose enrollment has been approved by the Secretary of the Interior, and by persons duly identified by the Commission to the Five Civilized Tribes as Mississippi Choctaws, and by none others.

16. When a selection of land has been made by a citizen, freedman or identified Mississippi Choctaw, and the land so selected is claimed by a person whose rights as a citizen or freedman have not been finally determined, contest for the land so selected may be instituted by the person claiming the land, formal application for the land being first made as is required by the Rules of Practice in Choctaw and Chickasaw allotment contest cases.

THE COMMISSION TO THE FIVE CIVILIZED TRIBES.
TAMS BIXBY, Chairman.

Muskogee, Indian Territory, March 24, 1903.

The above statement published prior to 1905, was established for what was supposed to be a set of guidelines when it came to allotments. But with supplemental agreements and Congressional legislation, time frames as well as rules and regulations often changed and were not the same for every tribe.

INTRODUCTION

The *Applications for Enrollment of Choctaw Newborn Act of 1905*, National Archive film M-1301, Rolls 50-57, are found under the heading of Applications for Enrollment of the Commission to the Five Civilized Tribes. For this series, I have transcribed the application forms filled out by individuals applying for enrollment in the Five Civilized Tribes under the Dawes Commission. These applications contain considerably more information than stated on the census cards found in series M-1186. M-1301 possesses its own numerical sequence, separate from M-1186. To find each party's roll number you would have to reference M-1186.

The Choctaw as well as the Chickasaw allotments were likely some of the most sought after properties in Indian Territory. There was supposed to be a 25-year restriction on the sale or lease of any Indian lands so as to insure that the owners wouldn't be swindled, but that isn't what happened. This fact is borne out in the Dawes Commission General Allotment Act, of February 8, 1887, Section 5, which "Provides that after an Indian person is allotted land, the United States will hold the land 'in trust [1] for the sole use and benefit of the Indian' (or his heirs if the Indian landowner dies) for a period of 25 years. (Land held in trust by the United States government cannot be sold or in anyway alienated by the Indian landowner, since the United States government considers the underlying ownership of the land held by itself and not the tribe. After the period of trust ends, the Indian landowner is free to sell the land and is free from any encumbrance from the United States.)"[1] Instead, Native Americans were exploited by the devious. The Choctaw and Chickasaw Districts both had huge asphalt and coal deposits, so there was pressure from outsiders to acquire them from the minute they were discovered. After repeated attacks throughout the years and many legislative changes, President "Roosevelt finally signed the Five Tribes Bill at noon on April 26, 1906, the forces seeking to end all restrictions were disappointed. Section 19 removed restrictions from the sale of all inherited land but directed that no full-bloods could sell their land for twenty-five years. The Act also prohibited leases for more than one year without the approval of the Secretary of the Interior."[2]

Angie Debo described the opportunists that wanted these Native American allotments as, "Grafters". The parents of the newborns enumerated within this series would no sooner receive the approval for their child's allotment than there would be someone there with cash in hand holding a new deed or lease for the parents to sign their child's birthright away. Angie Debo said it best, "As the business incapacity of the allottees became apparent, a horde of despoilers fastened themselves upon their property." According to Debo, "The term 'grafter' was applied as a matter of course to dealers in Indian land, and was frankly accepted by them. The speculative fever also affected Government employees so that it was almost impossible to prevent them from making personal investments."[3]

---

[1] General Allotment Act, Act of Feb. 8, 1887 (24 Stat. 388, ch. 119, 25 USCA 331)
[2] The Dawes Commission and the Allotment of the Five Civilized Tribes, 1893-1914 by Kent Carter, pg. 173
[3] And Still the Waters Run, Angie Debo, p. 92.

INTRODUCTION

According to the Department of Interior in 1905, "It is estimated that there will be added to the final rolls of the citizens and freedmen of the Choctaw and Chickasaw nations the names of 2,000 persons, including 1,500 new-born children to be enrolled under the provisions of the act of Congress approved March 3, 1905."[4]

The quote below explains, in detail, the requirements for qualifying as a newborn Choctaw, "By the act of Congress approved March 3, 1905 (H.R. 17474), entitled 'An act making appropriations for the current and contingent expenses of the Indian Department and for fulfilling treaty stipulations with various Indian tribes for the fiscal year ending June 30, 1906, and for other purposes,' it was provided as follows:

'That the Commission to the Five Civilized Tribes is hereby authorized for sixty days after the date of the approval of this act to receive and consider applications for enrollment of infant children born prior to September twenty-fifth, nineteen hundred and two, and who were living on said date, to citizens by blood of the Choctaw and Chickasaw tribes of Indians whose enrollment has been approved by the Secretary of the Interior prior to the date of the approval of this act; and to enroll and make allotments to such children.'

'That the Commission to the Five Civilized Tribes is authorized for sixty days after the date of the approval of this act to receive and consider applications for enrollment of children born subsequent to September twenty-fifth, nineteen hundred and two, and prior to March fourth, nineteen hundred and five, and who were living on said latter date, to citizens by blood of the Choctaw and Chickasaw tribes of Indians whose enrollment has been approved by the Secretary of the Interior prior to the date of the approval of this act; and to enroll and make allotments to such children.'

"Notice is hereby given that the Commission to the Five Civilized Tribes will, up to and inclusive of midnight, May 2, 1905, receive applications for the enrollment of infant children born prior to September 25, 1902, and who were living on said date, to citizens by blood of the Choctaw and Chickasaw tribes of Indians whose enrollment has been approved by the Secretary of the Interior prior to March 3, 1905."[5]

Following is the scope of these transcriptions: Besides the applications themselves, researchers will find the identities of other individuals within these applications -- doctors, lawyers, mid-wives, and other relatives -- that may help with you genealogical research.

Jeff Bowen
Gallipolis, Ohio
NativeStudy.com

---

[4] Annual Reports of the Department of the Interior For the Fiscal Year Ended June 30, 1905, p. 609.
[5] Annual Reports of the Department of the Interior For the Fiscal Year Ended June 30, 1905, p. 593.

Applications for Enrollment of Choctaw Newborn
Act of 1905   Volume XIX

Choc New Born 1398
    Minnie Briggs
    (Born Feb. 26, 1904)

BIRTH AFFIDAVIT.

DEPARTMENT OF THE INTERIOR.
COMMISSION TO THE FIVE CIVILIZED TRIBES.

IN RE APPLICATION FOR ENROLLMENT, as a citizen of the Choctaw Nation, of Minnie Briggs, born on the 26th day of February, 1904

Name of Father: Thomas J Briggs   a citizen of the white citizen ~~Nation~~.
Name of Mother: Jennie Briggs   a citizen of the Choctaw Nation.

      Postoffice   Whitefield, I.T.

AFFIDAVIT OF MOTHER.

UNITED STATES OF AMERICA, Indian Territory, ⎫
   Central   DISTRICT. ⎭

    I, Jennie Briggs, on oath state that I am thirty years of age and a citizen by blood, of the Choctaw Nation; that I am the lawful wife of Thomas J Briggs, who is a ~~citizen, by~~ white citizen of the United States ~~Nation~~; that a female child was born to me on 26th day of February, 1904; that said child has been named Minnie Briggs, and was living March 4, 1905.

                                        Jennie Briggs

Witnesses To Mark:
   { Emry[sic] Farrell
    William Agee

    Subscribed and sworn to before me this 27th day of April, 1905

                                Wm C. Carr
                                      Notary Public.

Applications for Enrollment of Choctaw Newborn
Act of 1905   Volume XIX

AFFIDAVIT OF ATTENDING PHYSICIAN OR MID-WIFE.

UNITED STATES OF AMERICA, Indian Territory, }
    Western   DISTRICT.

    I, J. Culbertson, a Physician, on oath state that I attended on Mrs. Jennie Briggs, wife of Thomas J Briggs on the 26th day of February, 1904; that there was born to her on said date a female child; that said child was living March 4, 1905, and is said to have been named Minnie Briggs

                              J Culbertson M.D.

Witnesses To Mark:
  { O N Williams
    W.W. Milton

    Subscribed and sworn to before me this 27 day of April, 1905

                              John H. Oliver
                              Notary Public.

                                                7-2532.

                Muskogee, Indian Territory, May 4, 1905.

Thomas J. Briggs,
    Whitefield, Indian Territory.

Dear Sir:

    Receipt is hereby acknowledged of the affidavits of Jennie Briggs and J. Culbertson to the birth of Minnie Briggs, daughter of Thomas J. and Jennie Briggs, February 26, 1904, and the same have been filed with our records as an application for the enrollment of said child.

                          Respectfully,

                                          Chairman.

Applications for Enrollment of Choctaw Newborn
Act of 1905   Volume XIX

Choc New Born 1399
   William L. Swink
   (Born Nov. 8, 1902)

NEW-BORN AFFIDAVIT.

Number..............

Choctaw Enrolling Commission.

IN THE MATTER OF THE APPLICATION FOR ENROLLMENT, as a citizen of the Choctaw   Nation, of   William Lenard Swink

born on the   8th day of   November   190 2

Name of father   David R Swink   a citizen of   Choctaw
Nation final enrollment No   92
Name of mother   Lena B Swink   a citizen of   Choctaw
Nation final enrollment No   4992

                    Postoffice   Swink I.T.

AFFIDAVIT OF MOTHER.

UNITED STATES OF AMERICA, ⎫
    INDIAN TERRITORY,   ⎬
   Central   DISTRICT   ⎭

   I   Lena B Swink   on oath state that I am 33 years of age and a citizen by   Blood   of the   Choctaw   Nation, and as such have been placed upon the final roll of the   Choctaw   Nation, by the Honorable Secretary of the Interior my final enrollment number being   4992 ; that I am the lawful wife of   David R Swink   , who is a citizen of the   Choctaw   Nation, and as such has been placed upon the final roll of said Nation by the Honorable Secretary of the Interior, his final enrollment number being   92   and that a   Male   child was born to me on the 8th day of   November   190 2 ; that said child has been named   William Lenard Swink   , and is now living.

                              Lena B Swink

WITNESSETH:
  Must be two   ⎫ S.W. Byram
  Witnesses who   ⎬
  are Citizens.   ⎭ N.E. Swink

       Subscribed and sworn to before me this   2   day of   January   190 5

                         William Swink
                                Notary Public.
My commission expires   Dec 6th 1906

3

Applications for Enrollment of Choctaw Newborn
Act of 1905 Volume XIX

Affidavit of Attending Physician or Midwife

UNITED STATES OF AMERICA,
   INDIAN TERRITORY,
Central   DISTRICT

I, Mrs Lizzie Pettey a Mid Wife on oath state that I attended on Mrs. Lena B Swink wife of David R Swink on the 8th day of November, 190 2, that there was born to her on said date a male child, that said child is now living, and is said to have been named William Lenard Swink

                        Mrs Lizzie Pettey   Mi Dwife

Subscribed and sworn to before me this the 21 day of January 1905

                        William Swink
                                Notary Public.

WITNESSETH:
Must be two witnesses who are citizens and know the child. { S.W. Byram
N.E. Swink

We hereby certify that we are well acquainted with Mrs Lizzie Pettey a Mid Wife and know her to be reputable and of good standing in the community.

                  Must be two citizen witnesses. { S.W. Byram
N.E. Swink

BIRTH AFFIDAVIT.

DEPARTMENT OF THE INTERIOR.
COMMISSION TO THE FIVE CIVILIZED TRIBES.

IN RE APPLICATION FOR ENROLLMENT, as a citizen of the Choctaw Nation, of William L. Swink, born on the 8th day of November, 1902

Name of Father: David R Swink   a citizen of the Choctaw Nation.
Name of Mother: Lena B Swink   a citizen of the Choctaw Nation.

                    Postoffice   Swink I.T.

Applications for Enrollment of Choctaw Newborn
Act of 1905   Volume XIX

AFFIDAVIT OF MOTHER.

UNITED STATES OF AMERICA, Indian Territory, }
Central   DISTRICT.

I, Lena B Swink, on oath state that I am 33 years of age and a citizen by Blood, of the Choctaw Nation; that I am the lawful wife of David R Swink, who is a citizen, by Intermarriage of the Choctaw Nation; that a male child was born to me on 8th day of November, 1902; that said child has been named William L Swink, and was living March 4, 1905.

          Lena B Swink

Witnesses To Mark:
{

Subscribed and sworn to before me this 29 day of April, 1905

          William Swink
          Notary Public.

AFFIDAVIT OF ATTENDING PHYSICIAN OR MID-WIFE.

UNITED STATES OF AMERICA, Indian Territory, }
Central   DISTRICT.

I, Mrs Lizzie Pettey, a Mid wife, on oath state that I attended on Mrs. Lena B Swink, wife of David R Swink on the 8th day of November, 1902; that there was born to her on said date a male child; that said child was living March 4, 1905, and is said to have been named William L Swink

          Mrs Lizzie Pettey

Witnesses To Mark:
{

Subscribed and sworn to before me this 29 day of April, 1905

          William Swink
          Notary Public.

Applications for Enrollment of Choctaw Newborn
Act of 1905   Volume XIX

Choc New Born 1400
    Gency Elapashabbe
    (Born Jan. 2, 1905)

BIRTH AFFIDAVIT.

DEPARTMENT OF THE INTERIOR.
COMMISSION TO THE FIVE CIVILIZED TRIBES.

IN RE APPLICATION FOR ENROLLMENT, as a citizen of the Chocktaw[sic] Nation, of Gency Elapashabbe, born on the second day of January, 1905

Name of Father: Barnett Elapashabbe   a citizen of the Chocktaw Nation.
Name of Mother: Louisa Elapashabbe   a citizen of the Chocktaw Nation.

Postoffice   Corinne, Ind. Ter.

AFFIDAVIT OF MOTHER.

UNITED STATES OF AMERICA, Indian Territory,
    Central   **DISTRICT.**

    I, Louisa Elapashabbe, on oath state that I am 23 years of age and a citizen by Blood, of the Chocktaw Nation; that I am the lawful wife of Barnett Elapashabbe, who is a citizen, by Blood of the Chocktaw Nation; that a Female child was born to me on second day of January, 1902; that said child has been named Gency Elapashabbe, and was living March 4, 1905.

                                      Louisa Elapashabbe

Witnesses To Mark:
    Alfred Holman
        Columbus Tims

    Subscribed and sworn to before me this fourth day of April, 1905

My commission
expires Dec 12 1908
                                  Jno. E. Talbert
                                  Notary Public.

Applications for Enrollment of Choctaw Newborn
Act of 1905 Volume XIX

AFFIDAVIT OF ATTENDING PHYSICIAN OR MID-WIFE.

UNITED STATES OF AMERICA, Indian Territory,
Central DISTRICT.

I, Sillien Campbell , a Midwife , on oath state that I attended on Mrs. Louisa Elapashabbe , wife of Barnett Elapashabbe on the second day of January , 1905; that there was born to her on said date a Female child; that said child was living March 4, 1905, and is said to have been named Gency Elapashabbe

                                              her
                                    Sillien x Campbell
Witnesses To Mark: mark
   { Alfred Holman
     Columbus Tims

Subscribed and sworn to before me this fourth day of April , 1905

My commission
expires Dec 12 1908   Jno. E. Talbert
                              Notary Public.

BIRTH AFFIDAVIT.

DEPARTMENT OF THE INTERIOR.
COMMISSION TO THE FIVE CIVILIZED TRIBES.

IN RE APPLICATION FOR ENROLLMENT, as a citizen of the Chocktaw[sic] Nation, of Gency Elapashabbe , born on the 2d day of January , 1905

Name of Father: Barnett Elapashabbe   a citizen of the Chocktaw Nation.
Name of Mother: Louisa Pickens   a citizen of the Chocktaw Nation.

                        Postoffice   Corinne I.T.

AFFIDAVIT OF MOTHER.

UNITED STATES OF AMERICA, Indian Territory,
Central DISTRICT.

I, Louisa Pickens , on oath state that I am 23 years of age and a citizen by Blood , of the Chocktaw Nation; that I am the lawful wife of Barnett Elapashabbe , who is a citizen, by Blood of the Chocktaw Nation; that a Female child was born to me on second day of January , 1902; that said child has been named Gency Elapashabbe , and was living March 4, 1905.

                                    Louisa Pickens

Applications for Enrollment of Choctaw Newborn
Act of 1905   Volume XIX

Witnesses To Mark:
- James B Tims
- Columbus Tims

Subscribed and sworn to before me this 25 day of April , 1905

My Com Expires
Dec 12 1908

Jno. E. Talbert
Notary Public.

AFFIDAVIT OF ATTENDING PHYSICIAN OR MID-WIFE.

UNITED STATES OF AMERICA, Indian Territory,
Central DISTRICT.

I, Sillien Campbell , a Midwife , on oath state that I attended on Mrs. Louisa Pickens , wife of of Barnett Elapashabbe on the second day of January , 1905; that there was born to her on said date a Female child; that said child was living March 4, 1905, and is said to have been named Gency Elapashabbe

Sillien x Campbell
her mark

Witnesses To Mark:
- James B Tims
- Columbus Tims

Subscribed and sworn to before me this 25 day of April , 1905

My Com Expires
Dec 12 1908

Jno. E. Talbert
Notary Public.

BIRTH AFFIDAVIT.

DEPARTMENT OF THE INTERIOR,
COMMISSIONER TO THE FIVE CIVILIZED TRIBES.

ENROLLMENT OF MINORS.   ACT OF CONGRESS, APPROVED APRIL 26, 1906.

IN RE APPLICATION FOR ENROLLMENT, as a citizen of the Choctaw Nation, of Jincy Push , born on the 10 day of May , 1905

Name of Father: Burnett Push   a citizen of the Choctaw Nation.
Name of Mother: Louisa Campbell   a citizen of the Choctaw Nation.

Tribal enrollment of father ………………… Tribal enrollment of mother …………………

Postoffice   Corrine, I.T.

Applications for Enrollment of Choctaw Newborn
Act of 1905   Volume XIX

AFFIDAVIT OF ~~MOTHER~~ *Acquaintance*.

UNITED STATES OF AMERICA, Indian Territory, }
Central   District.   }

I, Sophie Bobb , on oath state that I am 39 years of age and a citizen by blood , of the Choctaw Nation; that I am ~~the lawful wife of~~ *personally acquainted with Louisa Campbell wife of Burnett Push* , who is a citizen, by blood of the Choctaw Nation; that a Female child was born to me on 10th day of May , 1905 , that said child has been named Jincy Push , and was living March 4, 1906.

                                                             her
                                            Sophie x Bobb

WITNESSES TO MARK: mark
{ T.J. Cephus
{ *(Name Illegible)*

Subscribed and sworn to before me this 24 day of *(Illegible)* , 1906.

                                     W. H. McKinney
                                            Notary Public.

AFFIDAVIT OF ~~ATTENDING PHYSICIAN OR MID-WIFE~~ *Acquaintance*.

UNITED STATES OF AMERICA, Indian Territory, }
Central   District.   }

I, Wilmon Nanomantube , ~~a~~ Acquaintance , on oath state that I ~~attended on~~ *am personally acquainted with Louisa Campbell* , wife of *wife of Burnett Push & that* on the 10 day of May , 1905 ; that there was born to her on said date a Female child; that said child was living March 4, 1906, and is said to have been named Jincy Push

                                       Wilmon Nanomantube

WITNESSES TO MARK:
{

Subscribed and sworn to before me this 24 day of *(Illegible)* , 1906.

                                     W. H. McKinney
                                           Notary Public.

Applications for Enrollment of Choctaw Newborn
Act of 1905   Volume XIX

DEPARTMENT OF THE INTERIOR,
COMMISSIONER TO THE FIVE CIVILIZED TRIBES.
Corrinne[sic], Indian Territory, January 29, 1907.

In the matter of the application for enrollment as a minor citizen of the Choctaw Nation (Act April 26, 1906) of Jincy Push, card No. 890; and as a New Born citizen of the Choctaw Nation (Act March 3, 1905) of Gency Elapashabbe, card No. 1400.

TESTIMONY TAKEN NEAR CORRINNE, I. T.

Barnett Elapashabbe being duly sworn testifies as follows:

Emerson D. Willis official interpreter.

EXAMINATION BY THE COMMISSIONER:
Q What is your name? A Barnett Elapashabbe.
Q What is your post office address? A Corrinne.
Q How old are you? A About twenty-two years old.
Q Have you a child named Gency Elapashabbe? A Yes sir.
Q When was Gency born? A January 2, 1905.
Q What is the name of the mother of the child? A On the roll as Louisa Pickens.
Q Is she now your wife? A Yes sir.
Q Was she ever known by the name of Louisa Campbell? A Yes sir, she used to be Campbell.
Q Have you already selected an allotment of land for this child, Gency Elapashabbe? A Yes sir.
Q You present here homestead and allotment certificate issued to Gency Elapashabbe, Choctaw New Born, roll No. 1224; is this the child to whom you refer? A Yes sir.
Q On June 24, 1906, Sophie Bobb and Wilmon Nanomantube made affidavits before W. H. McKinney, Notary Public, relative to the birth on May 10, 1905, of a child, Jincy Push, the child of Burnett Push and Louisa Campbell: Is this the same child as Gency Elapashabbe who has already been enrolled and for whom whom[sic] you have selected an allotment? A Yes sir, same child.
Q The date of birth of this child given as May 10, 1905, is wrong, is it? A Yes sir.
Q You are the same person named in these affidavits as Burnett Push? A Yes sir, same person.
Q Are you sometimes known by the name of Push? A Yes sir; before I was enrolled they called me Push but it is Elapashabbe on the roll.
Q And the Louisa Campbell named in the affidavits of Sophie Bobb and Wilmon Nanomantube is the same person as your wife, Louisa Elapashabbe, who was Louisa Pickens? A Yes sir, same person.

Frank L. Doble on oath states that the above and foregoing is a full, true and correct transcript of his stenographic notes taken in the above entitled cause near Corrinne[sic], Indian Territory, on January 29, 1907.

Frank L. Doble

Applications for Enrollment of Choctaw Newborn
Act of 1905   Volume XIX

Subscribed and sworn to before me this January 30, 1907.

(Name Illegible)
Notary Public.

$W^m O.B.$

COMMISSIONERS:
TAMS BIXBY,
THOMAS B. NEEDLES,
C.R. BRECKINBRIDGE.

DEPARTMENT OF THE INTERIOR,
COMMISSIONER TO THE FIVE CIVILIZED TRIBES.

REFER IN REPLY TO THE FOLLOWING:

WM. O. BEALL
Secretary

ADDRESS ONLY THE
COMMISSION TO THE FIVE CIVILIZED TRIBES.

Muskogee, Indian Territory, April 12, 1905.

Barnett Elapashabbe,
    Corinne, Indian Territory.

Dear Sir:

    Receipt is hereby acknowledged of the affidavits of Louisa Elapashabbe and Sillien Campbell to the birth of Gency Elapashabbe, daughter of Barnett and Louisa Elapashabbe, January 2nd, 1905.

    It appears from the affidavit of the mother that she is a citizen by blood of the Choctaw Nation. If this is correct, you are requested to state the name under which she was enrolled, the names of her parents, and if she has selected an allotment of the lands of the Choctaw and Chickasaw Nations, please give her roll number as the same appears upon her certificate of allotment.

Respectfully,

T.B. Needles

Commissioner in Charge.

Applications for Enrollment of Choctaw Newborn
Act of 1905   Volume XIX

Muskogee, Indian Territory, August 4, 1906.

J. T. Tims,
    Corrinne[sic], Indian Territory.

Dear Sir:-

    In the matter of the application for the enrollment of Jincy Push, child of Burnnett[sic] Push and Louisa Campbell, you are requested to advise this office where and under what name application was made for the enrollment of Burnnett Push and Louisa Campbell, the names of this parents, and if they have selected allotments of land in the Choctaw or Chickasaw Nation give their roll numbers as they appear upon their allotment certificates.

                      Respectfully,

                                  Commissioner.

                                  Refer in reply
                      to the following 7-NB-1400

                      Corinne, I. Terr.

                      Aug. 27, 1906

T. Bixby,

    Dear Sir:

    I will tell you about this matter of the application for the enrollment of Gency Elapushabbee[sic]. I have filed a land for this child and she got Townsite money.
    I have file all Choctaw land
Her name is Gency Elapushabbee and you put Jincy Push.

    Homestead certificate

    Certificate
    No. 15535.

    Roll number
    Choctaw NB 1224.

    Allotment certificate
    No. 19335
    Choctaw land.

Applications for Enrollment of Choctaw Newborn
Act of 1905   Volume XIX

Gency Elapushabbee
from Barnett Elapushabbee.

Homestead

NW of Sec 36 Town 4s Range 19 E. Acre 160

   Allotment certificate.

SW of Sec. 25, 35, 34, Town 4s Range 19E Acre 160-40
                                                360 acre.

                      Please answer soon.
                              From

                      Barnett Elapushabbee.

23-890
7-NB-1400

                    Muskogee, Indian Territory, September 5, 1906.

Barnett Esapushabbe[sic],
    Corinne, Indian Territory.

Dear Sir:

    Receipt is hereby acknowledged of your letter of August 27, 1906, giving information relative to the parents of Jincy Push to whose birth affidavits were received at this office July 25, 1906.

    You are advised that from the information contained in your letter it seems that Jincy Push is identical with Gency Elapashabbe. You are requested, however, to advise this office the number and names of the children of Barnett and Eliza Elapashabbe.

                    Respectfully,

                                      Acting Commissioner.

Applications for Enrollment of Choctaw Newborn
Act of 1905 Volume XIX

7NB1400
23-89o

Muskogee, Indian Territory, December 28, 1906.

J. B. Tims,
    Corinne, I.T.

Dear Sir:

    Affidavits have been received at this office to the birth of Jincy Push, child of Burnett Push and Louisa Campbell, May 10, 1905, an applicant for enrollment under the Act of Congress approved April 26, 1906.

    It appears from the records of this office that application was also made under the Act of Congress approved March 3, 1905, for the enrollment of Gency Elapashabbe, child of Barnett and Louisa Elapashabbe, born January 2, 1905.

    From the information in the possession of this office it is believed that Jincy Push, referred to above, is the same child as Gency Elapashabbe and I have to request that if possible you ascertaimin[sic] definitely whether this is the same child and the Burnett Push and Louisa Campbell, named as the parents of Jincy Push, are identical with Barnett and Louisa Elapashabbe who appear as the parents of Gency Elapashabbe.

        Respectfully,

                Acting Commissioner.

23-890

Muskogee, Indian Territory, February 2, 1907.

Chief Clerk,
    Choctaw Land Office,
        Atoka, Indian Territory.

Dear Sir:

    Referring to minor Choctaw New born card No. 890, (Act of April 26, 1906) you are advised that a red line has been drawn through the name of No. 1 thereon Jincy Push, the large "Cancelled" stamp has been placed transversely across the face of the card, the date Feb. 1, 1907 and the following notation in red ink has been placed on said card:

    "No. 1 is duplicate of Gency Elapashabbe on Choctaw NB card
    (Act of March 3, 1905) #1400."

Applications for Enrollment of Choctaw Newborn
Act of 1905   Volume XIX

You are therefore directed to make duplicate card of this number in your possession conform to the information thereon and eliminate the name of this person from your list of undetermined applicants for enrollment in the Choctaw Nation.

Respectfully,

Commissioner.

Choc New Born 1401
    Annie Lawechobe[sic]
    (Born Jan. 28, 1905)

BIRTH AFFIDAVIT.

DEPARTMENT OF THE INTERIOR.
COMMISSION TO THE FIVE CIVILIZED TRIBES.

IN RE APPLICATION FOR ENROLLMENT, as a citizen of the Choctaw Nation, of Annie Lawechubbee, born on the 28 day of Jan, 1905

Name of Father: Hopel T. Lawechubbee   a citizen of the Choctaw Nation.

Name of Mother: Tennessee Lawechubbee *née Jefferson* a citizen of the Choctaw Nation.

Postoffice   Goodwater I.T.

AFFIDAVIT OF MOTHER.

UNITED STATES OF AMERICA, Indian Territory,
    Central   DISTRICT.

I, Tennessee Lawechubbee, on oath state that I am 27 years of age and a citizen by Blood, of the Choctaw Nation; that I am the lawful wife of Hopel T. Lawechubbee, who is a citizen, by Blood of the Choctaw Nation; that a Female child was born to me on 28th day of January, 1905; that said child has been named Annie Lawechubbee, and was living March 4, 1905.

                              her
                        Tennessee x Lawechubbee
Witnesses To Mark: mark
    { L.G. Battiest
      Daniel Jefferson

Applications for Enrollment of Choctaw Newborn
Act of 1905   Volume XIX

Subscribed and sworn to before me this 10th day of   April   , 1905

                                        (Name Illegible)
                                        Notary Public.

AFFIDAVIT OF ATTENDING PHYSICIAN OR MID-WIFE.

UNITED STATES OF AMERICA, Indian Territory, }
    Central   DISTRICT.

   I, Wincey Thompson   and   Sophie Going , on oath state that I attended on Mrs. Tennessee Lawechubbee , wife of Hopel T. Lawechubbee   on the 28 day of January   , 1905; that there was born to her on said date a   Female   child; that said child was living March 4, 1905, and is said to have been named   Annie Lawechubbee

                                1   Sophie Going
Witnesses To Mark: 2   Wincey Thompson
{

   Subscribed and sworn to before me this 10 day of   April   , 1905

                                        (Name Illegible)
                                        Notary Public.

Choc New Born 1402
        Annie Quinton
        (Born Nov. 8, 1903)

Applications for Enrollment of Choctaw Newborn
Act of 1905   Volume XIX

NEW-BORN AFFIDAVIT.

Number............

...Choctaw Enrolling Commission...

IN THE MATTER OF THE APPLICATION FOR ENROLLMENT, as a citizen of the Choctaw Nation, of Annie Quinton born on the 8th day of ___November___ 190 3

Name of father Joel Quinton   a citizen of   Choctaw
Nation final enrollment No. 8783
Name of mother Katie Quinton   a citizen of   Choctaw
Nation final enrollment No. ....

                                             Postoffice   Featherston IT

AFFIDAVIT OF MOTHER.

UNITED STATES OF AMERICA
INDIAN TERRITORY
  Western   DISTRICT

I Katie Quinton, on oath state that I am 30 years of age and a citizen by white of the ——— Nation, and as such have been placed upon the final roll of the ———-Nation, by the Honorable Secretary of the Interior my final enrollment number being ——— ; that I am the lawful wife of Joel Quinton, who is a citizen of the Choctaw Nation, and as such has been placed upon the final roll of said Nation by the Honorable Secretary of the Interior, his final enrollment number being 8783 and that a female child was born to me on the 8th day of November 190 3; that said child has been named Annie Quinton, and is now living.

Witnesseth.   Katie Quinton
  Must be two ⎤ T.J. Walls
  Witnesses who ⎦
  are Citizens.   T.D. Dyer

Subscribed and sworn to before me this .... day of .... 190........

                          (Name Illegible)
                                Notary Public.

My commission expires:

Applications for Enrollment of Choctaw Newborn
Act of 1905   Volume XIX

AFFIDAVIT OF ATTENDING PHYSICIAN OR MIDWIFE

UNITED STATES OF AMERICA
INDIAN TERRITORY
Western   DISTRICT

I,   Elizabeth Quinton   a   midwife on oath state that I attended on Mrs. Katie Quinton   wife of Joel Quinton on the   8th   day of   November, 190 3, that there was born to her on said date a female child, that said child is now living, and is said to have been named   Annie Quinton

Elizabeth Quinton

Subscribed and sworn to before me this, the   4   day of January   190 5

John M Lentz   Notary Public.

WITNESSETH:
Must be two witnesses who are citizens { Sam Bench
James Quinton

We hereby certify that we are well acquainted with   Elizabeth Quinton a   midwife   and know   her   to be reputable and of good standing in the community.

James Quinton

T. D. Dyer

BIRTH AFFIDAVIT.

DEPARTMENT OF THE INTERIOR.
COMMISSION TO THE FIVE CIVILIZED TRIBES.

IN RE APPLICATION FOR ENROLLMENT, as a citizen of the   Choctaw   Nation, of Annie Quinton, born on the 8th day of November, 1903

Name of Father: Joel Quinton   a citizen of the   Choctaw   Nation.
Name of Mother: Katie Quinton   a citizen of the   Choctaw   Nation.

Postoffice   Quinton, Indian Territory.

Applications for Enrollment of Choctaw Newborn
Act of 1905   Volume XIX

AFFIDAVIT OF MOTHER.

UNITED STATES OF AMERICA, Indian Territory, }
Western   DISTRICT.

I, Katie Quinton, on oath state that I am 31 years of age and a citizen by intermarriage, of the Choctaw Nation; that I am the lawful wife of Joel Quinton, who is a citizen, by blood of the Choctaw Nation; that a Female child was born to me on 8th day of November, 1903; that said child has been named Annie Quinton, and was living March 4, 1905.

Katie Quinton

Witnesses To Mark:
{

Subscribed and sworn to before me this 1st day of May, 1905

Guy A. Curry
Notary Public.

AFFIDAVIT OF ATTENDING PHYSICIAN OR MID-WIFE.

UNITED STATES OF AMERICA, Indian Territory, }
Western   DISTRICT.

I, Elizabeth Quinton, a mid-wife, on oath state that I attended on Mrs. Katie Quinton, wife of Joel Quinton on the 8th day of November, 1903; that there was born to her on said date a Female child; that said child was living March 4, 1905, and is said to have been named Annie Quinton

Elizabeth Quinton

Witnesses To Mark:
{

Subscribed and sworn to before me this 1st day of May, 1905

Guy A. Curry
Notary Public.

Applications for Enrollment of Choctaw Newborn
Act of 1905   Volume XIX

Choc New Born 1403
    Kemble Hancock
    (Born Dec. 24, 1903)

BIRTH AFFIDAVIT.

DEPARTMENT OF THE INTERIOR.
COMMISSION TO THE FIVE CIVILIZED TRIBES.

IN RE APPLICATION FOR ENROLLMENT, as a citizen of the Choctaw Nation, of Kemble Hancock, born on the 24 day of Dec, 1903

Name of Father: Albert Hancock   a citizen of the Choctaw Nation.
Name of Mother: Viola Hancock   a citizen of the Choctaw Nation.

    Postoffice   Featherston Ind Ter

AFFIDAVIT OF MOTHER.

UNITED STATES OF AMERICA, Indian Territory,
    Central   DISTRICT.

    I, Viola Hancock, on oath state that I am 24 years of age and a citizen by marriage, of the Choctaw Nation; that I am the lawful wife of Albert Hancock, who is a citizen, by blood of the Choctaw Nation; that a male child was born to me on 24 day of December, 1903; that said child has been named Kemble Hancock, and was living March 4, 1905.

                                      her
                            Viola x Hancock
Witnesses To Mark: mark
    { Aug. Timmerman
    { Bessie Boatright

    Subscribed and sworn to before me this 28 day of April, 1905

                            J.C. Hubert
My commission expires   Notary Public.
Nov 25 1908

Applications for Enrollment of Choctaw Newborn
Act of 1905   Volume XIX

AFFIDAVIT OF ATTENDING PHYSICIAN OR MID-WIFE.

UNITED STATES OF AMERICA, Indian Territory, }
.... DISTRICT. }

    I,   Urban T. Kemble   , a   Physician   , on oath state that I attended on Mrs.   Viola Hancock   , wife of   A Lee Hancock   on the   24   day of   December   , 1903; that there was born to her on said date a   male   child; that said child was living March 4, 1905, and is said to have been named   Kemble Hancock

                                       Urban T. Kemble

Witnesses To Mark:
{

    Subscribed and sworn to before me this   26th   day of   April   , 1905

                                (Name Illegible)
commission expires   Notary Public.
Feb. 14, 1909

                                                                                7--3227.

                      Muskogee, Indian Territory, May 5, 1905.

Albert Hancock,
    Featherston, Indian Territory.

Dear Sir:

    Receipt is hereby acknowledged of the affidavits of Viola Hancock and Urban T. Kemale[sic] to the birth of Kemble Hancock, son of Albert and Viola Hancock, December 24, 1903, and the same have been filed with our records as an application for the enrollment of said child.
                                Respectfully,

                                                Commissioner in Charge.

Applications for Enrollment of Choctaw Newborn
Act of 1905   Volume XIX

Choc New Born 1404
    Frank Johnson
    (Born Feb. 22, 1905)

BIRTH AFFIDAVIT.

DEPARTMENT OF THE INTERIOR.
COMMISSION TO THE FIVE CIVILIZED TRIBES.

IN RE APPLICATION FOR ENROLLMENT, as a citizen of the Choctaw Nation, of Frank Johnson, born on the 22nd day of February, 1905

Name of Father: Esias Johnson *(Roll No. 9902)* a citizen of the Choctaw Nation.
Name of Mother: Sallie Johnson *(Roll No. 9903)* a citizen of the Choctaw Nation.

        Postoffice   Durant, I.T.

AFFIDAVIT OF MOTHER.

UNITED STATES OF AMERICA, Indian Territory,
    Central   **DISTRICT.**

    I, Sallie Johnson, on oath state that I am about 25 years of age and a citizen by blood, of the Choctaw Nation; that I am the lawful wife of Esias Johnson, who is a citizen, by blood of the Choctaw Nation; that a male child was born to me on 22nd day of February, 1905; that said child has been named Frank, and was living March 4, 1905.

                                    her
                            Sallie x Johnson
Witnesses To Mark: mark
    { D.W. Cochnauer
    { P.L. Cain
    Esias Johnson
    Subscribed and sworn to before me this 29th day of April A D, 1905

                                    Notary Public.

Applications for Enrollment of Choctaw Newborn
Act of 1905 Volume XIX

AFFIDAVIT OF ATTENDING PHYSICIAN OR MID-WIFE.

UNITED STATES OF AMERICA, Indian Territory, }
Central DISTRICT. }

I, Eliza Nail , a mid wife , on oath state that I attended on Mrs. Sallie Johnson , wife of Esias Johnson on the 22nd day of February , 1905; that there was born to her on said date a male child; that said child was living March 4, 1905, and is said to have been named Frank

                      her
                   Eliza x Nail

Witnesses To Mark: mark
{ D.W. Cochnauer
{ P.L. Cain
Esias Johnson

Subscribed and sworn to before me this 29th day of April A D , 1905

                  SH Kyle
                      Notary Public.

BIRTH AFFIDAVIT.

DEPARTMENT OF THE INTERIOR.
COMMISSION TO THE FIVE CIVILIZED TRIBES.

IN RE APPLICATION FOR ENROLLMENT, as a citizen of the Choctaw Nation, of Frank Johnson , born on the 22" day of February , 1905

Name of Father: Esias Johnson *(Roll No. 9902)* a citizen of the Choctaw Nation.
Name of Mother: Sallie Johnson *(Roll No. 9903)* a citizen of the Choctaw Nation.

              Postoffice Durant, I.T.

AFFIDAVIT OF MOTHER.

UNITED STATES OF AMERICA, Indian Territory, }
Central DISTRICT. }

I, Sallie Johnson , on oath state that I am about 25 years of age and a citizen by blood , of the Choctaw Nation; that I am the lawful wife of Esias Johnson , who is a citizen, by blood of the Choctaw Nation; that a male child was born to me on 22" day of February , 1905; that said child has been named Frank Johnson , and was living March 4, 1905.

                  her
              Sallie x Johnson
                mark

Applications for Enrollment of Choctaw Newborn
Act of 1905   Volume XIX

Witnesses To Mark:
{ W C Smith
  A.N. Jefferson

Subscribed and sworn to before me this 8th day of August , 1905

Lewis T Martin
Notary Public.

7-3474

Muskogee, Indian Territory, May 5, 1905.

Esias Johnson,
    Durant, Indian Territory.

Dear Sir:

    Receipt is hereby acknowledged of the affidavits of Sallie Johnson and Eliza Nail to the birth of Frank Johnson, son of Esias and Sallie Johnson, February 22, 1905, and the same have been filed with our records as an application for the enrollment of said child.

Respectfully,

Chairman.

7-NB-1404.

Muskogee, Indian Territory, June 3, 1905.

Esias Johnson,
    Durant, Indian Territory.

Dear Sir:

    There is enclosed you herewith for execution the mother's affidavit, in the matter of the enrollment of your infant child, Frank Johnson, born February 22, 1905.

    In the application heretofore filed in this office the Notary Public failed to sign the mother's affidavit. It will, therefore, be necessary that this affidavit be re-executed.

    In having the affidavit executed care should be exercised to see that all names are written in full, as they appear in the body of the affidavit. Signature by mark must be attested by two witnesses. Each affidavit must be executed before a Notary Public and the notarial seal and signature of the officer must be attached to each separate affidavit.

Applications for Enrollment of Choctaw Newborn
Act of 1905   Volume XIX

Respectfully,

VR 3-3. [sic]

7-NB-1404

Muskogee, Indian Territory, July 28, 1905.

Esias Johnson,
    Durant, Indian Territory.

Dear Sir:

    Your attention is called to a communication addressed to you by the Commission to the Five Civilized Tribes, under date od[sic] June 3, 1905, with which there was inclosed for execution, the mother's affidavit, in the matter of the enrollment of your infant child, Frank Johnson, born February 22, 1905.

    In said letter you were advised that in the application heretofore filed in this office, the Notary Public failed to sign the mother's affidavit, and you are requested to have said affidavit properly executed and return to this office.

    This matter should receive your immediate attention as no further action can be taken relative to the enrollment of your said child until the evidence heretofore requested has been supplied.

Respectfully,

Commissioner.

DC-36999

Durant, Ind. Ter., Aug. 2nd. 1905.

Tams Bixby,
    Commissioner,
        Muskogee, Ind. Ter.

Dear Sir:

    Referring to 7-NB-1404, yours of the 28th ult. addressed to Esias Johnson calling my attention to a communication addressed to me by the Commission to the Five Civilized Tribes under date of June 3, 1905, with which there was enclosed for execution, the mother's affidavit, in the matter of the enrollment of my infant child, Frank Johnson, born February 22, 1905 In your letter to me of the 28th you tell me that in the application heretofore filed the Notary Public failed to sign the mother's affidavit.

Applications for Enrollment of Choctaw Newborn
Act of 1905   Volume XIX

I beg to advise you that I never received the communication under date of June 3, 1905, and I don't understand why I didn't get it, and I wish you would send me another affidavit for my wife, the mother of said Frank Johnson to sign. My wife's name is Sallie Johnson. Please address it to me at Durant, I. T. at your earliest opportunity.

                Yours truly,
                  (signed) Esias Johnson.

Send my mail to Durant, I. T., Lock Box 336.

                Esias Johnson.

7-NB-1404

                Muskogee, Indian Territory, August 5, 1905.

Esias Johnson,
    Lock Box 336,
        Durant, Indian Territory.

Dear Sir:

    Receipt is hereby acknowledged of your letter of August 2, 1905, in which you state that you did not receive a communication from the Commission to the Five Civilized Tribes of June 3, 1905, enclosing for execution the affidavit of the mother in the matter of the enrollment of your infant child Frank Johnson born February 22, 1905, and you request another blank to be forwarded you.

    In compliance with your request an affidavit partially filled out is inclosed herewith for execution by your wife Sallie Johnson to the birth of your child Frank Johnson.

                Respectfully,

                              Commissioner.

KB 1-5

Applications for Enrollment of Choctaw Newborn
Act of 1905   Volume XIX

7-NB-1404

Muskogee, Indian Territory, August 12, 1905.

Esias Johnson,
    Box 336,
        Durant, Indian Territory.

Dear Sir:

    Receipt is hereby acknowledged of your letter of August 8, 1905, enclosing affidavit of Sallie Johnson to the birth of Frank Johnson, son of Esias Johnson and Sallie Johnson, February 22, 1905, and the same has been filed in the matter of the enrollment of said child.

                Respectfully,

                Acting Commissioner.

Choc New Born 1405
    Myrtle Gladys Miller
    (Born Nov. 11, 1902)
    James Gordon Miller   Choc. N.B. 1229
    (Born July 28, 1904)

BIRTH AFFIDAVIT.
DEPARTMENT OF THE INTERIOR.
COMMISSION TO THE FIVE CIVILIZED TRIBES.

IN RE APPLICATION FOR ENROLLMENT, as a citizen of the Choctaw Nation, of Myrtle Gladys Miller, born on the 11th day of November, 1902

Name of Father: Samuel G. Miller   a citizen of the Choctaw Nation.
Name of Mother: Hattie Miller   a citizen of the Choctaw Nation.

            Postoffice   Antlers, Ind. Ter.

Applications for Enrollment of Choctaw Newborn
Act of 1905   Volume XIX

AFFIDAVIT OF MOTHER.

UNITED STATES OF AMERICA, Indian Territory,
Central DISTRICT.

I, Hattie Miller, on oath state that I am 22 years of age and a citizen by blood, of the Choctaw Nation; that I am the lawful wife of Samuel G. Miller, who is a citizen, by blood of the Choctaw Nation; that a female child was born to me on 11th day of November, 1902; that said child has been named Myrtle Gladys Miller, and was living March 4, 1905.

Hattie Miller

Witnesses To Mark:
{

Subscribed and sworn to before me this 28th day of April, 1905

Wirt Franklin
Notary Public.

AFFIDAVIT OF ATTENDING PHYSICIAN OR MID-WIFE.

UNITED STATES OF AMERICA, Indian Territory,
Central DISTRICT.

I, W.B. Pigg, a physician, on oath state that I attended on Mrs. Hattie Miller, wife of Samuel G. Miller on the 11th day of November, 1902; that there was born to her on said date a female child; that said child was living March 4, 1905, and is said to have been named Myrtle Gladys Miller

W.B. Pigg M.D.

Witnesses To Mark:
{

Subscribed and sworn to before me this 1st day of May, 1905

Commission expires August 2, 1905

WG Skinner
Notary Public.

Applications for Enrollment of Choctaw Newborn
Act of 1905   Volume XIX

BIRTH AFFIDAVIT.

DEPARTMENT OF THE INTERIOR.
COMMISSION TO THE FIVE CIVILIZED TRIBES.

IN RE APPLICATION FOR ENROLLMENT, as a citizen of the Choctaw Nation, of James Gordon Miller, born on the 28th day of July, 1904

Name of Father: Samuel G. Miller   a citizen of the Choctaw Nation.
Name of Mother: Hattie Miller   a citizen of the Choctaw Nation.

Postoffice   Antlers, Ind. Ter.

AFFIDAVIT OF MOTHER.

UNITED STATES OF AMERICA, Indian Territory,
Central DISTRICT.

I, Hattie Miller, on oath state that I am 22 years of age and a citizen by blood, of the Choctaw Nation; that I am the lawful wife of Samuel G. Miller, who is a citizen, by blood of the Choctaw Nation; that a male child was born to me on 28th day of July, 1904; that said child has been named James Gordon Miller, and was living March 4, 1905.

Hattie Miller

Witnesses To Mark:

Subscribed and sworn to before me this 28th day of April, 1905

Wirt Franklin
Notary Public.

AFFIDAVIT OF ATTENDING PHYSICIAN OR MID-WIFE.

UNITED STATES OF AMERICA, Indian Territory,
Central DISTRICT.

I, H.C. Johnson, a physician, on oath state that I attended on Mrs. Hattie Miller, wife of Samuel G. Miller on the 28th day of July, 1904; that there was born to her on said date a male child; that said child was living March 4, 1905, and is said to have been named James Gordon Miller

HC Johnson

Witnesses To Mark:

Applications for Enrollment of Choctaw Newborn
Act of 1905 Volume XIX

Subscribed and sworn to before me this 2nd day of May , 1905

Wirt Franklin
Notary Public.

7-3163.

Muskogee, Indian Territory, May 6, 1905.

Samuel G. Miller,
    Antlers, Indian Territory.

Dear Sir:

    Receipt is hereby acknowledged of the affidavits of Hattie Miller and W. B. Pigg to the birth of Myrtle Gladys Miller, daughter of Samuel G. and Hattie Miller, November 11, 1902, and the same have been filed with our records as an application for the enrollment of said child.

    Respectfully,

Commissioner in Charge.

7-NB-1405

Muskogee, Indian Territory, July 27, 1905.

S. G. Miller,
    Antlers, Indian Territory.

Dear Sir:

    Receipt is hereby acknowledged of your letter of July 2, 1905, asking if your child James Gordon Miller has been enrolled.

    In reply to your letter you are advised that the names of your children Myrtle Gladys Miller and James Gordon Miller have been placed upon a schedule of citizens by blood of the Choctaw Nation which has been forwarded the Secretary of the Interior and you will be notified when their enrollment is approved by the Department.

    Respectfully,

Commissioner.

Applications for Enrollment of Choctaw Newborn
Act of 1905   Volume XIX

Choc New Born 1406
    Eller Summer
    (Born Oct. 8, 1902)

BIRTH AFFIDAVIT.

DEPARTMENT OF THE INTERIOR.
COMMISSION TO THE FIVE CIVILIZED TRIBES.

IN RE APPLICATION FOR ENROLLMENT, as a citizen of the Chocktaw[sic] Nation, of Eller Summers[sic], born on the 8th day of Oct, 1902

Name of Father: James Summers   a citizen of the Chocktaw Nation.
Name of Mother: Amanda L M Summers   a citizen of the Chocktaw Nation.

Postoffice _____

AFFIDAVIT OF MOTHER.

UNITED STATES OF AMERICA, Indian Territory,
  Southern   DISTRICT.

    I, Ammanda[sic] L. M. Summers, on oath state that I am 25 years of age and a citizen by Blood, of the Chocktaw Nation; that I am the lawful wife of James Summers, who is a citizen, by Marriage of the Chocktaw Nation; that a Female child was born to me on 8th day of Oct., 1902; that said child has been named Eller Summers, and was living March 4, 1905.

                                           her
                                Amanda L x M Summers

Witnesses To Mark: mark
    { SE Whitford   Linn I.T.
    { J R Thomas   Linn I T

    Subscribed and sworn to before me this 25th day of April, 1905.

                            H.F. Fultz
                                Notary Public.

Applications for Enrollment of Choctaw Newborn
Act of 1905   Volume XIX

AFFIDAVIT OF ATTENDING PHYSICIAN OR MID-WIFE.

UNITED STATES OF AMERICA, Indian Territory, } Central DISTRICT.

I, Nancey[sic] L Parker, a Midwife, on oath state that I attended on Mrs. Amanda L M Summers, wife of James Summers on the 8th day of Oct, 1905; that there was born to her on said date a Female child; that said child was living March 4, 1905, and is said to have been named Eller Summers

Caney I.T.

Nancey L. Parker
x
her mark

Witnesses To Mark:
{ H. T. Parker Caney I.T.
{ Alpho Parker Caney I.T

Subscribed and sworn to before me this 28th day of April, 1905

Charles S Lewis
Notary Public.

BIRTH AFFIDAVIT.

DEPARTMENT OF THE INTERIOR.
COMMISSION TO THE FIVE CIVILIZED TRIBES.

IN RE APPLICATION FOR ENROLLMENT, as a citizen of the Choctaw Nation, of Eller Summer, born on the 8th day of Oct, 1902

Name of Father: James Summer   a citizen of the Choctaw Nation.
Name of Mother: Amanda L M Summer   a citizen of the Choctaw Nation.

Postoffice   Linn Ind Ter

AFFIDAVIT OF MOTHER.

UNITED STATES OF AMERICA, Indian Territory, } Southern DISTRICT.

I, Amanda L.M. Summer, on oath state that I am 25 years of age and a citizen by blood, of the Choctaw Nation; that I am the lawful wife of James Summer, who is a citizen, ~~by~~ ——— of the United States Nation; that a female child was born to me on 8th day of Oct, 1902; that said child has been named Eller Summer, and was living March 4, 1905.

her
Amanda L M x Summer
mark

32

Applications for Enrollment of Choctaw Newborn
Act of 1905 Volume XIX

Witnesses To Mark:
{ LE Fultz
{ J.E. Whitford

    Subscribed and sworn to before me this 14th day of July , 1905

                                H.F. Fultz
                                Notary Public.

AFFIDAVIT OF ATTENDING PHYSICIAN OR MID-WIFE.

UNITED STATES OF AMERICA, Indian Territory, }
   Central   DISTRICT. }

    I, M.E. Baawner , a Midwife , on oath state that I attended on Mrs. Amanda L M Summer , wife of James Summer on the 8th day of Oct , 1902; that there was born to her on said date a female child; that said child was living March 4, 1905, and is said to have been named Eller Summer

                              her
                        Nancy x Parker
Witnesses To Mark: mark
{ H. T. Parker
{ Alpho Parker

    Subscribed and sworn to before me this 6th day of July , 1905

                              Charles S Lewis
                              Notary Public.

BIRTH AFFIDAVIT.
DEPARTMENT OF THE INTERIOR.
COMMISSION TO THE FIVE CIVILIZED TRIBES.

    IN RE APPLICATION FOR ENROLLMENT, as a citizen of the Choctaw Nation, of Eller Summer , born on the 8th day of October , 1902

Name of Father: James Summer   a citizen of the U.S. Nation.
Name of Mother: Amanda L M Summer   a citizen of the Choctaw Nation.

                    Postoffice   Linn, I. T.

Applications for Enrollment of Choctaw Newborn
Act of 1905   Volume XIX

AFFIDAVIT OF MOTHER.

UNITED STATES OF AMERICA, Indian Territory, }
.... DISTRICT. }

I, ..., on oath state that I am .... years of age and a citizen by ...., of the .... Nation; that I am the lawful wife of ...., who is a citizen, by .... of the .... Nation; that a .... child was born to me on ..... day of ...., 1......., that said child has been named ...., and was living March 4, 1905.

Witnesses To Mark:
{ ....
  .... }

Subscribed and sworn to before me this .... day of ...., 1905.

                                                                                    Notary Public.

AFFIDAVIT OF ATTENDING PHYSICIAN OR MID-WIFE.

UNITED STATES OF AMERICA, Indian Territory, }
    Central   DISTRICT. }

I,   Nancy L Parker , a   mid-wife   , on oath state that I attended on Mrs.   Amanda L M Summer , wife of   James Summer   on the 8th   day of   October , 1902; that there was born to her on said date a   female   child; that said child was living March 4, 1905, and is said to have been named   Eller Summer

                                            Nancy L. Parker

Witnesses To Mark:
{ .... }

Subscribed and sworn to before me this 23 day of   July , 190**6**

                                            Charles S Lewis
                                            Notary Public.

Applications for Enrollment of Choctaw Newborn
Act of 1905   Volume XIX

7-NB-1406.

Muskogee, Indian Territory, June 15, 1905.

James Summer,
    Linn, Indian Territory.

Dear Sir:

There is enclosed herewith for execution application for the enrollment of your infant child, Eller Summer.

In the mother's affidavit of April 25, 1905, the date of the applicant's birth appears as October 8, 1902, while the midwife in her affidavit of April 28, 1905, gives the date of birth as October 8, 1905.

In the enclosed application the date of birth is left blank. Please insert the correct date and when the affidavits are properly executed return them to this office.

In having these affidavits executed care should be exercised to see that all names are written in full, as they appear in the body of the affidavit, and in the event either of the persons signing the affidavit are unable to write, signatures by mark must be attested by two witnesses. Each affidavit must be executed before a Notary Public and the notarial seal and signature of the officer must be attached to each separate affidavit.

Respectfully,

Chairman.

7-NB-1406

Muskogee, Indian Territory, July 28, 1905.

James Summer,
    Leon, Indian Territory.

Dear Sir:

Receipt is hereby acknowledged of the affidavits of Amanda L. Summer and Nancy Parker to the birth of Eller Summer, daughter of James and Amanda L. M. Summer, October 8, 1902, and the same have been filed with the records of this office in the matter of the enrollment of said child.

Respectfully,

Commissioner.

Applications for Enrollment of Choctaw Newborn
Act of 1905 Volume XIX

7-NB-1406.

Muskoge[sic], Indian Territory, August 19, 1905.

James Sumer,
    Linn, Indian Territory.

Dear Sir:

    On July 27, 1905, you filed with this office the affidavit of your wife Amanda L. M. Summer and what purports to be the affidavit of Nancy Parker as to the birth of your daughter Eller Summer, born October 8, 1902. This office acknowledged receipt of said affidavits on July 28, 1905, and informed you that the same had been filed with the records of this office in the matter of the enrollment of your said daughter.

    However upon examination the affidavit of said Nancy Parker, as to the birth of your said daughter, is defective inasmuch as the name of the affiant appears in the body of the affidavit as M. E. Baawner while the signature of the affiant is that of Nancy Parker.

    For the purpose of correcting this discrepancy there is inclosed herewith an affidavit to be executed by Nancy L. Parker who, it appears from the record in this case, was the midwife that attended at the birth of said Eller Summer. In having the same executed be careful to see that the notary public before whom the affidavit is sworn to attaches both his name and seal to the affidavit, and if the said Nancy L. Parker signs the affidavit by mark that two disinterested witnesses who can write ~~have~~ attested such signature.

    Please give this matter your immediate attention.

        Respectfully,

            Acting Commissioner.

CTD-2.
Env.

Applications for Enrollment of Choctaw Newborn
Act of 1905   Volume XIX

> CHOCTAW BY BLOOD
>
> NB 1406
>
> See letter dated
> 5/5/05 giving
> age of Eller
> Summer filed
> in (illegible)
> #375

Choc New Born 1407
    Crystal Locke
    (Born Jan. 28, 1905)

BIRTH AFFIDAVIT.

DEPARTMENT OF THE INTERIOR.
COMMISSION TO THE FIVE CIVILIZED TRIBES.

    IN RE APPLICATION FOR ENROLLMENT, as a citizen of the Choctaw Nation, of Crystal Locke, born on the 28th day of January, 1905

Name of Father: Wilson Locke   a citizen of the Choctaw Nation.
Name of Mother: Susan Locke   a citizen of the Choctaw Nation.

    Postoffice   Antlers, Ind. Ter.

AFFIDAVIT OF MOTHER.

UNITED STATES OF AMERICA, Indian Territory,
    Central   DISTRICT.

    I, Susan Locke, on oath state that I am 18 years of age and a citizen by blood, of the Choctaw Nation; that I am the lawful wife of Wilson Locke, who is a citizen, by blood of the Choctaw Nation; that a female child

Applications for Enrollment of Choctaw Newborn
Act of 1905   Volume XIX

was born to me on   28th   day of   January   , 1905; that said child has been named   Crystal Locke   , and was living March 4, 1905.

Susan Locke

Witnesses To Mark:
{

   Subscribed and sworn to before me this   25th   day of   April   , 1905

Wirt Franklin
Notary Public.

AFFIDAVIT OF ATTENDING PHYSICIAN OR MID-WIFE.

UNITED STATES OF AMERICA, Indian Territory, }
   Central   DISTRICT.

   I,   M. J. Wise   , a mid-wife   , on oath state that I attended on Mrs.   Susan Locke   , wife of   Wilson Locke   on the 28th   day of   January   , 1905; that there was born to her on said date a   female   child; that said child was living March 4, 1905, and is said to have been named   Crystal Locke

M. J. Wise

Witnesses To Mark:
{

   Subscribed and sworn to before me this   25th   day of   April   , 1905

Wirt Franklin
Notary Public.

7-NB-1407

Muskogee, Indian Territory, August 1, 1905.

Wilson Locke,
   Antlers, Indian Territory.

Dear Sir:

   Receipt is hereby acknowledged of your letter of July 24, 1905, asking relative to the enrollment of your child Crystal Locke.

   In reply to your letter you are advised that the name of your child Crystal Locke has been placed upon a schedule of citizens by blood of the Choctaw Nation which has

Applications for Enrollment of Choctaw Newborn
Act of 1905   Volume XIX

been forwarded the Secretary of the Interior and you will be notified when her enrollment is approved by the Department.

Respectfully,

Commissioner.

Choc New Born 1408
    Benjamin Williams
    (Born April 6, 1903)

BIRTH AFFIDAVIT.

DEPARTMENT OF THE INTERIOR,
COMMISSION TO THE FIVE CIVILIZED TRIBES.

IN RE APPLICATION FOR ENROLLMENT, as a citizen of the Choctaw Nation, of Benjamin William[sic], born on the 6th day of April, 190 3

Name of Father: Abel Williams   a citizen of the Choctaw Nation.
Name of Mother: Sillin Williams   a citizen of the Choctaw Nation.

Post-Office: Talihina I.T.

AFFIDAVIT OF MOTHER.

UNITED STATES OF AMERICA,
  INDIAN TERRITORY,
Central   District.

I, Sillin Williams, on oath state that I am 23 years of age and a citizen by Blood, of the Choctaw Nation; that I am the lawful wife of Abel Williams, who is a citizen, by blood of the Choctaw Nation; that a male child was born to me on the 6th day of April, 190 3, that said child has been named Benjamin Williams, and is now living.

her
Sillin x Williams
mark

WITNESSES TO MARK:
    C A Welch
    Benjamin Willis

Applications for Enrollment of Choctaw Newborn
Act of 1905 Volume XIX

Subscribed and sworn to before me this 25th day of April, 1904

CA Welch
NOTARY PUBLIC.

AFFIDAVIT OF ATTENDING PHYSICIAN OR MID-WIFE.

UNITED STATES OF AMERICA,
INDIAN TERRITORY,
Central   District.

I, Abel Williams, a husband, on oath state that I attended on Mrs. Sillin Williams, wife of Abel Williams on the 6th day of April, 190 3; that there was born to her on said date a Male child; that said child is now living and is said to have been named Benjamin Williams

Abel Williams

WITNESSES TO MARK:

Subscribed and sworn to before me this 25 day of April, 1904

CA Welch
NOTARY PUBLIC.

BIRTH AFFIDAVIT.   7-NB-1408

DEPARTMENT OF THE INTERIOR.
COMMISSION TO THE FIVE CIVILIZED TRIBES.

IN RE APPLICATION FOR ENROLLMENT, as a citizen of the Choctaw Nation, of Benjamin Williams, born on the 6 day of April, 1903

Name of Father: Abel Williams   a citizen of the Choctaw Nation.
Formerly Columbus
Name of Mother: Celin Williams   a citizen of the Choctaw Nation.

Postoffice   Talihina

Applications for Enrollment of Choctaw Newborn
Act of 1905   Volume XIX

AFFIDAVIT OF MOTHER.

UNITED STATES OF AMERICA, Indian Territory,
Central   DISTRICT.

I, Celin Williams, on oath state that I am 24 years of age and a citizen by blood, of the Choctaw Nation; that I am the lawful wife of Abel Williams deceased, who is was a citizen, by blood of the Choctaw Nation; that a male child was born to me on 6 day of April, 1903; that said child has been named Benjamin Williams, and was living March 4, 1905.

                her
                Celin x Williams
                mark

Witnesses To Mark:
{ Wesley Woods
{ Sam T Roberts Jr

Subscribed and sworn to before me this 26th day of Aug, 1905

                Jno J Thomas
                Notary Public.

AFFIDAVIT OF ATTENDING PHYSICIAN OR MID-WIFE.

UNITED STATES OF AMERICA, Indian Territory,
Central   DISTRICT.

we are acquainted with We, E.P. Pitchlynn and Henry Johnson, on oath state that ~~I attended on~~ Mrs. Celin Williams, wife of Abel Williams, dec^d *and that* on *or about* the 6th day of April, 1903; that there was born to her on said date a male child; that said child was living March 4, 1905, and is said to have been named Benjamin Williams ; *that we are not related to the applicant nor interested in this case.*

                E P Pitchlynn
Witnesses To Mark: Henry Johnson
{

Subscribed and sworn to before me this 26 day of Aug, 1905

                Jno J Thomas
                Notary Public.

Applications for Enrollment of Choctaw Newborn
Act of 1905 Volume XIX

7-2041

Muskogee, Indian Territory, April 28, 1904.

Abel Williams,
    Talihina, Indian Territory.

Dear Sir:

    Receipt is hereby acknowledged of your affidavit and that of Silin[sic] Williams, relative to the birth of your infant son, Benjamin Williams, April 6, 1903, which it is presumed have been forwarded to this office as an application for enrollment of said child as a citizen by blood of the Choctaw Nation.

    You are informed that under the provisions of the Act of Congress, approved July 1, 1902, the Commission is now without authority to receive or consider the original application for enrollment of any person whomsoever as a citizen of the Choctaw or Chickasaw Nation.

Respectfully,

Chairman.

$W^m O.B.$

COMMISSIONERS:
TAMS BIXBY,
THOMAS B. NEEDLES,
C.R. BRECKINRIDGE.

DEPARTMENT OF THE INTERIOR,
COMMISSIONER TO THE FIVE CIVILIZED TRIBES.

REFER IN REPLY TO THE FOLLOWING:

WM. O. BEALL
Secretary

ADDRESS ONLY THE
COMMISSION TO THE FIVE CIVILIZED TRIBES.

Muskogee, Indian Territory, March 30, 1905.

Abel Williams,
    Talihina, Indian Territory.

Dear Sir:

    Referring to the affidavits heretofore forwarded relative to the birth of Benjamin Williams son of Abel and Sillin Williams, April 6, 1903, it is stated in the affidavit of the mother that she is a citizen by blood of the Choctaw Nation.

    If this is correct you are requested to state the names of her parents, the name under which she was listed for enrollment, the names of any of the other members of her family who may have applied for enrollment at the same time and such other information as will enable us to identify Sillin Williams upon our records as a citizen by blood of the Choctaw Nation.

Applications for Enrollment of Choctaw Newborn
Act of 1905   Volume XIX

Respectfully,
Tams Bixby
Chairman.

(The letter below typed as given.)

(COPY)

Talihina, I. T
April 29, 1905.

The Commission to the Five Civilized Tribes,
Muscogee, Ind Ty.

Gentlemen:-

The attached letter was handed to me by Cilin Williams for reply as she cannot write and her husban Abel Williams is dead.

In reply she states that she was enrolled at Alikchi, I T as Cilin Columbus, with Tecumseh Columbus, her fathers name was Moses McCoy and her mothers Louisa McCoy She did not have her certificates and does not seem to know what had become of them or her number would have been secured She says that Abel Williams did her fileing for her. she has a brother named Holman McCoy and one named Elias McCoy also a Sister named Sallie or Sallie Ann who is married to Rufus Hudson.

Trusting the above will enable you to locate the party

I remain

Respectfully,

Sam T. Roberts.

7--NB--1408

Muskogee, Indian Territory, June 2, 1905.

Abel Williams,
Talihina, Indian Territory.

Dear Sir:

Referring to the application for the enrollment of your minor child Benjiman[sic] Williams, born April 6, 1903, it is noted from the affidavits heretofore filed in this office that you were the only one in attendance upon your wife at the time of the birth of the applicant.

Applications for Enrollment of Choctaw Newborn
Act of 1905   Volume XIX

In this event it will be necessary that the affidavits of two persons, who are disinterested and not related to the applicant, who have actual knowledge to the facts that the child was born, the date of his birth; that he was living on March 4, 1905, and that Sillin Williams is his mother be filed in this office.

This matter should receive your immediate attention as no further action can be taken relative to the enrollment of your child until the Commission is furnished these affidavits.

Respectfully,

[sic]

7-NB-1408

Muskogee, Indian Territory, July 28, 1905.

Celin Williams,
    Talihina, Indian Territory.

Dear Madam:

There is inclosed you herewith for execution application for the enrollment of your infant child, Benjamin Williams, born April 6, 1903.

It appears from the evidence filed in this case, that your husband, Abel Williams, was the only one in attendance upon you at the time of the birth of the applicant, and that your husband is dead; it further appears from said evidence that the child was living April 25, 1904.

It is necessary for the child to be enrolled, that he was living March 4, 1905, and that you supply the affidavits of two disinterested persons who are not related to the applicant, and who have actual knowledge of the facts, that the child was born, the date of his birth, that he was living March 4, 1905, and that you are his mother. The inclosed application is prepared to cover the case.

You are requested to have the affidavits properly executed and return to this office immediately as no further action can be taken relative to the enrollment of your said child, until the evidence requested is supplied.

Respectfully,

LM 4/28   Commissioner.

Applications for Enrollment of Choctaw Newborn
Act of 1905 Volume XIX

7- N B 1408

Muskogee, Indian Territory, August 30, 1905.

Celin Williams,
　　Talihina, Indian Territory.

Dear Madam:

　　Receipt is hereby acknowledged of your affidavit and the affidavits of E. P. Pitchlynn and Henry Johnson, of August 26, 1905, relative to the birth of Benjamin Williams and same have been filed with the records of this office and will receive consideration in the disposition of the application for the enrollment of Benjaman[sic] Williams as a new-born citizen by blood of the Choctaw Nation.

　　　　　　　　　　Respectfully,

　　　　　　　　　　　　　　Commissioner.

7-NB-1408

Muskogee, Indian Territory, November 7, 1905.

John J. Thomas,
　　Talihina, Indian Territory.

Dear Sir:

　　Receipt is hereby acknowledged of your letter of November 3, 1905, asking if the enrollment of Benjamin Williams has been approved.

　　In reply to your letter you are advised that the name of Benjamin Williams has not yet been placed upon a schedule of citizens by blood of the Choctaw Nation prepared for forwarding to the Secretary of the Interior. In event further evidence is necessary to enable this office to pass upon the rights of this child to enrollment you will be duly notified.

　　　　　　　　　　Respectfully,

　　　　　　　　　　　　　　Commissioner.

Applications for Enrollment of Choctaw Newborn
Act of 1905   Volume XIX

7-NB-1408

Muskogee, Indian Territory, January 3, 1906.

Cillin Williams,
 Talihina, Indian Territory.

Dear Madam:

Receipt is hereby acknowledged of your letter of December 29, 1905, asking if your child Benjamin Williams has been enrolled.

In reply to your letter you are advised that the name of your child Benjiman[sic] Williams has not yet been placed upon a schedule of new born citizens of the Choctaw Nation prepared for forwarding to the Secretary of the Interior, but if further evidence is necessary to enable this office to determine the right of your child to enrollment you will be duly notified.

Respectfully,

Commissioner.

Choc New Born 1409
 Julia Ann Colbert
 (Born April 5, 1903)

BIRTH AFFIDAVIT.

DEPARTMENT OF THE INTERIOR.
COMMISSION TO THE FIVE CIVILIZED TRIBES.

IN RE APPLICATION FOR ENROLLMENT, as a citizen of the   Choctaw   Nation, of Julia Ann Colbert   , born on the 5th   day of   April , 1903

Name of Father: Davidson Colbert   a citizen of the   Choctaw   Nation.
Name of Mother: Levina Colbert   a citizen of the   Choctaw   Nation.

Postoffice   **LUKFATA IND TER**

Applications for Enrollment of Choctaw Newborn
Act of 1905   Volume XIX

AFFIDAVIT OF MOTHER.

UNITED STATES OF AMERICA, Indian Territory, }
Central   DISTRICT.

    I, Levina Colbert, on oath state that I am 36 years of age and a citizen by Blood, of the Choctaw Nation; that I am the lawful wife of Davidson Colbert, who is a citizen, by Blood of the Choctaw Nation; that a Female child was born to me on 5th day of April, 1905[sic]; that said child has been named Julia Ann Colbert, and was living March 4, 1905.

                                         her
                                 Levina x Colbert

Witnesses To Mark: mark
  { David Dyer Jr
  { *(Name Illegible)*

    Subscribed and sworn to before me this 10th day of April, 1905

                                  J.W. Costelow
                                  Notary Public.

AFFIDAVIT OF ATTENDING PHYSICIAN OR MID-WIFE.

UNITED STATES OF AMERICA, Indian Territory, }
Central   DISTRICT.

    I, Davidson Colbert, a Husband, on oath state that I attended on Mrs. Levina Colbert, wife of *my own wife* on the 5th day of April, 1905; that there was born to her on said date a Female child; that said child was living March 4, 1905, and is said to have been named Julia Ann Colbert *I was the only one present at the time of the birth of this child*

                                  Davidson Colbert

Witnesses To Mark:

  {

    Subscribed and sworn to before me this 10th day of April, 1905

                                  J.W. Costilow
                                  Notary Public.

Applications for Enrollment of Choctaw Newborn
Act of 1905   Volume XIX

BIRTH AFFIDAVIT.

DEPARTMENT OF THE INTERIOR.
COMMISSION TO THE FIVE CIVILIZED TRIBES.

IN RE APPLICATION FOR ENROLLMENT, as a citizen of the Choctaw Nation, of Julia Ann Colbert, born on the _____ day of _____, 1____

Name of Father: Davison[sic] Colbert   a citizen of the Choctaw Nation.
Name of Mother: Levina Colbert   a citizen of the Choctaw Nation.

Postoffice   Lukfata, Ind. Ter.

AFFIDAVIT OF MOTHER.

UNITED STATES OF AMERICA, Indian Territory, } Central DISTRICT.

I, Levina Colbert, on oath state that I am 36 years of age and a citizen by blood, of the Choctaw Nation; that I am the lawful wife of Davison Colbert, who is a citizen, by blood of the Choctaw Nation; that a female child was born to me on 5th day of April, 1903; that said child has been named Julia Ann Colbert, and was living March 4, 1905.

her
Levina x Colbert
mark

Witnesses To Mark:
{ R.P. Goforth
{ Harkin Franklin

Subscribed and sworn to before me this 19 day of June, 1905

J.L. Merry
Notary Public.

AFFIDAVIT OF ATTENDING PHYSICIAN OR MID-WIFE.

UNITED STATES OF AMERICA, Indian Territory, } Central DISTRICT.

I, Forbis Kanashambe, a _____, on oath state that I ~~attended on~~ *am acquainted with* Mrs. Levina Colbert, wife of Davison Colbert ~~on the~~ ~~day of~~ ~~1~~; that there was born to her on ~~said date~~ *the 5 day of April 1903* a Female child; that said child was living March 4, 1905, and is said to have been named Julia Ann Colbert

Forbis Kanashambe

Applications for Enrollment of Choctaw Newborn
Act of 1905 Volume XIX

Witnesses To Mark:

{

Subscribed and sworn to before me this 19 day of June, 1905

J.L. Merry
Notary Public.

BIRTH AFFIDAVIT.

DEPARTMENT OF THE INTERIOR.
COMMISSION TO THE FIVE CIVILIZED TRIBES.

IN RE APPLICATION FOR ENROLLMENT, as a citizen of the Choctaw Nation, of Julia Ann Colbert, born on the .... day of ...., 1......

Name of Father: Davison Colbert   a citizen of the Choctaw Nation.
Name of Mother: Levina Colbert   a citizen of the Choctaw Nation.

Postoffice   Lukfata, Ind. Ter.

AFFIDAVIT OF MOTHER.

UNITED STATES OF AMERICA, Indian Territory, } .... DISTRICT.

I, ..., on oath state that I am .... years of age and a citizen by ...., of the .... Nation; that I am the lawful wife of ...., who is a citizen, by .... of the .... Nation; that a .... child was born to me on ...... day of ...., 1......, that said child has been named ...., and was living March 4, 1905.

Witnesses To Mark:

{ ....

Subscribed and sworn to before me this ...... day of ...., 1905.

Notary Public.

Applications for Enrollment of Choctaw Newborn
Act of 1905   Volume XIX

AFFIDAVIT OF ATTENDING PHYSICIAN OR MID-WIFE.

UNITED STATES OF AMERICA, Indian Territory,
Central   DISTRICT.

I, Harkin Franklin, ~~a~~ *am acquainted with* Mrs. Levina Colbert, wife of Davison Colbert *that* on ~~attended on~~ *or about* the 5 day of April, 1903; that there was born to her on said date a female child; that said child was living March 4, 1905, and is said to have been named Julia Ann Colbert

Harkin Franklin

Witnesses To Mark:

Subscribed and sworn to before me this 19 day of June, 1905

J. L. Merry
Notary Public.

Choctaw 800.

Muskogee, Indian Territory, April 16, 1905.

Davidson Colbert,
   Lukfata, Indian Territory.

Dear Sir:

   Receipt is hereby acknowledged of the affidavits of Levina Colbert and Davison Colbert to the birth of Julia Ann Colbert, daughter of Davidson and Levina Colbert, April 5, 1905[sic], and you are requested to advise this office if the Levina Colbert referred to in the affidavit forwarded by you is the same person as Daviney Colbert, daughter of Alex Frazier, who appears upon our records as the wife of Davidson Colbert.

   You are advised that the date of the birth of Julia Ann Colbert appears in the application as ~~July~~ *April* 5, 1903, while in the affidavit of yourself and Levina Colbert the date of her birth is given as April 5, 1905.

   Please state the correct date of the birth of this child and also furnish the information requested above at the earliest date practicable.

Respectfully,

Chairman.

Applications for Enrollment of Choctaw Newborn
Act of 1905   Volume XIX

7--NB--1409

Muskogee, Indian Territory, June 3, 1905.

Davidson Colbert,
    Lukfata, Indian Territory.

Dear Sir:

   Referring to the application for the enrollment of your infant child, Julia Ann Colbert, heretofore filed in this office it is noted that you were the only one in attendance upon your wife at the time of the applicant's birth.

   In this event it will be necessary that the affidavits of two persons, who are disinterested and not related to the applicant, who have actual knowledge to the facts that the child was born, the date of her birth; that she was living on March 4, 1905, and that Levina Colbert is her mother be filed in this office. For this purpose there is enclosed you herewith blank affidavits.

   You are further advised that the application for the enrollment of this child heretofore filed with the Commission show the date of birth to be April 5, 1905 and April 5, 1903. For the purpose of securing the correct date of the birth of the applicant there is enclosed herewith an affidavit to be executed by the mother.

   In the enclosed affidavits the date of birth has been left blank and you are requested to insert the correct date and when the affidavits have been properly executed return to this office.

   In having these affidavits executed care should be exercised to see that all names are written in full, as they appear in the body of the affidavit, and in the event that either of the persons signing the affidavit are unable to write, signatures by mark must be attested by two witnesses. Each affidavit must be executed before a Notary Public and the notarial seal and signature of the officer must be attached to each separate affidavit.

   This matter should be given your immediate attention as no further action can be taken relative to the enrollment of said child until the Commission has been furnished these affidavits.

                     Respectfully,

Enc-FVK-25   [sic]

Applications for Enrollment of Choctaw Newborn
Act of 1905 Volume XIX

7 NB 1409

Muskogee, Indian Territory, June 23, 1905.

Davison Colbert,
    Glover, Indian Territory.

Dear Sir:

    Receipt is hereby acknowledged of the affidavits of Levina Colbert, Forbis Kanashambe and Harkin Franklin, to the birth of Julia Ann Colbert, daughter of Davison and Levina Colbert, April 5, 1903, and the same have been filed with our records in the matter of the enrollment of said child.

        Respectfully,

                Chairman.

(The letter below typed as given.)

(C O P Y)

Lukfata, I. T.   May 1st, 1905

Commission to the Five Civilized Tribes,
    Muskogee, I . T.

Gentlemen   Davidson Colbert handed me the enclosed letter yesterday and directed me to say in reply that his wife is the same Davina Colbert daughter of Alex Frazier mentioned in your letter. As to the mistake in the date of the birth of this child Colbert says is my mistake, which may be possible as I had no interpreter, but since have a good interpreter and he and his wife both state that the date of the birth of this child is April 5, 1903. Please write me what to do to correct the error and oblige

                J. W. Castilow,
                Notary Public.

Applications for Enrollment of Choctaw Newborn
Act of 1905   Volume XIX

Choc New Born 1410
    Joseph W. Thompson
    (Born March 5, 1903)

BIRTH AFFIDAVIT.

DEPARTMENT OF THE INTERIOR.
COMMISSION TO THE FIVE CIVILIZED TRIBES.

    IN RE APPLICATION FOR ENROLLMENT, as a citizen of the   Choctaw   Nation, of   Joseph W. Thompson   , born on the 5 day of March , 1903

Name of Father: Joseph P. Thompson   a citizen of the   Choctaw   Nation.
Name of Mother: Betsy Thompson   a citizen of the   Choctaw   Nation.

        Postoffice   Fort Towson Ind. Ter.

AFFIDAVIT OF MOTHER.

UNITED STATES OF AMERICA, Indian Territory, }
    Central   DISTRICT. }

    I,   Betsy Thompson   , on oath state that I am 34 years of age and a citizen by   Blood   , of the   Choctaw   Nation; that I am the lawful wife of   Joseph P Thompson   , who is a citizen, by Blood   of the   Choctaw   Nation; that a male   child was born to me on 5th day of   March   , 1903; that said child has been named   Joseph W Thompson   , and was living March 4, 1905.

                Betsy Thompson

Witnesses To Mark:
{

    Subscribed and sworn to before me this 29 day of   April   , 1905

                Thomas Fennell
                Notary Public.

AFFIDAVIT OF ATTENDING PHYSICIAN OR MID-WIFE.

UNITED STATES OF AMERICA, Indian Territory, }
    Central   DISTRICT. }

    I,   Emelin[sic] Tims   , a   midwife   , on oath state that I attended on Mrs.   Betsy Thompson   , wife of   Joseph P Thompson   on the 5th day of

Applications for Enrollment of Choctaw Newborn
Act of 1905   Volume XIX

March   , 1903; that there was born to her on said date a .... child; that said child was living March 4, 1905, and is said to have been named Joseph W Thompson

                                         Emeline Tims

Witnesses To Mark:
{

    Subscribed and sworn to before me this   29   day of   April   , 1905

                                      Thomas Fennell
                                        Notary Public.

Choc New Born 1411
    Newcomb Davenport Taylor
    (Born Jan. 10, 1903)

BIRTH AFFIDAVIT.
DEPARTMENT OF THE INTERIOR.
COMMISSION TO THE FIVE CIVILIZED TRIBES.

    IN RE APPLICATION FOR ENROLLMENT, as a citizen of the   Choctaw   Nation, of Newcomb Davenport Taylor   , born on the   10th   day of   January , 1903

Name of Father: Newcomb B. Taylor   a citizen of the   Choctaw   Nation.
Name of Mother: Zuelika[sic] Jane Taylor   a citizen of the   Choctaw   Nation.

                        Postoffice   Ardmore, Ind. Ter.

AFFIDAVIT OF MOTHER.

UNITED STATES OF AMERICA, Indian Territory, }
   Southern Judicial   DISTRICT.

    I,   Zuelika Jane Taylor   , on oath state that I am   22   years of age and a citizen by   blood   , of the   Choctaw   Nation; that I am the lawful wife of Newcomb B. Taylor   , who is a citizen, by intermarriage   of the   Choctaw   Nation; that a   male   child was born to me on   10th   day of   January   , 1903; that said child has been named   Newcomb Davenport Taylor   , and was living March 4, 1905.

                                     Zuleika Jane Taylor

Applications for Enrollment of Choctaw Newborn
Act of 1905   Volume XIX

Witnesses To Mark:
{

Subscribed and sworn to before me this 21st day of   April   , 1905

JR Mason
Notary Public.

AFFIDAVIT OF ATTENDING PHYSICIAN OR MID-WIFE.

UNITED STATES OF AMERICA, Indian Territory, }
   Southern Judicial   DISTRICT.}

I,   T. S. Booth   , a physician   , on oath state that I attended on Mrs.   Zuelika Jane Taylor   , wife of   Newcomb B. Taylor   on the   10th day of   January 1903   , 1........; that there was born to her on said date a   male   child; that said child was living March 4, 1905, and is said to have been named Newcomb Davenport Taylor

Witnesses To Mark:
{

Subscribed and sworn to before me this 21st day of   April, 1905.   , 190......

Notary Public.

BIRTH AFFIDAVIT.
DEPARTMENT OF THE INTERIOR.
COMMISSION TO THE FIVE CIVILIZED TRIBES.

IN RE APPLICATION FOR ENROLLMENT, as a citizen of the   Choctaw   Nation, of   Newcomb Davenport Taylor   , born on the   10th   day of   January   , 1903

Name of Father: Newcomb B. Taylor   Roll 7.W.1074 a citizen of the   Choctaw   Nation.
Name of Mother: Zuleika Taylor   Roll   477 a citizen of the   Choctaw   Nation.

Postoffice   Ardmore I.T.

55

Applications for Enrollment of Choctaw Newborn
Act of 1905 Volume XIX

AFFIDAVIT OF MOTHER.

UNITED STATES OF AMERICA, Indian Territory,
.... DISTRICT.

I, ..., on oath state that I am .... years of age and a citizen by ...., of the .... Nation; that I am the lawful wife of ...., who is a citizen, by .... of the .... Nation; that a .... child was born to me on ...... day of ...., 1......, that said child has been named ...., and was living March 4, 1905.

Witnesses To Mark:
{ ....

Subscribed and sworn to before me this ...... day of ...., 1905.

....
Notary Public.

AFFIDAVIT OF ATTENDING PHYSICIAN OR MID-WIFE.

UNITED STATES OF AMERICA, Indian Territory,
Southern DISTRICT.

I, T. S. Booth, a physician, on oath state that I attended on Mrs. Zuleika Taylor, wife of Newcomb B. Taylor on the 10th day of January, 1903; that there was born to her on said date a .... child; that said child was living March 4, 1905, and is said to have been named Newcomb Davenport Taylor

T.S. Booth M.D.

Witnesses To Mark:
{ JN Coleman
  Wm T. Bogel

Subscribed and sworn to before me this 21st day of January, 1907

John F Easley
Notary Public.

Applications for Enrollment of Choctaw Newborn
Act of 1905   Volume XIX

7-NB-1411.

Muskogee, Indian Territory, June 3, 1905.

Newcomb B. Taylor,
    Ardmore, Indian Territory.

Dear Sir:

    There is enclosed herewith for execution blank affidavit of the attending physician, in the matter of the enrollment of your infant child, Newcomb Davenport Taylor, born January 10, 1903.

    In the application heretofore filed in this office the affidavit of the attending physician was not executed.

    In having the affidavit executed care should be exercised to see that all the names are written in full, as they appear in the body of the affidavit. Signature by mark must be attested by two witnesses. Each affidavit must be executed before a Notary Public and the notarial seal and signature of the officer must be attached to each separate affidavit.

    Respectfully,

VR 3-2.   [sic]

7-NB-1411

Muskogee, Indian Territory, July 28, 1905.

Newcomb Taylor,
    Ardmore, Indian Territory.

Dear Sir:

    Your attention is called to a communication addressed to you by the Commission to the Five Civilized Tribes, under date of June 3, 1905, with which there was inclosed blank affidavit of the attending physician in the matter of the enrollment of your infant child, Newcomb Davenport Taylor, born January 10, 1903.

    In said letter you were advised that in the application heretofore filed in this office, the affidavit of the attending physician was not executed. No reply to this letter has been received.

    You are requested to have the affidavit properly executed and return to this office immediately, as no further action can be taken relative to the enrollment of said child, until the evidence requested is supplied.

Applications for Enrollment of Choctaw Newborn
Act of 1905   Volume XIX

Respectfully,

Commissioner.

---

7 nB
23-1411

Muskogee, Indian Territory, January 26, 1907.

Newcomb B. Taylor,
    Ardmore, Indian Territory.

Dear Sir:

    Receipt is hereby acknowledged of the affidavit of T. S. Booth and the same has been filed in the matter of the enrollment of your child Newcomb Davenport Taylor.

Respectfully,

Commissioner.

Choc New Born 1412
    Hickman Willis
    (Born Sep. 30, 1903)

BIRTH AFFIDAVIT.

DEPARTMENT OF THE INTERIOR.
COMMISSION TO THE FIVE CIVILIZED TRIBES.

IN RE APPLICATION FOR ENROLLMENT, as a citizen of the Choctaw Nation, of Hickman Willis, born on the 30 day of September, 1903

Name of Father: Allen Willis   a citizen of the Choctaw Nation.
Name of Mother: Sistie Willis   a citizen of the Choctaw Nation.

Postoffice   Bethel Ind Teritory[sic]

Applications for Enrollment of Choctaw Newborn
Act of 1905   Volume XIX

AFFIDAVIT OF MOTHER.

UNITED STATES OF AMERICA, Indian Territory, }
Central   DISTRICT.

I, Sistie Willis, on oath state that I am about 25 years of age and a citizen by Blood, of the Choctaw Nation; that I am the lawful wife of Allen Willis, who is a citizen, by Blood of the Choctaw Nation; that a male child was born to me on 30 day of September, 1903; that said child has been named Hickman Willis, and was living March 4, 1905.

Sistie Willis

Witnesses To Mark:
{ Paul Stephens Noah IT
{ Rayson John Bethel I.T.

Subscribed and sworn to before me this 25 day of April, 1905

J H Matthews
Notary Public.

AFFIDAVIT OF ATTENDING PHYSICIAN OR MID-WIFE.

UNITED STATES OF AMERICA, Indian Territory, }
Central   DISTRICT.

I, Allen Willis, a ...., on oath state that I attended on Mrs. Sistie Willis, wife of Allen Willis on the 30 day of Sept, 1903; that there was born to her on said date a male child; that said child was living March 4, 1905, and is said to have been named Hickman Willis

Allen Willis Bethel I.T.

Witnesses To Mark:
{ Rayson John Bethel I.T.
{ Paul Stephens Noah IT

Subscribed and sworn to before me this 25 day of April, 1905

J H Matthews
Notary Public.

Applications for Enrollment of Choctaw Newborn
Act of 1905   Volume XIX

7 - NB 1412

BIRTH AFFIDAVIT.

DEPARTMENT OF THE INTERIOR.
COMMISSION TO THE FIVE CIVILIZED TRIBES.

IN RE APPLICATION FOR ENROLLMENT, as a citizen of the Choctaw Nation, of Hickman Willis, born on the 30 day of Sept, 1903

Name of Father: Allen Willis — a citizen of the Choctaw Nation.
Name of Mother: Sistie Willis — a citizen of the Choctaw Nation.

Postoffice   Bethel Ind Ter

AFFIDAVIT OF MOTHER.

UNITED STATES OF AMERICA, Indian Territory, ... DISTRICT.

I, ..., on oath state that I am .... years of age and a citizen by ...., of the .... Nation; that I am the lawful wife of ...., who is a citizen, by .... of the .... Nation; that a child was born to me on .... day of ...., 1........, that said child has been named ...., and was living March 4, 1905.

Witnesses To Mark:
....
....

Subscribed and sworn to before me this ...... day of ...., 1905.

....
Notary Public.

AFFIDAVIT OF ATTENDING PHYSICIAN OR MID-WIFE.

UNITED STATES OF AMERICA, Indian Territory,
Central   DISTRICT.

we are acquainted with
We, *Isaac Jacob* and *Moses Williams*, on oath state that ~~I attended on~~ Mrs. Sistie Willis, wife of Allen Willis *and that* on *or about* the 30 day of Sept, 1903; that there was born to her on said date a male child; that said child was living March 4, 1905, and is said to have been named Hickman Willis *and that we are not related to the applicant*

Applications for Enrollment of Choctaw Newborn
Act of 1905   Volume XIX

Witnesses To Mark:
{

Isaac Jacob   PO Bethel IT
Morris Williams   Bethel IT

Subscribed and sworn to before me this   31   day of   July   , 1905

J.H. Matthews
Notary Public.

7-1040

Muskogee, Indian Territory, May 5, 1905.

Allen Willis,
    Bethel, Indian Territory.

Dear Sir:

    Receipt is hereby acknowledged of the affidavits of Sistie Willis and Allen Willis to the birth of Hickman Willis, son of Allen and Sistie Willis, September 30, 1903, and the same have been filed with our records as an application for the enrollment of said child.

Respectfully,

Commissioner in Charge.

7--NB--1412

Muskogee, Indian Territory, June 2, 1905.

Allen Willis,
    Bethel, Indian Territory.

Dear Sir:

    Referring to the application for the enrollment of your infant child, Hickman Willis, born September 30, 1903, it is noted from the affidavits heretofore filed in this office that you were the only one in attendance upon your wife at the time of the birth of the applicant.

    In this event it will be necessary that the affidavits of two persons who are disinterested and not related to the applicant, who have actual knowledge of the facts that the child was born, the date of his birth; that he was living on March 4, 1905, and that Sistie Willis is his mother be filed with the Commission.

Applications for Enrollment of Choctaw Newborn
Act of 1905   Volume XIX

This matter should receive your immediate attention as no further action can be taken relative to the enrollment of said child until the Commission is furnished these affidavits.

Respectfully,

[sic]

7-NB-1412

Muskogee, Indian Territory, July 28, 1905.

Allen Willis,
    Bethel, Indian Territory.

Dear Sir:

There is inclosed you herewith joint affidavit to be executed by two witnesses in the matter of the enrollment of your infant child, Hickman Willis, born September 30, 1903.

It is noted in the affidavits heretofore filed in this office, that you were the only one in attendance upon your wife at the time of the birth of the applicant. In this event it will be necessary that the affidavits of two persons who are disinterested and not related to the applicant, and who have actual knowledge of the facts, that the child was born, the date of his birth, that he was living March 4, 1905, and that Sistie Willis is his mother, be filed. The inclosed affidavit is prepared to cover the case.

Please have the same properly executed and return to this office immediately, as no further action can be taken relative to the enrollment of your said child, until the evidence requested is supplied.

Respectfully,

LM 3/28   Commissioner.

Applications for Enrollment of Choctaw Newborn
Act of 1905   Volume XIX

7-NB-1412

Muskogee, Indian Territory, August 8, 1905.

Allen Willis,
    Bethel, Indian Territory.

Dear Sir:

    Receipt is hereby acknowledged of the joint affidavit of Isaac Jacob and Morriw Williams to the birth of Hickman Willis, son of Allen and Sistie Willis, September 30, 1903, and the same has been filed with the records of this office in the matter of the enrollment of said child.

                Respectfully,

                Acting Commissioner.

Choc New Born 1413
    Della Williams
    (Born Feb. 12, 1904)

BIRTH AFFIDAVIT.

DEPARTMENT OF THE INTERIOR.
COMMISSION TO THE FIVE CIVILIZED TRIBES.

IN RE APPLICATION FOR ENROLLMENT, as a citizen of the Choctaw Nation, of Della Williams, born on the 12 day of February, 1904

Name of Father: John Williams   a citizen of the Choctaw Nation.
by intermarriage
Name of Mother: Minnie Williams   a citizen of the Choctaw Nation.

              Postoffice   Nashoba Ind Ter

Applications for Enrollment of Choctaw Newborn
Act of 1905   Volume XIX

AFFIDAVIT OF MOTHER.

UNITED STATES OF AMERICA, Indian Territory, }
Central   DISTRICT.

I, Minnie Williams, on oath state that I am 21 years of age and a citizen by blood, of the Choctaw Nation; that I am the lawful wife of John Williams, who is a citizen, by intermarriage of the Choctaw Nation; that a Female child was born to me on 12 day of February, 1904; that said child has been named Della Williams, and was living March 4, 1905.

            Minnie Williams

Witnesses To Mark:
{ Mary Wheat
{ J.W. Wheat

Subscribed and sworn to before me this 22 day of April, 1905

            F. M. Fuller
            Notary Public.

AFFIDAVIT OF ATTENDING PHYSICIAN OR MID-WIFE.

UNITED STATES OF AMERICA, Indian Territory, }
Central   DISTRICT.

I, Peggy Witt, a mid wife, on oath state that I attended on Mrs. Minnie Williams, wife of John Williams on the 12 day of February, 1904; that there was born to her on said date a Female child; that said child was living March 4, 1905, and is said to have been named Della Williams

              her
            Peggy x Witt
Witnesses To Mark: mark
{ John Williams
{ William Daden

Subscribed and sworn to before me this 22 day of April, 1905

            F. M. Fuller
            Notary Public.

my commission expires April 19th 1908

Applications for Enrollment of Choctaw Newborn
Act of 1905   Volume XIX

Choc New Born 1414
   Gladess Lee Reed
   (Born July 26, 1903)

NEW BORN AFFIDAVIT

No ....

CHOCTAW ENROLLING COMMISSION

IN THE MATTER OF THE APPLICATION FOR ENROLLMENT as a citizen of the Choctaw Nation, of   Glaydis[sic] Reid   born on the 26th [sic] day of   July   190 3

Name of father   M A Reid   a citizen of ———— Nation, final enrollment No. ——   *now Reid*

Name of mother   Inez Turnbull   a citizen of   Choctaw   Nation, final enrollment No.   10677

Matoy I.T.   Postoffice.

AFFIDAVIT OF MOTHER

UNITED STATES OF AMERICA
INDIAN TERRITORY
DISTRICT   Central

I   Inez Turnbull *now Reid*   , on oath state that I am   27   years of age and a citizen by   blood   of the   Choctaw   Nation, and as such have been placed upon the final roll of the   Choctaw   Nation, by the Honorable Secretary of the Interior my final enrollment number being   10677   ; that I am the lawful wife of   M A Reid   , who is a citizen of the   ————   Nation, and as such has been placed upon the final roll of said Nation by the Honorable Secretary of the Interior, his final enrollment number being ——   and that a   Female   child was born to me on the   26th   day of July   190 3; that said child has been named   Gladys Reid   , and is now living.

Inez Turnbull ^ *now* Reid

WITNESSETH:

Must be two witnesses   N J Tolbert
who are citizens   N A Perkins

Applications for Enrollment of Choctaw Newborn
Act of 1905   Volume XIX

Subscribed and sworn to before me this, the 14th day of February, 1905

A.E. Folsom
Notary Public.

My Commission Expires:
Jan 9-1909

Affidavit of Attending Physician or Midwife

UNITED STATES OF AMERICA, }
    INDIAN TERRITORY,
Central   DISTRICT

I, J H Armstrong a Practicing Physician on oath state that I attended on Mrs. Inez Turnbull now Reid wife of M A Reid on the 26th day of July, 1903, that there was born to her on said date a Female child, that said child is now living, and is said to have been named Glaydis Reid

J H Armstrong   M. D.

Subscribed and sworn to before me this the 14th day of February 1905

A.E. Folsom
Notary Public.

WITNESSETH:

Must be two witnesses who are citizens and know the child. { N J Tolbert
N. A. Perkins

We hereby certify that we are well acquainted with J H Armstrong a Physician and know him to be reputable and of good standing in the community.

Must be two citizen witnesses. { N J Tolbert
N.A. Perkins

Applications for Enrollment of Choctaw Newborn
Act of 1905 Volume XIX

BIRTH AFFIDAVIT.

DEPARTMENT OF THE INTERIOR.
COMMISSION TO THE FIVE CIVILIZED TRIBES.

IN RE APPLICATION FOR ENROLLMENT, as a citizen of the Choctaw Nation, of Gladess Lee Reed , born on the 26 day of July , 1903

Name of Father: M A Reed a citizen of the U S Nation.
Name of Mother: Inez (Turnbull) Reed a citizen of the Choctaw Nation.

Postoffice Matoy Ind Ter

AFFIDAVIT OF MOTHER.

UNITED STATES OF AMERICA, Indian Territory, }
Central DISTRICT.

I, Inez (Turnbull) Reed , on oath state that I am 28 years of age and a citizen by blood , of the Choctaw Nation; that I am the lawful wife of M A Reed , who is a citizen, by ——— of the U.S. Nation; that a Female child was born to me on 26 day of July , 1903; that said child has been named Gladess Lee Reed , and was living March 4, 1905.

Inez Turnbull Reid[sic]

Witnesses To Mark:
{

Subscribed and sworn to before me this 29 day of April , 1905

A Denton Phillips
Notary Public.

AFFIDAVIT OF ATTENDING PHYSICIAN OR MID-WIFE.

UNITED STATES OF AMERICA, Indian Territory, }
Central DISTRICT.

I, J H Armstrong , a M. D. , on oath state that I attended on Mrs. Inez Turnbull Reed , wife of M A Reed on the 26 day of July , 1903; that there was born to her on said date a Female child; that said child was living March 4, 1905, and is said to have been named Gladess Lee Reed

J H Armstrong M.D.

Witnesses To Mark:
{

Applications for Enrollment of Choctaw Newborn
Act of 1905   Volume XIX

Subscribed and sworn to before me this   29 day of   April   , 1905

                          A Denton Phillips
                          Notary Public.

Choc New Born 1415
    Raymond Arthur Lawrence
    (Born Feb. 2, 1905)

AFFIDAVIT OF ATTENDING PHYSICIAN OR MIDWIFE

UNITED STATES OF AMERICA
INDIAN TERRITORY
_____DISTRICT

   I,   E R Birdo   a   Physician
on oath state that I attended on Mrs. Sudie Lawrence   wife of Joseph R Lawrence
on the   2nd day of   February   , 190 5 , that there was born to her on said date a   Male child, that said child is now living, and is said to have been named   Raymond Arthur Lawrence

                          E. R. Birdo, M.D.

    Subscribed and sworn to before me this, the   8   day of   March   190 5

WITNESSETH: AJ Burns   Notary Public.
  Must be two witnesses
  who are citizens   Grayson Co Tex
        A F Manning

    We hereby certify that we are well acquainted with_____
a _____ and know _____ to be reputable and of good standing in the community.

        A F Manning

Applications for Enrollment of Choctaw Newborn
Act of 1905   Volume XIX

BIRTH AFFIDAVIT.

DEPARTMENT OF THE INTERIOR.
COMMISSION TO THE FIVE CIVILIZED TRIBES.

IN RE APPLICATION FOR ENROLLMENT, as a citizen of the   Choctaw   Nation, of   Raymond Arthur Lawrence   , born on the 2nd day of February , 1905

Name of Father: Joseph R Lawrence   a citizen of the   Choctaw   Nation.
Name of Mother: Sudie Lawrence   a citizen of the   Choctaw   Nation.

Postoffice   Atoka Ind Tery

AFFIDAVIT OF MOTHER.

UNITED STATES OF AMERICA, Indian Territory,
.... DISTRICT.

I,   Sudie Lawrence   , on oath state that I am   22   years of age and a citizen by   Marriage   , of the   Choctaw   Nation; that I am the lawful wife of   Joseph R Lawrence   , who is a citizen, by Blood   of the   Choctaw   Nation; that a   Male   child was born to me on 2nd day of   February   , 1905; that said child has been named   Raymond Author Lawrence   , and was living March 4, 1905.

Sudie Lawrence

Witnesses To Mark:

Subscribed and sworn to before me this 20   day of   April   , 1905.

JW Jones
Notary Public.

Applications for Enrollment of Choctaw Newborn
Act of 1905   Volume XIX

Choc New Born 1416
    Johnnie Campbell
    (Born April 3, 1904)

DEPARTMENT OF THE INTERIOR,
COMMISSIONER TO THE FIVE CIVILIZED TRIBES.

In the matter of the application for the enrollment as a citizen by blood of the Choctaw Nation..................OF....................

JOHNNIE CAMPBELL...7-N.B.-1416.

BIRTH AFFIDAVIT.

DEPARTMENT OF THE INTERIOR.
COMMISSION TO THE FIVE CIVILIZED TRIBES.

IN RE APPLICATION FOR ENROLLMENT, as a citizen of the Choctaw Nation, of Johnnie Campbell, born on the 3rd day of April, 1904

Name of Father: Ephraim F. Campbell   a citizen of the Choctaw Nation.
Name of Mother: Lucy Campbell   a citizen of the Choctaw Nation.

Postoffice   Peola, Ind. Ter.

AFFIDAVIT OF MOTHER.

UNITED STATES OF AMERICA, Indian Territory,
    Southern   DISTRICT.

    I, Lucy Campbell, on oath state that I am about 35 years of age and a citizen by intermarriage, of the Choctaw Nation; that I am the lawful wife of Ephraim F. Campbell, who is a citizen, by blood of the Choctaw Nation; that a female child was born to me on 3rd day of April, 1904; that said child has been named Johnnie Campbell, and was living March 4, 1905.

                                her
                          Lucy x Campbell
Witnesses To Mark: mark
    { Wm C. Bunn
      Harry C Risteen

Applications for Enrollment of Choctaw Newborn
Act of 1905   Volume XIX

Subscribed and sworn to before me this 2nd day of   May   , 1905

                                        H.C. Miller
                                        Notary Public.

AFFIDAVIT OF ATTENDING PHYSICIAN OR MID-WIFE.

UNITED STATES OF AMERICA, Indian Territory, }
   Southern   DISTRICT.}

      I,   H.P. Lovell   , a physician   , on oath state that I attended on Mrs.   Lucy Campbell   , wife of   Ephraim F. Campbell   on the 3rd   day of   April   , 1904; that there was born to her on said date a   female   child; that said child was living March 4, 1905, and is said to have been named   Johnnie Campbell

                                        H.P. Lovell

Witnesses To Mark:
{

Subscribed and sworn to before me this 2nd day of   May   , 1905

                                        H.C. Miller
                                        Notary Public.

DEPARTMENT OF THE INTERIOR,
COMMISSIONER TO THE FIVE CIVILIZED TRIBES.
Pauls Valley, Indian Territory.
May 24, 1906.

-oOo-

In the matter of the application for the enrollment of Johnnie Easter Campbell as a citizen by blood of the Choctaw Nation.

-oOo-

Lucy Morgan, after being duly sworn, testified as follows:

EXAMINATION BY THE COMMISSIONER

Q State your name, age and post office address? A Lucy Morgan, about thirty-six years old, post office Paoli, Indian Territory.
Q You are a white woman? A Yes, sir.
Q Were you ever the wife of a Choctaw Indian? A Yes, sir.
Q What was the name of that Indian? A Ephraim Campbell?[sic]

Applications for Enrollment of Choctaw Newborn
Act of 1905   Volume XIX

Q Is he dead? A I heard he was dead.
Q Have you married since then? A Yes, sir.
Q What is the name of your husband now? A John Morgan.
Q Is he a white man? A Yes, sir.
Q When were you married to him? A We haven't been married quiet three years.
Q Do you remember what month.[sic]   A   It was about the first of December, I thenk[sic]; we will be married three years in December.
Q You were married in December of what year? A Well, I dont[sic] know; we hven't[sic] been married quite three years.
Q Was that child Johnnie Easter Campbell born after you were married to John Morgan? A Yes, sir.
Q When did you last see Ephraim alive? A I don't remember just how how[sic] long it has been, but I think it was right at the last of July or the first of August.
Q Of what year? A L903[sic].
Q Where were you living at that time? A At Sulphur Springs.
Q Isn't it a fact that you have been separated from Ephriam[sic] Campbell
A Yes, sir; we have been separated.
Q How long have you been separated from him? A I don't know just how long it has been, about a year or two years.
Q Isn't-- at the time you were living with Ephraim Campbell where did you live.[sic]
A Down close to Red River, near Albany?[sic]
Q When did you leave Albany? A It has been three or four years since I have lived at Albany, I reckon.
Q What was your post office address in 1902? A I don't remember.
Q Isn't it a fact that you were living in Dougherty in 1902? A No, sir; I never lived in Dougherty.
Q Didn't you live near Dougherty? A Yes, sir.
Q And that was your post office? A Yes, sir.
Q Did you ever appear before the Commission at the time your post office was Dougherty? A Yes, sir.
Q Where did you appear before the Commission at that time? A I know the name of the place, if I could speak it.
Q Where was your husband at that time? A I don't know where he was at that time?[sic]
Q Isn't it a matter [sic] at that time you were separated from your husband? A No, sir; we were not separated, but I don't know ehere[sic] he was.
Q How soon after that did you see him? A I never saw him any more only that time at Sulphur.
Q How often did you see him at Sulphur? A I never saw him but once.
Q Isn't it a matter of fact that you haven't seen your husband since December, 1902? A I don't know exactly just when it was.
Q How long did you see your husband in 1903? A I don't know just how long I saw him.
Q How often did you see him after December, 1902? A I don't know.
Q And you never saw him any more until in July, 1903? A No, sir.
Q July before this child was born? A Yes, sir.
Q How long have you been living with Mr. Morgan? A About three years?[sic]
Q How long had you known him when you last saw your husband? A Not very long.

Applications for Enrollment of Choctaw Newborn
Act of 1905   Volume XIX

Q How long? A About two or three months.
Q Did you ever apply for this child before now.[sic] A Yes, sir.
Q Where? [sic] Down at Atoka. No it was at Ardmore.
Q When was that, last year? A Yes, sir.
Q Did they refuse to accept the application at that time? A No, sir; they took it alright, but we never heard anything from it.
Q Was Ephriam[sic] Campbell under indictment for something? A Yes, sir.
Q For what? A I don't know just what you would call it.
Q Whisky? A No.
Q Murder? A No, sir.
Q Well, what caused you and him to separate? A He just simply stole a horse and ran away.
Q And what became of him? A I don't know; I heard he was dead.
Q How did he die? A I heard that he was killed by some marshals.
Q Where did you get acquainted with Mr. Morgan? A At Sulphur.
Q How long had he lived there? A I don't know just how long he had lived there.
Q Were you and Ephriam Campbell ever divorced? A No, I just heard that he was dead is the only way.
Q When did you first make up your mind that he was dead? A I made up my mind when I heard he was dead.
Q And in three or four weeks after you heard he was dead you married Morgan? A Yes, sir; some where long there.
Q Did any body see Ephriam Campbell at Sulphur in 1903? A I don't know whether any body saw him or not; he didn't want any body to see him.
Q As a matter of fact you and Ephriam Campbell have not lived together as husband and wife since 1902, have you? A I has been a long time since we kept house together.

Witness excused.

Vester W Rose, stenographer to the Commissioner to the Five Civilized Tribes, states on oath that he reported the proceedings had in the above entitled case and that the above is a true copy of his stenographic notes taken in said case.

Vester W Rose

Subscribed and sworn to before me this the 24th day of May, 1906.

D Conway Lloyd
Notary Public.

Applications for Enrollment of Choctaw Newborn
Act of 1905   Volume XIX

BIRTH AFFIDAVIT.

DEPARTMENT OF THE INTERIOR,
COMMISSIONER TO THE FIVE CIVILIZED TRIBES.

ENROLLMENT OF MINORS. ACT OF CONGRESS, APPROVED APRIL 26, 1906.

IN RE APPLICATION FOR ENROLLMENT, as a citizen of the Choctaw Nation, of Johnnie Easter Campbell, born on the 3 day of April, 1904

Name of Father: Ephraim Campbell   a citizen of the Choctaw Nation.
    Campbell)   by JW
Name of Mother: Lucy Morgan (formerly)   a citizen of the Choctaw Nation.

Tribal enrollment of father Choc bbld #10936 Tribal enrollment of mother Choct I W #143
Father & mother listed on Choc filed Card #3882

Postoffice   Paoli I.T.

AFFIDAVIT OF MOTHER.

UNITED STATES OF AMERICA, Indian Territory, }
Southern   District.   }

I, Lucy Morgan (formerly Campbell), on oath state that I am 36 years of age and a citizen by intermarriage, of the Choctaw Nation; that I ~~am was~~ the lawful wife of Ephraim Campbell, who is a citizen, by blood of the Choctaw Nation; that a female child was born to me on 3rd day of April, 1904, that said child has been named Johnnie Easter Campbell, and was living March 4, 1906.

                                her
                        Lucy x Morgan formerly Campbell
                              mark

WITNESSES TO MARK:
{ J T Hockman
{ Vester W Rose

Subscribed and sworn to before me this 24 day of May, 1906.

                        D Conway Lloyd
                              Notary Public.

Applications for Enrollment of Choctaw Newborn
Act of 1905   Volume XIX

AFFIDAVIT OF ATTENDING PHYSICIAN OR MID-WIFE.

UNITED STATES OF AMERICA, Indian Territory,
Southern   District.

I,   H. P. Lovell   , a   physician   , on oath state that I attended on   Mrs Lucy Morgan (formerly Campbell)   , wife of   Ephraim Campbell   on the   3"   day of   April   , 190 4; that there was born to her on said date a   female child; that said child was living March 4, 1906, and is said to have been named   Johnnie Easter Campbell

H.P. Lovell M.D.

WITNESSES TO MARK:

{

Subscribed and sworn to before me this   24   day of   May   , 1906.

D Conway Lloyd
Notary Public.

United States of America,
 The Indian Territory,
  Southern Judicial District.

DEPARTMENT OF THE INTERIOR,

COMMISSIONER TO THE FIVE CIVILIZED TRIBES.

In the matter of the application for the enrollment of Johnnie Easter Campbell, as a citizen by blood of the Choctaw Nation.

On this day personally appeared before me, the undersigned authority, Lucy Morgan, who, after being first duly sworn, upon her oath deposes and says:

My name is Lucy Morgan. I am about thirty-six years old. My postoffice is Paoli, I.T. I was married to my present husband, John Morgan, during the month of September, 1903. Prior to that time I was the wife of Ephriam Campbell. Ephriam Campbell was a member of the Choctaw Tribe of Indians by blood, and I am enrolled as a member of said tribe of Indians by reason of my marriage to Ephriam Campbell. Ephriam Campbell and myself lived together as husband and wife until sometime during the fall of 1902, when he was charged with horse stealing, and commenced to hid[sic] himself out to keep from being arrested by the officers. I did not see him from that time, sometime during the fall of 1902, until during the month of ~~June~~, *July* 1903. I was living at Sulphur, Chickasaw Nation, Indian Territory, and Ephriam Campbell came to my house where I was living, and stayed part of one night. My remembrance is, he was there on the night of the 9th day of July, 1903. We had intercourse that night, and it was the last time I ever saw him. Something like a month after that, or sometime during the month of August, I was informed by what I considered reliable source that Ephriam

Applications for Enrollment of Choctaw Newborn
Act of 1905 Volume XIX

Campbell had been killed by the officers. Since that time I have not seen or heard of him, and during the following September I married John Morgan. During the month of April, 1904, a child was born to me. It is now living and is named Johnnie Easter Campbellz[sic]. It is the child of Ephriam Campbell and myself, and Ephriam Campbell is the father of said child. I made application for the enrollment of said child during the summer of 1905, being made to the Commissioner at Ardmore, I.T. I again appeared before the representative of the Commissioner on the 24th day of May, 1906, at Pauls Valley and gave my evidence at said time. In my application at Ardmore in 1905 I also gave evidence. I make this statement in additin[sic] to the evidence given on thos different occasions in order to make the matter perfectly clear.

Witnesses to mark
WN Lewis
(Name Illegible)

      her
Lucy x Morgan
      mark

Subscribed and sworn to before me this June 25 1906.

WN Lewis
Notary Public.

Southern District }
Indian Territory }

On this day before me the undersigned authority within and for the Southern District of the Indian Territory, appeared in person W.B. Farris of Davis, I.T. Who being by me first duly sworn deposes and says:

That he was well acquainted with Ephriam Campbell. Have known him ten years or more. I knew him before he married Lucy, now Lucy Morgan, wife of John Morgan.

During the Summer of 1903 I was living in Sulphur, I.T. and Ephriam Campbell's wife, Lucy Campbell, also lived in Sulphur. Ephriam Campbell himself was an outlaw, and was dodging the officers and going from place to place. Lucy Campbell lived between my house and the business part of town, during the Summer referred to, 1903, and I would pass her house on my way to town. One night during that Summer, my recollection is, that it was in July 1903, I passed her house and saw Ephriam Campbell there in the house. I recognized him but as we had some time prior to this, I did not go in and speak to him. But I know it was Ephriam Campbell. I do not know how long he stayed with his wife. He was gone next day and I have never seen him since.

Applications for Enrollment of Choctaw Newborn
Act of 1905   Volume XIX

In September 1903, Lucy Campbell married John Morgan, her present husband.

W B Farris

Subscribed and sworn to before me on this June 25th, 1906.

WN Lewis
Notary Public.

7-NB-1416.
O.L.J.

DEPARTMENT OF THE INTERIOR,
COMMISSIONER TO THE FIVE CIVILIZED TRIBES.

In the matter of the application for the enrollment of Johnnie Campbell as a citizen by blood of the Choctaw Nation.

- DECISION -

It appears from the record herein that on May 2, 1905, application was made to the Commission to the Five Civilized Tribes for the enrollment of Johnnie Campbell as a citizen by blood of the Choctaw Nation under the provisions of the Act of Congress approved March 3, 1905 (33 Stats., 1060).

It further appears from the record herein that said applicant was born on April 3, 1904, and is the daughter of Ephraim F. Campbell whose name appears opposite No. 10936 upon the final roll of citizens by blood of the Choctaw Nation approved by the Secretary of the Interior February 4, 1903, and Lucy Campbell whose name appears opposite No. 143 upon the final roll of citizens by intermarriage of the Choctaw Nation approved by the Secretary of the Interior June 13, 1903, and that said applicant was living on March 4, 1905.

I am, therefore, of the opinion that Johnnie Campbell should be enrolled as a citizen by blood of the Choctaw Nation, under the provisions of the Act of Congress approved March 3, 1905 (33 Stats., 1060), and it is so ordered.

Tams Bixby   Commissioner.

Muskogee, Indian Territory.
FEB 19 1907

Applications for Enrollment of Choctaw Newborn
Act of 1905   Volume XIX

7-NB-1416.

COPY

Muskogee, Indian Territory, February 27, 1907.

Lucy Morgan,
    Paoli, Indian Territory.

Dear Madam:-

    Inclosed herewith you will find a copy of the decision of the Commissioner to the Five Civilized Tribes, rendered February 19, 1907, granting the application for the enrollment of Johnnie Campbell as a citizen by blood of the Choctaw Nation.

    You are further advised that the names of the persons granted in said decision have been placed upon a schedule of citizens by blood of the Choctaw Nation, to be submitted to the Secretary of the Interior for his approval. You will be notified of Departmental action thereon.

    Respectfully,

SIGNED *Tams Bixby*

    Commissioner.

Registered.
Incl. 7-NB-1416.

7-NB-1416.

COPY

Muskogee, Indian Territory, February 27, 1907.

Ledbetter, Bledsoe & Thompson,
    Attorneys at Law,
        Pauls Valley, Indian Territory.

Gentlemen:

    You are hereby notified that the Commissioner to the Five Civilized Tribes on February 19, 1907, rendered his decision granting the application for the enrollment of Johnnie Campbell, as a citizen by blood of the Choctaw Nation.

    You are further advised that the names of the persons granted in said decision have been placed upon a schedule of citizens by blood of the Choctaw Nation, to be submitted to the Secretary of the Interior for his approval. You will be notified of Departmental action thereon.

Applications for Enrollment of Choctaw Newborn
Act of 1905 Volume XIX

Respectfully,

SIGNED *Tams Bixby*

Commissioner.

Registered.
Incl. 7-NB-1416.

7-NB-1416.

COPY

Muskogee, Indian Territory, February 27, 1907.

Mansfield, McMurray & Cornish,
    Attorneys at Law,
        South McAlester, Indian Territory.

Gentlemen:

    Inclosed herewith you will find a copy of the decision of the Commissioner to the Five Civilized Tribes, rendered February 19, 1907, granting the application for the enrollment of Johnnie Campbell as a citizen by blood of the Choctaw Nation.

    You are further advised that the names of the persons granted in said decision have been placed upon a schedule of citizens by blood of the Choctaw Nation, to be submitted to the Secretary of the Interior for his approval. You will be notified of Departmental action thereon.

Respectfully,

SIGNED *Tams Bixby*

Commissioner.

Registered.
Incl. 7-NB-1416.

(The letter below typed as given.)

COPY

Davis, Ind. Ter., June 12th, 1905.

Paul B. Taylor,
    Ardmore, I. T.
Friend Paul:-

    Not knowing the name of the Chief Clerk of the Land Office I will rite you, a few lines and ask you to refer this letter to the proper purson, I am in formed that one Mrs. Lucy Campbell, who is an inter married citizen the wife of Ephram Campbell a

Applications for Enrollment of Choctaw Newborn
Act of 1905   Volume XIX

Chocktaw by blood, and has one child Annie Campbell, who is some 5 years old, and now has another child by her second husband, a Mr Morgan, who is not a cotizen of either of the tribes, has registered the last child as a child of Campbell, and the age of the child is, borne April 1st, 1904 or about then, if this is a fact the matter should be investigated at once and as the Gran-Jury is now in session at Pauls-Valley, you will please examine the records and write me or Albert Rennie Assistant U. S. Attorney at Pauls-Valley, and please write as soon as possible as the G. J. will soon adjourn, I am reliably in formed that this a fact, and the same is worth investigating, and examining the records Morgan has told this to confidential friends. This child is name is Johnie Morgan but is supposed to be enrolled as Johnie Campbell.

Respectfully,
Ed House
Deputy U. S. Marshal.

INDORSED: Indexed   Commission to the Five Tribes.   No. 29644   1905

Received Jun 15 1905.
House, Ed, Davis, I. T. Chickasaw Nation, June 12, 1905.
Desires information relative to application for enrollment of Johnie Morgan alias Johnie Campbell.

C O P Y

Ardmore, Indian Territory, June 13, 1905.

Commission to the Five Civilized Tribes,
   Muskogee, Indian Territory.

Gentlemen:

  There is herewith transmitted, for consideration and appropriate action, letter received at this office from the following named person:

  Ed House, Deputy U. S. Marshal, Davis, Indian Territory.

Respectfully,
Fred T. Marr
Chief Clerk.

CY-13/4

INDORSED: Indexed   Commission to the Five Tribes   No. 29705   1905
Received Jun 15 1905.

Chickasaw Land Office, Ardmore, I. T. June 13, 1905.
Transmits, for appropriate action, letter of Ed House.

Applications for Enrollment of Choctaw Newborn
Act of 1905   Volume XIX

Muskogee, Indian Territory June 19, 1905.

Ed House,
    Deputy U. S. Marshal,
        Davis, Indian Territory.

Dear Sir:

    Receipt is hereby acknowledged of your letter of the 12th inst. addressed to Paul B. Taylor, Ardmore, Indian Territory, which has been referred to this office for reply. In your letter you state "that one Mrs. Luch[sic] Campbell, who is an intermarried citizen, the wife of Ephram[sic] Campbell a Choctaw by blood, and has one child Annie Campbell, who is some 5 years old, and now has another child by her second husband, a Mr. Morgan, who is not a citizen of either of the tribes, has registered the last child as a child of Campbell, "that the child was born April 1st "or about then"; that you have reliable information about this and that the matter is worthy investigation; that Morgan has told this to confidential friends, the child is named Johnie Morgan but is supposed to have been enrolled as Johnie Campbell.

    You desire that the records be examined and information be furnished you relative to the enrollment of this child as you desire to bring the matter before the grand jury now in session at Pauls Valley.

    In reply to your letter you are informed that on May 2, 1905 Lucy Campbell appeared before the Chickasaw Land Office of the Commission at Ardmore, Indian Territory and made application for the enrollment, as a citizen by blood of the Choctaw Nation, of her infant child Johnnie Campbell, born April 3, 1904. At that time she made affidavit that she was about thirty-five years of age and a citizen by blood of the Choctaw Nation intermarriage of the Choctaw Nation and the lawful wife of Ephraim F. Campbell, a citizen by blood; that a female child was born to her on the 3rd day of April 1904, and that said child has been named Johnnie Campbell and was living March 4, 1905. At the same time there was presented the affidavit of H. P. Lovell, a physician, executed May 2, 1905 in which he alleges that he attended Mrs. Lucy Campbell, wife of Ephraim F. Campbell on April 3, 1904; that a female child was born to her on that date and that said child was living March 4, 1905 and is said to have been named Johnnie Campbell.

    The affidavits above referred to were executed on the date given before H. C. Miller, a notary public and an employee of the Commission at the Chickasaw Land Office, Ardmore, Indian Territory. The signature of Lucy Campbell to the affidavit executed by her is signed by mark and her signature is witnesses[sic] by Wn[sic]. C. Bunn and Harry C. Risteen also employees of the Commission at the Chickasaw Land Office.

Applications for Enrollment of Choctaw Newborn
Act of 1905   Volume XIX

There are inclosed you herewith certified copies of the affidavits above referred to and the Commission will thank you for any further information that you may obtain in this matter.

         Respectfully,

               Chairman.

CTD-1.

                   7--NB--1416.

       Muskogee, Indian Territory, June 20, 1905.

Albert Rennie,
  Assistant United States Attorney,
    Pauls Valley, Indian Territory.

Dear Sir:

  The Commission is in receipt of a communication dated June 12, 1905, from Mr. Ed House, Deputy United States Marshal to Paul B. Taylor, Ardmore, Indian Territory, and referred to this office for reply.

  In his letter, Mr. House states that he is in possession of reliable information that Lucy Campbell, an enrolled citizen by intermarriage of the Choctaw Nation, formerly wife of Ephraim F. Campbell, a citizen by blood of the Choctaw Nation and now the wife of a Mr. Morgan, a white man, made application to the Commission for the enrollment of her child, Johnnie Campbell, born April 1, 1904; that the child is by her second husband, Morgan, and is not entitled to enrollment; that the real name of the child is Johnnie Morgan, 'but is supposed to be enrolled as Johnnie Campbell; that the man Morgan has told his confidential friends of this".   Mr. House requests that the records of the Commission be examined and that you be advised in the premises.

  You are informed that the records of the Commission show that on May 2, 1905, Lucy Campbell appeared before the Chickasaw Land Office of the Commission to the Five Civilized Tribes at Ardmore, Indian Territory, and made application for the enrollment of her infant child, Johnnie Campbell, as a citizen by blood of the Choctaw Nation.

  At that time she made affidavit before H. C. Miller, a Notary Public and an employe[sic] of the Chickasaw Land Office, that she was thirty five years of age, a citizen by intermarriage of the Choctaw Nation and the lawful wife of Ephraim F. Campbell a citizen by blood of the Choctaw Nation; that there was born to her on the third day of April, 1904, a female child which has been named Johnnie Campbell and that said child was living on March 4, 1905. The affidavit is signed by mark and is witnessed by Wm. C. Bunn and Harry C. Risteen who are employes[sic] of the Chickasaw Land Office.

Applications for Enrollment of Choctaw Newborn
Act of 1905 Volume XIX

At the same time there was presented the affidavit of H. C. Lovell a physician in which he alleges that he attended upon Mrs. Lucy Campbell, wife of Ephraim F. Campbell, on the third day of April, 1904 and that a female child was born to her on said date; that said child was living on March 4, 1905, and is said to have been named Johnnie Campbell. This affidavit was also executed before H. C. Miller, Notary Public.

There are enclosed you herewith original affidavits above referred to, and the Commission will thank you to advise them of the result of any investigation that may be made of this matter.

When the affidavits have served your purpose kindly return them to this office.

Respectfully,

Chairman.

FVK Enc-1

DEPARTMENT OF JUSTICE.
OFFICE OF
UNITED STATES ATTORNEY,
SOUTHERN DISTRICT OF INDIAN TERRITORY.
Pauls Valley, Ind. Ter. July 15, 1905.

Hon. Tams Bixby,
    Commission to the Five Civilized Tribes.
        Muskogee, I.T.

Honorable Sir:

Re 7---- N B ---1416.

This matter was referred to this office by the Honorable Commission to the Five Civilized Tribes for appropriate action, under date of June 20, 1905.

The investigation of the writer shows, in addition to the roll card information which you are in possession of, that Lucy Campbell was married to John Morgan, a white man, on September 3, 1903; that her Choctaw husband, Ephraim F. Campbell and she had been separated for two or three years, that she did not know his whereabouts, and that she heard he was dead; that when these parties talked of making application for enrollment of Johnnie Campbell, they were told by Robert Morgan, a nephew of John Morgan, not to make the application that it would get them into the penitentiary; that John Morgan took Lucy to Ardmore knowing that she was going before the Commission to make application for enrollment of the child; that he did not go to the land office, but let her go by herself; presumably to hide the fact that she was married again, and she was

Applications for Enrollment of Choctaw Newborn
Act of 1905   Volume XIX

not asked by the "roll clerk" if she had married again, as she swore "I am the lawful wife of Ephraim F. Campbell"; that Robert Morgan told these people recently they they[sic] would certainly ne[sic] caught in the transaction, and that John Morgan advised with Robert Morgan as to whether or not he had better run.

The writer swore out a warrant for the arrest of Lucy Campbell for Perjury based on her sworn statement, "I am the lawful wife of Ephraim f. Campbell," and for the arrest of John Morgan for Subornation of Perjury. It appears that Lucy Campbell was asked "If Ephriam F. Campbell was the father of Johnnie?" only as a preliminary question and was not required to swear to that fact, and such fact does not appear in the affidavit proper.

These parties were arrested at their home in Paoli on yesterday morning. A preliminary examination was held before Hon. William Pfieffer, United States Commission, at Ardmore, with the result that the Honorable Commissioner held Lucy Campbell and discharged John Morgan.

Herewith I return the original affidavit, which this office will require as evidence before the Grand Jury at Ardmore in December, 1905.

                        Respectfully,
                          Albert Rennie,
                        Assistant United States Attorney.

Substitute

7 N B 1416

                    Muskogee, Indian Territory, July 22, 1905.

Albert Rennie,
    Assistant United States Attorney,
        Pauls Valley, Indian Territory.

Dear Sir:

Receipt is hereby acknowledged of your letter of July 15, returning the application for the enrollment of Johnnie Campbell as a citizen by blood of the Choctaw Nation, and stating that Lucy Campbell, the mother of said child, has been arrested for perjury.

You state that the original affidavits returned by you will be required as evidence before the Grand Jury at Ardmore, Indian Territory, in December, 1905.

You are advised that the same will be returned to you on request for the purpose indicated.

Applications for Enrollment of Choctaw Newborn
Act of 1905 Volume XIX

Respectfully,

Commissioner.

7-NB-1416

Received of the Commissioner to the Five Civilized Tribes one copy of the testimony of Lucy Morgan of May 24, 1906, to be used in the matter of the enrollment of her child as a new born citizen of the Choctaw Nation.

Ledbetter, Bledsoe & Thompson

Muskogee, Indian Territory.
June 7, 1906.

7-NB-1416

Muskogee, Indian Territory, June 6, 1906.

Ledbetter, Bledsoe & Thompson,
    Attorneys at Law,
        Pauls Valley, Indian Territory.

Gentlemen:

Receipt is hereby acknowledged of your letter of May 26, 1906, asking for a copy of the testimony in the matter of the application of Lucy Campbell formerly wife of Ephriam Campbell, for the enrollment of her child as a new born citizen of the Choctaw Nation.

In compliance with your request there is inclosed herewith copy of the testimony of Lucy Morgan of May 24, 1906, together with receipt therefor which please sign and return to this office.

Respectfully,

EB 3-6

Commissioner.

Applications for Enrollment of Choctaw Newborn
Act of 1905   Volume XIX

7-3882

Muskogee, Indian Territory, July 19, 1906.

Ledbetter, Bledsoe & Thompson,
    Attorneys at Law,
        Pauls Valley, Indian Territory.

Dear Sirs:

Receipt is hereby acknowledged of your letter of June 28, 190₃, enclosing affidavits of W. B. Farris and Lucy Morgan in the matter of the application for the enrollment of Johnnie Easter Campbell, and [sic] same have been filed in the matter of the enrollment of said child.

        Respectfully,

                Commissioner.

Choc New Born 1417
    Bettie Johnson
    (Born Feb. 24, 1903)

NEW-BORN AFFIDAVIT.

    Number................

...Choctaw Enrolling Commission...

IN THE MATTER OF THE APPLICATION FOR ENROLLMENT, as a citizen of the Choctaw Nation, of Bettie Johnson

born on the 24 day of __Feb__ 190 3

Name of father   Louis Johnson   a citizen of   Choctaw
Nation final enrollment No.   1931
Name of mother   Liley Johnson   a citizen of   Choctaw
Nation final enrollment No.   1932

        Postoffice   Hochatown, I.T.

Applications for Enrollment of Choctaw Newborn
Act of 1905   Volume XIX

AFFIDAVIT OF MOTHER.

UNITED STATES OF AMERICA
INDIAN TERRITORY
Central   DISTRICT

I   Liley Johnson   , on oath state that I am   31   years of age and a citizen by   blood   of the   Choctaw   Nation, and as such have been placed upon the final roll of the   Choctaw   Nation, by the Honorable Secretary of the Interior my final enrollment number being _____ ; that I am the lawful wife of   Louis Johnson   , who is a citizen of the   Choctaw   Nation, and as such has been placed upon the final roll of said Nation by the Honorable Secretary of the Interior, his final enrollment number being _____ and that a   female   child was born to me on the   24   day of   Feb   190 3; that said child has been named   Bettie Johnson   , and is now living.

Liley Johnson

Witnesseth.

Must be two Witnesses who are Citizens.   } Sampson Jefferson
Davis Ebahatubbi

Subscribed and sworn to before me this   21   day of   Jan   190 5

W.A. Shoney
Notary Public.

My commission expires: Jan 10, 1909

AFFIDAVIT OF ATTENDING PHYSICIAN OR MIDWIFE

UNITED STATES OF AMERICA
INDIAN TERRITORY
Central   DISTRICT

I,   Nancy Ibahotubbe   a   Midwife   on oath state that I attended on Mrs.   Liley Johnson   wife of   Louis Johnson   on the   24   day of   Feb   , 190 3 , that there was born to her on said date a   Bettie Johnson[sic]   child, that said child is now living, and is said to have been named   Bettie Johnson

her
Nancy x Ibahotubbe
mark

Subscribed and sworn to before me this, the   21   day of   Jan   190 5

W.A. Shoney   Notary Public.

WITNESSETH:

Must be two witnesses who are citizens   { Sampson Jefferson
Davis Ebahatubbi

Applications for Enrollment of Choctaw Newborn
Act of 1905   Volume XIX

a   We hereby certify that we are well acquainted with
       and know   to be reputable and of good standing in the community.

    Sampson Jefferson   _____

    Davis Ebahatubbi   _____

BIRTH AFFIDAVIT.

DEPARTMENT OF THE INTERIOR.
COMMISSION TO THE FIVE CIVILIZED TRIBES.

IN RE APPLICATION FOR ENROLLMENT, as a citizen of the Choctaw Nation, of Bettie Johnson, born on the 24th day of February, 1903

Name of Father: Louis Johnson   a citizen of the Choctaw Nation.
Name of Mother: Lila Johnson   a citizen of the Choctaw Nation.

    Postoffice   Hochatown Ind Ter

AFFIDAVIT OF MOTHER.

UNITED STATES OF AMERICA, Indian Territory,
Central   DISTRICT.

I, Lila Johnson, on oath state that I am 31 years of age and a citizen by blood, of the Choctaw Nation; that I am the lawful wife of Louis Johnson, who is a citizen, by blood of the Choctaw Nation; that a female child was born to me on 24th day of February, 1903; that said child has been named Bettie Johnson, and was living March 4, 1905.

                          her
                      Lila x Johnson

Witnesses To Mark: mark
  { Davis J Ebahatubbi
  { Marsie Sampson

Subscribed and sworn to before me this 21st day of July, 1905

                W.P. Wilson
                    Notary Public.

My commission expires Dec 1st 1905

Applications for Enrollment of Choctaw Newborn
Act of 1905 Volume XIX

AFFIDAVIT OF ATTENDING PHYSICIAN OR MID-WIFE.

UNITED STATES OF AMERICA, Indian Territory, }
Central   DISTRICT.

    I, Nancy Ibahotubbe, a midwife, on oath state that I attended on Mrs. Lila Johnson, wife of Louis Johnson on the 24th day of February, 1903; that there was born to her on said date a female child; that said child was living March 4, 1905, and is said to have been named Bettie Johnson

                                                                          her
                                              Nancy x Ibahotubbe
Witnesses To Mark: mark
  { Davis J Ebahatubbi
    Marsie Sampson

    Subscribed and sworn to before me this 21st day of July, 1905

                                     W.P. Wilson
                                           Notary Public.
My commission expires Dec 1st 1905

                                                            7--NB--1417

                           Muskogee, Indian Territory, June 2, 1905.

Louis Johnson,
        Hochatown, Indian Territory.

Dear Sir:

    There is enclosed you herewith for execution application for the enrollment of your infant child, Bettie Johnson, born February 24, 1903.

    The affidavits heretofore filed with the Commission show the child was living January 21, 1905. It is necessary, for the child to be enrolled, that she was living on March 4, 1905.

    In having these affidavits executed care should be exercised to see that all names are written in full, as they appear in the body of the affidavit, and in the event that either of the persons signing the affidavit are unable to write, signatures by mark must be attested by two witnesses. Each affidavit must be executed before a Notary Public and the notarial seal and signature of the officer must be attached to each separate affidavit.

    This matter should be given your immediate attention as no further action can be taken relative to the enrollment of this child until the Commission has been furnished these affidavits.

Applications for Enrollment of Choctaw Newborn
Act of 1905   Volume XIX

FVK-Enc-1   Respectfully,   [sic]

7-NB-1417

Muskogee, Indian Territory, July 28, 1905.

Louis Johnson,
    Hochatown, Indian Territory.

Dear Sir:

    Your attention is called to a communication addressed to you by the Commission to the Five Civilized Tribes under date of June 2, 1905, with which there was inclosed application to be executed for the enrollment of your infant child, Bettie Johnson, born February 24, 1903.

    In said letter you were advised that the affidavits heretofore filed with the Commission to the Five Civilized Tribes, show the child was living January 24, 1905, and that it was necessary for her to be enrolled that she was living March 4, 1905. No reply to this letter has been received.

    You should have the affidavits properly executed and return to this office immediately, as no further action can be taken relative to the enrollment of your said child, until the evidence requested is supplied.

Respectfully,

Commissioner.

7-NB-1417

Muskogee, Indian Territory, July 31, 1905.

Louis Johnson,
    Hochatown, Indian Territory.

Dear Sir:

    Receipt is hereby acknowledged of the affidavits of Lila Johnson and Nancy Ibahotubbe to the birth of Bettie Johnson, daughter of Louis and Lila Johnson, and the same have been filed with the records of this office in the matter of the enrollment of said child.

Respectfully,

Commissioner.

Applications for Enrollment of Choctaw Newborn
Act of 1905   Volume XIX

7-NB-1417

                                Muskogee, Indian Territory, August 10, 1905.
Lewis[sic] Johnson,
    Hochotown[sic], Indian Territory.

Dear Sir:

    Receipt is hereby acknowledged of your letter of August 4, 1905, asking if the enrollment of your child Bettie Johnson has been received.

    In reply to your letter you are advised that the affidavits to the birth of Bettie Johnson which were forwarded with office letter of July 28, 1905, have been returned and filed with the record in the matter of her application for enrollment as a citizen by blood of the Choctaw Nation. In event further evidence is necessary to enable this office to determine her right to enrollment you will be advised.

                            Respectfully,

                                              Acting Commissioner.

Choc New Born 1418
    Nancy S. Patterson
    (Born Sep. 26, 1904)

NEW BORN AFFIDAVIT

No _____

CHOCTAW ENROLLING COMMISSION

IN THE MATTER OF THE APPLICATION FOR ENROLLMENT as a citizen of the Choctaw Nation, of   Nancy S. Patterson   born on the 26 day of September 190 4

Name of father   E.L. Patterson   a citizen of   non   Nation,
final enrollment No. ———   *ne Jefferson*

Name of mother   Isabelle Patterson   a citizen of   Choctaw   Nation,
final enrollment No.   14738

Applications for Enrollment of Choctaw Newborn
Act of 1905 Volume XIX

Page I.T.   Postoffice.

AFFIDAVIT OF MOTHER

UNITED STATES OF AMERICA
    INDIAN TERRITORY
DISTRICT   Central

I   Isabelle Patterson ^ *(nee Jefferson)* *(deceased)*, on oath state that I am 21 years of age and a citizen by   blood   of the   Choctaw   Nation, and as such have been placed upon the final roll of the   Choctaw   Nation, by the Honorable Secretary of the Interior my final enrollment number being   14738 ; that I am the lawful wife of   E.L. Patterson , who is a citizen of the   non   Nation, and as such has been placed upon the final roll of said Nation by the Honorable Secretary of the Interior, his final enrollment number being   — and that a   female   child was born to me on the   26   day of   September   190 4; that said child has been named   Nancy S Patterson , and is now living.

                                                                   his

WITNESSETH: Isabelle Patterson x   *(deceased)*
Must be two witnesses { Charles T Perry   mark
who are citizens   { Israel Jefferson   *by E.L. Patterson*

Subscribed and sworn to before me this, the 16 day of   Feb , 190 5

                                  James Bower
                                              Notary Public.

My Commission Expires:
    Sept 23 - 1907

Affidavit of Attending Physician or Midwife

UNITED STATES OF AMERICA,
    INDIAN TERRITORY,
Central   DISTRICT

I,   J.N. Daily   a   Physician   on oath state that I attended on Mrs. Isabelle Patterson   wife of E.L. Patterson   on the   26 day of   September , 190 4, that there was born to her on said date a   female   child, that said child is now living, and is said to have been named   Nancy S Patterson

                                J.N. Daily   M. D.

Subscribed and sworn to before me this the   23rd day of   Feby   1905

                              (Name Illegible)
                                        Notary Public.

Applications for Enrollment of Choctaw Newborn
Act of 1905   Volume XIX

WITNESSETH:

Must be two witnesses who are citizens and know the child. { Charles T Perry / Israel Jefferson

We hereby certify that we are well acquainted with J N Daily a Physician and know him to be reputable and of good standing in the community.

Must be two citizen witnesses. { Charles T Perry / Israel Jefferson

BIRTH AFFIDAVIT.

DEPARTMENT OF THE INTERIOR.
COMMISSION TO THE FIVE CIVILIZED TRIBES.

IN RE APPLICATION FOR ENROLLMENT, as a citizen of the Choctaw Nation, of Nancy S Patterson, born on the 26th day of September, 1904

Name of Father: E.L. Patterson   a citizen of the ————Nation.
Name of Mother: Isabelle Patterson (Deceased)   a citizen of the   Choctaw   Nation.

Postoffice   Page, Ind Ter

AFFIDAVIT OF MOTHER.

UNITED STATES OF AMERICA, Indian Territory, DISTRICT.

I, W. R. Chapman, on oath state that I ~~am~~ *was acquainted with* ~~years of age and a citizen by~~, ~~of the~~ *Isabelle Patterson during her lifetime* ~~Nation~~; that ~~I am~~ *she was* the lawful wife of E.L. Patterson ~~, who is a citizen, by~~ ~~of the~~ ~~————Nation~~; that a female child was born to ~~me~~ *her* on 26th day of September, 1904; that said child has been named Nancy S. Patterson, and was living March 4, 1905.

W.R. Chapman

Witnesses To Mark:

Subscribed and sworn to before me this 17 day of June, 1905.

E W Moore
Notary Public.

Applications for Enrollment of Choctaw Newborn
Act of 1905 Volume XIX

BIRTH AFFIDAVIT.

DEPARTMENT OF THE INTERIOR.
COMMISSION TO THE FIVE CIVILIZED TRIBES.

IN RE APPLICATION FOR ENROLLMENT, as a citizen of the Choctaw Nation, of Nancy S Patterson, born on the 26th day of September, 1904

Name of Father: E.L. Patterson a citizen of the ———Nation.
Name of Mother: Isabelle Patterson (Deceased) a citizen of the Choctaw Nation.

Postoffice Page, Ind Ter

AFFIDAVIT OF MOTHER.

UNITED STATES OF AMERICA, Indian Territory, } DISTRICT.

I, Marthey Davis, on oath state that I ~~am~~ *was acquainted with* ~~years of age and a citizen by~~, ~~of the~~ *Isabelle Patterson during her lifetime* ~~Nation~~; that ~~I am~~ *she was* the lawful wife of E.L. Patterson, ~~who is a citizen, by~~ ~~of the~~ ~~Nation~~; that a female child was born to ~~me~~ *her* on 26th day of September, 1904; that said child has been named Nancy S. Patterson, and was ~~said to be~~ living March 4, 1905.

              her
           Marthey x Davis
Witnesses To Mark: mark
{ E.W. Moore
{ *(Name Illegible)*

Subscribed and sworn to before me this 20 day of June, 1905

         E W Moore
          Notary Public.

AFFIDAVIT OF ATTENDING PHYSICIAN OR MID-WIFE.

UNITED STATES OF AMERICA, Indian Territory, } DISTRICT.

I, J.N. Daily, a physician, on oath state that I attended on Mrs. Isabelle Patterson, wife of E.L. Patterson on the 26th day of September, 1904; that there was born to her on said date a female child; that said child was ~~said to be~~ living March 4, 1905, and is said to have been named Nancy S Patterson

          Dr. J.N. Daily

Applications for Enrollment of Choctaw Newborn
Act of 1905   Volume XIX

Witnesses To Mark:

Subscribed and sworn to before me this   20   day of   June   , 1905

          E W Moore
            Notary Public.

O. J. M. BREWER
GENERAL MERCHANDISE
AND
...LIVE STOCK...

HEAVENER, I.T.   June 22"   190 5

I James T McDaniel, on oath state I was acquainted with Isabelle Patterson during her lifetime, that she was the lawful wife of E L Patterson, that a female child was born to her on the 26" day of September 1904, that said child has been named Nancy S Patterson and was living Mch 4 - 1905

          J.T. McDaniel

Subscribed and sworn to before me this the 22" day of June 1905

         E.W. Moore
          Notary Public.

My Com expire Mch 6 - 1906

Applications for Enrollment of Choctaw Newborn
Act of 1905   Volume XIX

7 NB 1418

Muskogee, Indian Territory, May 20, 1905.

Elic L. Patterson,
    Heavener, Indian Territory.

Dear Sir:

    Receipt is hereby acknowledged of your affidavit and the affidavit of John R. Fox to the death of your daughter Nancy S. Patterson which occurred March 8, 1905, and the same have been filed with our records in the matter of the enrollment of said child

    Respectfully,

    Chairman.

7-NB-1418.

Muskogee, Indian Territory, June 3, 1905.

E. L. Patterson,
    Page, Indian Territory.

Dear Sir:

    There are enclosed you herewith for execution affidavits, in the matter of the enrollment of your infant child, Nancy S. Patterson, born September 26, 1904.

    The affidavit of the physician, heretofore filed in this office, shows that the child was living on February 16, 1904. It is necessary, for the child to be enrolled, that she was living on March 4, 1905.

    It is also noted that Isabelle Patterson, the mother of the applicant, is dead. It will, therefore, be necessary that you secure the affidavits of two persons, who are disinterested and not related to the applicant, who have actual knowledge of the facts that the child was born, the date of her birth; that she was living on March 4, 1905, and that Isabelle Patterson was her mother, for which purpose blanks are enclosed.

    This matter should receive your immediate attention, as no further action can be taken until these affidavits are filed with the Commission.

    Respectfully,

    Commissioner in Charge.

Applications for Enrollment of Choctaw Newborn
Act of 1905   Volume XIX

7 NB 1418

Muskogee, Indian Territory, June 29, 1905.

E. L. Patterson,
    Page, Indian Territory.

Dear Sir:

Receipt is hereby acknowledged of the affidavits of J. T. McDaniel, Marthy Davis, Dr. J. N. Dailey and W. R. Chapman, to the birth of Nancy S. Patterson, daughter of E. L. and Isabelle Patterson, September 26, 1904, and the same have been filed with our records in the matter of the enrollment of said child.

Respectfully,

Chairman.

Choc New Born 1419
    Floyd Rosenthal
    (Born Aug. 12, 1904)

    Died prior to March 4, 1905.

    No. 1 hereon dismissed under order
      of the Commissioner to the
      Five Civilized Tribes of
      July 18, 1905.

    Notice of decision forwarded
      applicant's father Aug. 23, 1905.

Applications for Enrollment of Choctaw Newborn
Act of 1905 Volume XIX

NEW-BORN AFFIDAVIT.

Number 3845

...Choctaw Enrolling Commission...

IN THE MATTER OF THE APPLICATION FOR ENROLLMENT, as a citizen of the Choctaw Nation, of Floyd Rosenthal

born on the 12th day of August 1904

Name of father   Jacob Rosenthal   a citizen of The Choctaw Nation
Nation final enrollment No. 3846
Name of mother   Birdie Rosenthal   a citizen of Choctaw
Nation final enrollment No. not required

Postoffice   Spencerville I.T.

AFFIDAVIT OF MOTHER.

UNITED STATES OF AMERICA
INDIAN TERRITORY
Central   DISTRICT

I   Birdie Rosenthal   , on oath state that I am 21 years of age and a citizen by Intermarriage of the Choctaw Nation Nation, and as such have *not yet* been placed upon the final roll of the Choctaw Nation, by the Honorable Secretary of the Interior my final enrollment number being *not yet read* ; that I am the lawful wife of Jacob Rosenthal , who is a citizen of the Choctaw Nation, and as such has been placed upon the final roll of said Nation by the Honorable Secretary of the Interior, his final enrollment number being 3846 and that a Male child was born to me on the 12th day of August 1904; that said child has been named Floyd Rosenthal , and is now *Dead* ~~living~~.

Witnesseth.   Birdie Rosenthal

Must be two Witnesses who are Citizens.   } (Name Illegible) x his mark
                                            Charley Thomas

Subscribed and sworn to before me this 11th day of February 1905

Fred Everett
Notary Public.
Cent. Jud. Dist.
Ind. Ter.

My commission expires:
Dec 5th 1906

Applications for Enrollment of Choctaw Newborn
Act of 1905   Volume XIX

It appearing from the within affidavits that Floyd Rosenthal, born August 12, 1904, for whose enrollment as a citizen by blood of the Choctaw Nation, application was made under the provisions of the Act of Congress approved March 3, 1905 (33 Stats., 1071), died prior to March 4, 1905, it is hereby ordered that the application for the enrollment of said Floyd Rosenthal as a citizen by blood of the Choctaw Nation be dismissed.

                              Tams Bixby
                                      Commissioner.

        Muskogee, Indian Territory.
            AUG 23 1905

AFFIDAVIT OF ATTENDING PHYSICIAN OR MIDWIFE

UNITED STATES OF AMERICA
INDIAN TERRITORY
   Central   DISTRICT

    I,   Dr T.D. Shannon   a   Practicing Physician on oath state that I attended on Mrs. Birdie Rosenthal   wife of   Jacob Rosenthal on the 12th day of August, 190 4, that there was born to her on said date a   male   child, that said child is now living *Dead*, and is said to have been named   Floyd Rosenthal

                                    T.D. Shannon   M.D.

WITNESSETH:
Must be two witnesses who are citizens and know the child.
{ Charley Thomas
  (Name Illegible) x his mark

                Subscribed and sworn to before me this, the   11th day of   February   190 5

                                  Fred Everett   Notary Public.
                                  Central Dist. I.T.

    We hereby certify that we are well acquainted with   T D Shannon a   Physician   and know   him   to be reputable and of good standing in the community.

                                      { Charley Thomas
                                        (Name Illegible) x his mark

Applications for Enrollment of Choctaw Newborn
Act of 1905   Volume XIX

7-NB-1419

COPY

Muskogee, Indian Territory, August 23, 1905.

Jacob Rosenthal,
    Spencerville, Indian Territory.

Dear Sir:

    You are hereby advised that it appearing from the record of this office that your child, Floyd Rosenthal died prior to March 4, 1905, the Commissioner to the Five Civilized Tribes, on August 23, 1905, dismissed the application for the enrollment of said child as a citizen by blood of the Choctaw Nation.

                                Respectfully,
                                SIGNED
                                Tams Bixby
                                Commissioner.

7-NB-1419

COPY

Muskogee, Indian Territory, August 23, 1905.

Mansfield, McMurray & Cornish,
    Attorneys for Choctaw and Chickasaw Nations,
        South McAlester, Indian Territory.

Gentlemen:

    You are hereby advised that it appearing from the records of this office that Floyd Rosenthal died prior to March 4, 1905, the Commissioner to the Five Civilized Tribes on August 23, 1905, dismissed the application for the enrollment of said child as a citizen by blood of the Choctaw Nation.

                                Respectfully,
                                SIGNED
                                  Tams Bixby
                                Commissioner.

Applications for Enrollment of Choctaw Newborn
Act of 1905   Volume XIX

Choc New Born 1420
    Betsey Green
    (Born Oct. 25, 1904)

BIRTH AFFIDAVIT.

DEPARTMENT OF THE INTERIOR.
COMMISSION TO THE FIVE CIVILIZED TRIBES.

IN RE APPLICATION FOR ENROLLMENT, as a citizen of the Choctaw Nation, of Betsey Green, born on the 25th day of October, 1904

Name of Father: Silas Folsom   a citizen of the Choctaw Nation.
Name of Mother: Ida Green   *Roll 15002*   a citizen of the Choctaw Nation.

Postoffice   Cabiness I.T.

AFFIDAVIT OF MOTHER.

UNITED STATES OF AMERICA, Indian Territory,
.... DISTRICT.

I, ..., on oath state that I am .... years of age and a citizen by ...., of the .... Nation; that I am the lawful wife of ...., who is a citizen, by .... of the .... Nation; that a .... child was born to me on ...... day of ...., 1......, that said child has been named ...., and was living ~~March 4, 1905~~.

Witnesses To Mark:
  { ....
    ....

Subscribed and sworn to before me this ...... day of ...., 1905.

....
Notary Public.

AFFIDAVIT OF ATTENDING PHYSICIAN OR MID-WIFE.

UNITED STATES OF AMERICA, Indian Territory,
  Central   DISTRICT.

I, ..., a midwife, on oath state that I attended on M~~iss~~. Ida Green, wife of ——— on the 25 day of October, 1904;

Applications for Enrollment of Choctaw Newborn
Act of 1905   Volume XIX

that there was born to her on said date a   female   child; that said child was living March 4, 1905, and is said to have been named Betsey Green

                                              her
                              Susan x Brown
Witnesses To Mark: mark
  { Ben Alberson
    Levi Orphan

      Subscribed and sworn to before me this   26   day of   Jany   , 1905

        Commission expires May 11 1909   WG Weimer
                                            Notary Public.

BIRTH AFFIDAVIT.
DEPARTMENT OF THE INTERIOR.
COMMISSION TO THE FIVE CIVILIZED TRIBES.

      IN RE APPLICATION FOR ENROLLMENT, as a citizen of the   Choctaw   Nation, of Betsey Green   , born on the   25   day of   October   , 1904

Name of Father: Silas Folsom   a citizen of the   Choctaw   Nation.
Name of Mother: Ida Green   a citizen of the   Chickasaw   Nation.

                     Postoffice   Cabiness I.T.

                     AFFIDAVIT OF MOTHER.

UNITED STATES OF AMERICA, Indian Territory, }
     Central   **DISTRICT.**

      I,   Ida Green   , on oath state that I am   32   years of age and a citizen by blood   , of the   Chickasaw   Nation; that I am *not* the lawful wife of   Silas Folsom   , who is a citizen, by blood   of the   Choctaw   Nation; that a Female   child was born to me on 25th day of   October   , 1904; that said child has been named   Betsey Green   , and was living March 4, 1905.
                                              her
                                   Ida x Green
Witnesses To Mark: mark
  { Lake Collins
    OL Johnson

      Subscribed and sworn to before me this   28   day of   April   , 1905

                                     OL Johnson
                                       Notary Public.

Applications for Enrollment of Choctaw Newborn
Act of 1905   Volume XIX

AFFIDAVIT OF ATTENDING PHYSICIAN OR MID-WIFE.

UNITED STATES OF AMERICA, Indian Territory,
   Central   DISTRICT.

I, Susan Brown, a midwife, on oath state that I attended on M~~iss~~. Ida Green, wife of Silas Folsom on the 25 day of October, 1904; that there was born to her on said date a female child; that said child was living March 4, 1905, and is said to have been named Betsey Green

Witnesses To Mark:

Subscribed and sworn to before me this ...... day of ...., 1905.

Notary Public.

DEPARTMENT OF THE INTERIOR,
COMMISSION TO THE FIVE CIVILIZED TRIBES.
SOUTH McALESTER, IND. TER. APRIL ~~25, 19~~05
28

In the matter of the application for the enrollment of Betsey Green as a citizen by blood of the Chickasaw Nation.

Ida Green being first duly sworn testifies as follows:

EXAMINATION BY THE COMMISSION:

Q What is your name? A Ida Green.
Q How old are you? A Thirty-two.
Q What is your post office address? A Cabiness.
Q You have this day made application for your child Betsey Green; when was she born? A 25th day of October 1904.
Q Was she living on March 4, 1905? A Yes, sir.
Q Who is the father of this child, Betsey Green? A Silas Folsom.
Q Of what nation is he a citizen? A Choctaw.
Q Of what nation are you a citizen? A Chickasaw.
Q In case it should be determined that this child is entitled to be enrolled in either the Choctaw or Chickasaw Nation in which nation do you desire to have her enrolled? A Chickasaw.
                    Witness excused.

Applications for Enrollment of Choctaw Newborn
Act of 1905 Volume XIX

  Chas. T. Difendafer being first duly sworn states that the above and foregoing is a full, true and correct transcript of his stenographic notes taken in said cause on said date.

Chas. T. Difendafer

Subscribed and sworn to before me this 29th day of April 1905.

OL Johnson
Notary Public.

7-NB-1420.

Muskogee, Indian Territory, June 3, 1905.

Ida Green,
  Cabiness, Indian Territory.

Dear Madam:

  There is enclosed herewith for execution blank affidavit of the attending midwife, in the matter of the enrollment of your infant child, Betsey Green, born October 25, 1904.

  In the application heretofore filed in this office the affidavit of the attending midwife was not executed.

  In having the affidavit executed care should be exercised to see that all the names are written in full, as they appear in the body of the affidavit. Signature by mark must be attested by two witnesses. Each affidavit must be executed before a Notary Public and the notarial seal and signature of the officer must be attached to each separate affidavit.

Respectfully,

VR 3-1.   [sic]

<u>Choc New Born 1421</u>
  Preston Lee Black
  (Born Sep. 2, 1904)

Applications for Enrollment of Choctaw Newborn
Act of 1905   Volume XIX

DEPARTMENT OF THE INTERIOR
COMMISSION TO THE FIVE CIVILIZED TRIBES.

IN RE Application for the enrollment of Preston Lee Black as a citizen by blood of the Choctaw Nation.

STATEMENT OF MOTHER.

The physician, Dr. Cluckler, who attended me upon the birth of Preston Lee Black, resides in the Choctaw Nation. His affidavit in support of this application will be supplied as soon as practicable.

Fannie Black

NEW-BORN AFFIDAVIT.

Number..................

...Choctaw Enrolling Commission...

IN THE MATTER OF THE APPLICATION FOR ENROLLMENT, as a citizen of the Choctaw Nation, of Preston Lee Black

born on the 2nd day of Sept 190 4

Name of father   Thomas Black   a *non* citizen of   Choctaw
Nation final enrollment No.   ——
Name of mother   Fannie Bee   a citizen of   Choctaw
Nation final enrollment No.   9138

Postoffice   Hartshorne, I.T.

AFFIDAVIT OF MOTHER.

UNITED STATES OF AMERICA
INDIAN TERRITORY
   Central   DISTRICT

I   Fannie Black (*nee Bee*)   , on oath state that I am 28 years of age and a citizen by blood of the Choctaw Nation, and as such have been placed upon the final roll of the Choctaw Nation, by the Honorable Secretary of the Interior my final enrollment number being 9138 ; that I am the lawful wife of Thomas Black , who is a *non* citizen of the Choctaw Nation, and as such has *not* been placed upon the final roll of said Nation by the Honorable Secretary of the Interior, his final enrollment number being —— and that a Male child was born to me

Applications for Enrollment of Choctaw Newborn
Act of 1905 Volume XIX

on the 2nd day of September 190 4; that said child has been named Preston Lee Black , and is now living.

Fannie Black (nee Bee)

Witnesseth.
Must be two Witnesses who are Citizens. } *(Name Illegible)*
(Name Illegible)

Subscribed and sworn to before me this 16th day of Jan 190 5

Wm J Hulsey
Notary Public.

My commission expires: 1908

AFFIDAVIT OF ATTENDING PHYSICIAN OR MIDWIFE

UNITED STATES OF AMERICA
INDIAN TERRITORY
Central DISTRICT

I, W.H. Cleckler a physician on oath state that I attended on Mrs. Fannie Black wife of Thomas Black on the 2nd day of Sept , 190 4 , that there was born to her on said date a male child, that said child is now living, and is said to have been named Preston Lee Black

W.H. Cleckler *m.D.*

Subscribed and sworn to before me this, the 16th day of January 190 5

Wm J Hulsey Notary Public.

WITNESSETH:
Must be two witnesses who are citizens { William Bee
JD Chastain

We hereby certify that we are well acquainted with W.H. Cluckler a physician and know him to be reputable and of good standing in the community.

William Bee

JD Chastain

Applications for Enrollment of Choctaw Newborn
Act of 1905   Volume XIX

BIRTH AFFIDAVIT.

DEPARTMENT OF THE INTERIOR.
COMMISSION TO THE FIVE CIVILIZED TRIBES.

IN RE APPLICATION FOR ENROLLMENT, as a citizen of the   Choctaw   Nation, of Preston Lee Black   , born on the 2nd day of   September   , 1904

Name of Father: Thomas Black   ~~a~~ non citizen of the   ———   Nation.
Name of Mother: Fannie Black   a citizen of the   Choctaw   Nation.

Postoffice   Lone Grove I.T.

AFFIDAVIT OF MOTHER.

UNITED STATES OF AMERICA, Indian Territory,
    Southern   DISTRICT.

I,   Fannie Black   , on oath state that I am   28   years of age and a citizen by blood   , of the   Choctaw   Nation; that I am the lawful wife of   Thomas Black   , who is a citizen, ~~by~~ .... of the   U.S.   ~~Nation~~; that a   male   child was born to me on 2nd day of   September   , 1904; that said child has been named Preston Lee Black   , and was living March 4, 1905.

Fannie Black

Witnesses To Mark:
{

Subscribed and sworn to before me this 1st day of   May   , 1905

T. L. Kelley
Notary Public.

(The affidavit below typed as given.)

United States of America
Southern Dist Ind Ter.
                Department of Interior
Commission to The Five Civilized Tribes
I - J E McCarty of Lone Grove Ind Ter. State that I am personly accuainted with Thomas Black and Fannie Black and I know that they are the Father and Mother of Preston Lee Black and state on the (4) Forth day of March - 1905 That the said Preston Lee Black was liveing and is liveing at the present date.

Applications for Enrollment of Choctaw Newborn
Act of 1905   Volume XIX

J E McCarty

United States Southern Dist
Ind. Ter.

Be It Know That on this (8) Eighth day of June - 1905 Before me the undersigned Notary Public in and for the Southern Dist Ind Ter personly appeared J E McCarty to me known to be the person named in and whose name is signed to the within and foregoing instrument and acknowledged that he executed the same on the day and year therein mentioned

W W Winans
Notary Public

Term expires Jan 20-1909.

(The affidavit below typed as given.)

United States }
Southern Dist }
Ind Ter. }

Department of Interior
Commision of the five Civilized Tribes

I - J N Cummings of Lone Grove Ind Ter state that I am personly accuainted with Thomas Black and Fannie Black and I know that they are the Father and Mother of Preston Lee Black and state on the (4) Fourth day of March 1905 that the said Preston Lee Black was liveing and is liveing at the present date.

J. N. Cumming

Subscribed and sworn to before me this (8) Eighth day June 1905

W W Winans
Notary Public

My term expires Jan 20-1909

Applications for Enrollment of Choctaw Newborn
Act of 1905 Volume XIX

BIRTH AFFIDAVIT.

DEPARTMENT OF THE INTERIOR.
COMMISSION TO THE FIVE CIVILIZED TRIBES.

IN RE APPLICATION FOR ENROLLMENT, as a citizen of the Choctaw Nation, of Preston Lee Black, born on the 2 day of Sept, 1904

Name of Father: Thomas Black   a citizen of the U.S. ~~Nation~~.
Name of Mother: Fannie Black Roll 9138   a citizen of the Choctaw Nation.
  nee Bee

Postoffice Lonegrove I.T.

AFFIDAVIT OF MOTHER.

UNITED STATES OF AMERICA, Indian Territory,
.... DISTRICT.

I, ..., on oath state that I am .... years of age and a citizen by ...., of the .... Nation; that I am the lawful wife of ...., who is a citizen, by .... of the .... Nation; that a .... child was born to me on ...... day of ...., 1......, that said child has been named ...., and was living March 4, 1905.

Witnesses To Mark:
  ....
  ....

Subscribed and sworn to before me this ...... day of ...., 1905.

....
Notary Public.

AFFIDAVIT OF ATTENDING PHYSICIAN OR MID-WIFE.

UNITED STATES OF AMERICA, Indian Territory,
  Central   DISTRICT.

I, W H Cleckler, a physician, on oath state that I attended on Mrs. Fannie Black, wife of Thomas Black on the 2^d day of Sept, 1904; that there was born to her on said date a male child; that said child was living March 4, 1905, and is said to have been named Preston Lee Black

W H Cleckler

Applications for Enrollment of Choctaw Newborn
Act of 1905   Volume XIX

Witnesses To Mark:
{

    Subscribed and sworn to before me this   19th   day of   June   , 1905

(Name Illegible)
Notary Public.

My term expires Jan 7-1908

Muskogee, Indian Territory, May 6, 1905.

Thomas Black,
    Lonegrove, Indian Territory.

Dear Sir:

    Receipt is hereby acknowledged of the affidavit of Fannie Black to the birth of Preston Lee Black, son of Thomas and Fannie Black, September 2, 1904.

    It is stated in the affidavit of the mother that she is a citizen by blood of the Choctaw Nation. If this is correct you are requested to state the name under which she was enrolled, the names of her parents, and if she has selected an allotment of the lands of the Choctaw or Chickasaw Nation please give her roll number as it appears upon her allotment certificate.

    Respectfully,

Commissioner in Charge.

7-NB-1421.

Muskogee, Indian Territory, June 2, 1905.

Thomas Black,
    Lone Grove, Indian Territory.

Dear Sir:

    There is enclosed you herewith for execution blank affidavit of the attending physician, in the matter of the enrollment of your infant child, Preston Lee Black.

    The affidavit of the attending physician, W. H. Clickler[sic], heretofore filed in this office, shows that the child was living January 16, 1905. It is necessary, for the enrollment of the child, that he was living on March 4, 1905.

    In having the affidavit executed care should be exercised to see that all names are written in full, as they appear in the body of the affidavit. Signature by mark must be

Applications for Enrollment of Choctaw Newborn
Act of 1905 Volume XIX

attested by two witnesses. Each affidavit must be executed before a Notary Public and the notarial seal and signature of the officer must be attached to each separate affidavit.

Respectfully,

VR 2-14.   Commissioner in Charge.

7-NB-1421.

Muskogee, Indian Territory, June 14, 1905.

Thomas Black,
    Lone Grove, Indian Territory.

Dear Sir:

    Receipt is hereby acknowledged of the affidavits of J. E. McCarty and J. N. Cummings to the birth of Preston Lee Black, son of Thomas and Fannie Black. These affidavits fail to state the date of the applicant's birth.

    If you cannot secure the physician's affidavit to the birth of this child, it will be necessary for you to file in this office, the affidavits of two persons who are disinterested and not related to the applicant, who have actual knowledge of the facts; that the child was born, the <u>date</u> of his birth, that he was living on March 4, 1905, and that Fannie Black is his mother.

Respectfully,

Chairman.

---

7 NB 1421

Muskogee, Indian Territory, June 24, 1905.

Thomas Black,
    Lonegrove, Indian Territory.

Dear Sir:

    Receipt is hereby acknowledged of the affidavit of W. H. Cleckler to the birth of Preston Lee Black, son of Thomas and Fannie Black, September 2, 1904, and the same has been filed with our records in the matter of the enrollment of said child.

Respectfully,

Chairman.

Applications for Enrollment of Choctaw Newborn
Act of 1905   Volume XIX

Choc. New Born 1422
    Willie R. E. Coker
    (Born Feb. 7, 1903)

NEW BORN AFFIDAVIT

No ....

CHOCTAW ENROLLING COMMISSION

IN THE MATTER OF THE APPLICATION FOR ENROLLMENT as a citizen of the Choctaw Nation, of   Willie R. E. Coker   born on the 7th day of   Feby   190 3

Name of father   T[sic]. C. Coker   a citizen of   United States   ~~Nation~~,
final enrollment No. ....   (ne Herron)
Name of mother   Lula Coker   a citizen of   Choctaw   Nation,
final enrollment No.   7449

Celestine I.T.   Postoffice.

AFFIDAVIT OF MOTHER

UNITED STATES OF AMERICA }
    INDIAN TERRITORY
DISTRICT   Central

I   Lula Coker   (ne Herron)   , on oath state that I am   21   years of age and a citizen by   Blood   of the   Choctaw   Nation, and as such have been placed upon the final roll of the   Choctaw   Nation, by the Honorable Secretary of the Interior my final enrollment number being   7449   ; that I am the lawful wife of   T.C. Coker, who is a citizen of the   United States   Nation, and as such has been placed upon the final roll of said Nation by the Honorable Secretary of the Interior, his final enrollment number being ——— and that a   Female   child was born to me on the   7th day of   Feby   190 3; that said child has been named   Willie R. E. Coker   , and is now living.

                                        Lula Coker
WITNESSETH:
  Must be two witnesses   { L.W. McMarriet
  who are citizens   { Solen Mclellon

Applications for Enrollment of Choctaw Newborn
Act of 1905 Volume XIX

Subscribed and sworn to before me this, the 25 day of Feby , 190 5

CE Culbertson
Notary Public.

My Commission Expires: Dec 2nd 1905

Affidavit of Attending Physician or Midwife

UNITED STATES OF AMERICA,
   INDIAN TERRITORY,
Central   DISTRICT

I, Kittie McClellon[sic] a Midwife on oath state that I attended on Mrs. Lula Coker wife of T. E[sic] Coker on the 7th day of Feby , 190 3, that there was born to her on said date a Female child, that said child is now living, and is said to have been named Willie R.E. Coker

Kittie Mclellan[sic] ~~M. D.~~

Subscribed and sworn to before me this the 25th day of Feby 1905

C.E. Culbertson
Notary Public.

WITNESSETH:

Must be two witnesses who are citizens and know the child.
{ Solen Mclellon
  L.W. McMarriet

We hereby certify that we are well acquainted with Kittie McClellon a Midwife and know her to be reputable and of good standing in the community.

Must be two citizen witnesses.
{ Solen Mclellon
  L.W. McMarriet

BIRTH AFFIDAVIT.

DEPARTMENT OF THE INTERIOR.
COMMISSION TO THE FIVE CIVILIZED TRIBES.

IN RE APPLICATION FOR ENROLLMENT, as a citizen of the Choctaw Nation, of Willie R. E. Coker , born on the 7 day of Feb , 1904[sic]

Name of Father: G. C. Coker   a citizen of the .... Nation.
Name of Mother: Lula Coker   a citizen of the Choctaw Nation.

Applications for Enrollment of Choctaw Newborn
Act of 1905   Volume XIX

Postoffice   Ashland, I.T.

AFFIDAVIT OF MOTHER.

UNITED STATES OF AMERICA, Indian Territory, }
.... DISTRICT. }

I, Lula Coker , on oath state that I am 21 years of age and a citizen by blood , of the Choctaw Nation; that I am the lawful wife of G. C. Coker , who is a citizen, by .... of the .... Nation; that a female child was born to me on 7 day of February , 1904; that said child has been named Willie R. E. Coker , and was living March 4, 1905.

Lula Coker

Witnesses To Mark:
{

Subscribed and sworn to before me this 26 day of April , 1905

H.G. Rowley
Notary Public.

My commission expires 9th Mch 1909

AFFIDAVIT OF ATTENDING PHYSICIAN OR MID-WIFE.

UNITED STATES OF AMERICA, Indian Territory, }
.... DISTRICT. }

I, G. B. Fondren , a physician , on oath state that I attended on Mrs. Lula Coker , wife of G. C. Coker on the 7 day of February , 1904; that there was born to her on said date a female child; that said child was living March 4, 1905, and is said to have been named Willie R. E. Coker

G.B. Fondren

Witnesses To Mark:
{

Subscribed and sworn to before me this 26 day of April , 1905

H.G. Rowley
Notary Public.

Applications for Enrollment of Choctaw Newborn
Act of 1905   Volume XIX

BIRTH AFFIDAVIT.

DEPARTMENT OF THE INTERIOR.
COMMISSION TO THE FIVE CIVILIZED TRIBES.

IN RE APPLICATION FOR ENROLLMENT, as a citizen of the   Choctaw   Nation, of Willie R. E. Coker   , born on the   7   day of   Feb   , 1904[sic]

Name of Father: George C. Coker   a citizen of the   U. S.   Nation.
Name of Mother: Lula Coker *(Herron)*   a citizen of the   Choctaw   Nation.
Postoffice   Ashland, Ind. Ter.

AFFIDAVIT OF MOTHER.

UNITED STATES OF AMERICA, Indian Territory, }
.... DISTRICT. }

I,   Lula Coker *(Herron)*   , on oath state that I am   21   years of age and a citizen by   blood   , of the   Choctaw   Nation; that I am the lawful wife of George C. Coker   , who is a citizen, by   ———   of the   United States   Nation; that a female   child was born to me on   7   day of   February   , 1904; that said child has been named   Willie R. E. Coker   , and was living March 4, 1905.

Lula Coker

Witnesses To Mark:
{

Subscribed and sworn to before me this   28   day of   June   , 1905

H.G. Rowley
Notary Public.

My commission expires Mch 9 - 1909

AFFIDAVIT OF ATTENDING PHYSICIAN OR MID-WIFE.

UNITED STATES OF AMERICA, Indian Territory, }
     Central   DISTRICT. }

I,   G. B. Fondren   , a   physician   , on oath state that I attended on Mrs.   Lula Coker   , wife of   George C. Coker   on the   7 day of February   , 1904; that there was born to her on said date a   female   child; that said child was living March 4, 1905, and is said to have been named   Willie R. E. Coker

G.B. Fondren

Witnesses To Mark:
{

Applications for Enrollment of Choctaw Newborn
Act of 1905   Volume XIX

Subscribed and sworn to before me this 28 day of June , 1905

H.G. Rowley
Notary Public.

My commission expires Mch 9 - 1909

Muskogee, Indian Territory, May 1, 1905.

G. C. Coker,
     Ashland, Indian Territory.

Dear Sir:

    Receipt is hereby acknowledged of the affidavits of Lula Coker and G. B. Fondren to the birth of Willie R. e. Coker, son of G. C. and Lula Coker, February 7, 1904.

    It is stated in the affidavit of the mother that she is a citizen by blood of the Choctaw Nation. If this is correct you are requested to state the name under which she was enrolled, the names of her parents, and if she has selected an allotment of the lands of the Choctaw or Chickasaw Nation please give her roll number as it appears upon her allotment certificate.

Respectfully,

Chairman.

7-NB-1422.

Muskogee, Indian Territory, June 15, 1905.

Lula Coker,
     Celestine, Indian Territory.

Dear Madam:

    There is enclosed herewith for execution application for the enrollment of your infant child, Willie R. E. Coker.

    In the affidavits of February 25, 1905, heretofore filed in this office, the name of the applicant's father is given as T. C. Coker and in the midwife's affidavit as T. E. Coker, and the date of the applicant's birth is given in both affidavits as February 7, 1903, while in the affidavits of April 26, 1905, the father's name is given as G. C. Coker and the date f birth as February 7, 1904.

Applications for Enrollment of Choctaw Newborn
Act of 1905   Volume XIX

In the enclosed affidavits the father's name and the date of birth are left blank. Please insert the correct name and date of birth, and when the affidavits are properly executed return them to this office.

In having these affidavits executed care should be exercised to see that all names are written in full, as they appear in the body of the affidavit, and in the event either of the persons signing the affidavit are unable to write, signatures by mark must be attested by two witnesses. Each affidavit must be executed before a Notary Public and the notarial seal and signature of the officer must be attached to each separate affidavit.

Respectfully,

Chairman.

DeB--4/15.

7-NB-1422

Muskogee, Indian Territory, July 5, 1905.

Lula Coker,
  Ashland, Indian Territory.

Dear Madam:

Receipt is hereby acknowledged of your affidavit and the affidavits of G. B. Fondren to the birth of Willie R. E. Coker, daughter of George C. Coker and Lula Coker (Herron) February 7, 1904, and the same have been filed with the records of this office in the matter of the enrollment of said child.

Respectfully,

Commissioner.

Choc. New Born 1423
  Murray Muncrief Anderson
  (Born May 4, 1903)

Applications for Enrollment of Choctaw Newborn
Act of 1905 Volume XIX

BIRTH AFFIDAVIT.

DEPARTMENT OF THE INTERIOR.
COMMISSION TO THE FIVE CIVILIZED TRIBES.

IN RE APPLICATION FOR ENROLLMENT, as a citizen of the Chocktaw[sic] Nation, of Murray Muncrief Anderson, born on the 4th day of May, 1903

Name of Father: Charles E. Anderson   a citizen of the Chocktaw Nation.
Name of Mother: Georgie Muncrief Anderson   a citizen of the Chocktaw Nation.

Postoffice   Maysville I.T.

AFFIDAVIT OF MOTHER.

UNITED STATES OF AMERICA, Indian Territory,
Southern   DISTRICT.

I, Georgie Muncrief Anderson, on oath state that I am 23 years of age and a citizen by blood, of the Chocktaw Nation; that I am the lawful wife of Charles E. Anderson, who is a citizen, by Intermarriage of the Chocktaw Nation; that a Male child was born to me on 4th day of May, 1903; that said child has been named Murray Muncrief Anderson, and was living March 4, 1905.

Georgia Muncrief Anderson

Witnesses To Mark:

Subscribed and sworn to before me this 21st day of April, 1905

F C Cook
My commission   Notary Public.
expires Nov 21st 1906

AFFIDAVIT OF ATTENDING PHYSICIAN OR MID-WIFE.

UNITED STATES OF AMERICA, Indian Territory,
Southern   DISTRICT.

I, Mrs. J. J. Lamb, a Midwife, on oath state that I attended on Mrs. Georgia M Anderson, wife of Charles E Anderson on the 4th day of May, 1903; that there was born to her on said date a Male child; that said child was living March 4, 1905, and is said to have been named Murray Muncrief Anderson

J J Lamb

Applications for Enrollment of Choctaw Newborn
Act of 1905   Volume XIX

Witnesses To Mark:
{

      Subscribed and sworn to before me this   21st day of   April   , 1905

                                    F C Cook

My commission   Notary Public.
expires Nov 21st 1906

Choc. New Born 1424
      Wilson Tims
      (Born May 11, 1904)

                                                  7--NB--1424

                        Muskogee, Indian Territory, June 3, 1905.

Willie Tims,
      Fort Towson, Indian Territory.

Dear Sir:

      There is enclosed you herewith for execution application for the enrollment of your infant child, Wilson Tims.

      In the affidavit of the mother of this applicant executed April 29, 1905, the date of the applicant's birth is given a May 11, 1904, while in the affidavit of the attending physician executed on same date the date of the birth of the applicant is given as May 11, 1905. In the enclosed application the date of birth has been lef[sic] blank. Please insert the correct date and when the affidavits have been properly executed return to this office.

                                Respectfully,

                                                               [sic]

Applications for Enrollment of Choctaw Newborn
Act of 1905   Volume XIX

7 N B 1424

Kinta Ind. Ter., Sept. 25, 1905.

Honorable Tams Bixby, Commissioner,
Muskogee, Indian Territory.

Sir:-

    I am in receipt of a letter from Willis Tims, a Choctaw by blood whose post office address is Ft. Towson, I. T., stating that he had made an affidavit to the effect that Wilson Tims, a new born, was living on the 4th day of March, 1905, when in truth and in fact said child Wilson Tims, was at that time deceased, and that he made this mistake in the affidavit ignorantly, and wants to make the proper correction in order that the childs[sic] name may be stricken from the rolls that has been duly approved by the Department. Please forward him blank affidavit with proper instructions or forward same to this office and I will take occasion to have him make affidavit to that effect.

                  Yours truly,
                  Green McCurtain
                  Prin Chief C. N.

Muskogee, Indian Territory, September 28, 1905.

Chief Clerk,
    Chickasaw Land Office,
        Ardmore, Indian Territory.

Dear Sir:

    This office is in receipt of a communication from Green McCurtain, Principal Chief of the Choctaw Nation, under date of September 25, 1905, in which he states that he has been informed by Willie Tims, a Choctaw by blood, of Fort Towson, Indian Territory, that he (Tims) had made an affidavit to the effect that Wilson Tims, a new born, was living on the 4th day of March, 1905, when as a matter of fact the said Wilson Tims was at that time deceased.

    You are advised that it appears that the name of Wilson Tims appears opposite No. 1101 of the approved roll of new born citizens of the Choctaw Nation and that his enrollment as such was approved by the Secretary of the Interior July 22, 1905.

    You are hereby directed to take no further action relative to an allotment to the said Wilson Tims pending an investigation for the purpose of ascertaining the exact date of his death.

                  Respectfully,
                  Commissioner.

Applications for Enrollment of Choctaw Newborn
Act of 1905   Volume XIX

BIRTH AFFIDAVIT.

DEPARTMENT OF THE INTERIOR.
COMMISSION TO THE FIVE CIVILIZED TRIBES.

IN RE APPLICATION FOR ENROLLMENT, as a citizen of the Choctaw Nation, of Wilson Tims, born on the 11 day of May, 1904

Name of Father: Willie Tims   a citizen of the Choctaw Nation.
Name of Mother: Mary Tims   a citizen of the Choctaw Nation.

Postoffice   Fort Towson Ind. Ter.

AFFIDAVIT OF MOTHER.

UNITED STATES OF AMERICA, Indian Territory, }
    Central   DISTRICT.

I, Mary Tims, on oath state that I am 25 years of age and a citizen by Blood, of the Choctaw Nation; that I am the lawful wife of Willie Tims, who is a citizen, by Blood of the Choctaw Nation; that a Male child was born to me on 11 day of May, 1904; that said child has been named Wilson Tims, and was living March 4, 1905.

                                                  her
                                           Mary x Tims
Witnesses To Mark: mark
  { Robert Tims
  { Johnney Tims

Subscribed and sworn to before me this 29 day of April, 1905

                                     Thomas Fennell
                                       Notary Public.

AFFIDAVIT OF ATTENDING PHYSICIAN OR MID-WIFE.

UNITED STATES OF AMERICA, Indian Territory, }
    Central   DISTRICT.

I, Nancy Lewis, a Midwife, on oath state that I attended on Mrs. Mary Tims, wife of Willie Tims on the 11 day of May, 1905[sic]; that there was born to her on said date a .... child; that said child was living March 4, 1905, and is said to have been named Wilson Tims

Applications for Enrollment of Choctaw Newborn
Act of 1905   Volume XIX

                                          her
                                    Nancy x Lewis

Witnesses To Mark: mark
{ Robert Tims
{ Johnney Tims

    Subscribed and sworn to before me this   29   day of   April   , 1905

                                    Thomas Fennell
                                    Notary Public.

BIRTH AFFIDAVIT.

DEPARTMENT OF THE INTERIOR.
COMMISSION TO THE FIVE CIVILIZED TRIBES.

IN RE APPLICATION FOR ENROLLMENT, as a citizen of the   Choctaw   Nation, of Wilson Tims   , born on the   11   day of   May   , 1904

Name of Father: Willie Tims   *Roll 3441*   a citizen of the   Choctaw   Nation.
Name of Mother: Mary Tims   "   *3442*   a citizen of the   Choctaw   Nation.

                          Postoffice   Fort Towson I.T.

AFFIDAVIT OF MOTHER.

UNITED STATES OF AMERICA, Indian Territory, }
....DISTRICT. }

    I,   Mary Tims   , on oath state that I am   25   years of age and a citizen by blood   , of the   Choctaw   Nation; that I am the lawful wife of   Willie Tims   , who is a citizen, by blood   of the   Choctaw   Nation; that a   male   child was born to me on   11   day of   May   , 1904; that said child has been named Wilson Tims   , and was living March 4, 1905.

                                    her
                                 Mary x Tims
Witnesses To Mark: mark
{ Willie Tims
{ Thos Fennell

    Subscribed and sworn to before me this   21   day of   May   , 1905

                                  Thomas Fennell
                                  Notary Public.

Applications for Enrollment of Choctaw Newborn
Act of 1905   Volume XIX

AFFIDAVIT OF ATTENDING PHYSICIAN OR MID-WIFE.

UNITED STATES OF AMERICA, Indian Territory, } DISTRICT.

I, Nancy Lewis, a midwife, on oath state that I attended on Mrs. Mary Tims, wife of Willie Tims on the 11 day of May, 1904; that there was born to her on said date a male child; that said child was living March 4, 1905, and is said to have been named Wilson Tims

                                          her
                              Nancy x Lewis
Witnesses To Mark: mark
  { Willie Tims
    Thos Fennell

Subscribed and sworn to before me this 21 day of May, 1905

                              Thomas Fennell
                              Notary Public.

DEPARTMENT OF THE INTERIOR.
COMMISSION TO THE FIVE CIVILIZED TRIBES.

In the matter of the death of Wilson Tims a citizen of the Choctaw Nation, who formerly resided at or near Fort Towson, Ind. Ter., and died on the 30 day of July, 1904

AFFIDAVIT OF RELATIVE.

UNITED STATES OF AMERICA, Indian Territory, } Central DISTRICT.

I, Willie Tims, on oath state that I am 28 years of age and a citizen by Blood, of the Choctaw Nation; that my postoffice address is Fort Towson, Ind. Ter.; that I am Father of Wilson Tims who was a citizen, by Blood, of the Choctaw Nation and that said Wilson Tims died on the 30 day of July, 1904

                              Willie Tims
Witnesses To Mark:
  {

Subscribed and sworn to before me this 16 day of Dec, 1905.

                              Thomas Fennell
                              Notary Public.

Applications for Enrollment of Choctaw Newborn
Act of 1905   Volume XIX

AFFIDAVIT OF ACQUAINTANCE.

UNITED STATES OF AMERICA, Indian Territory,
  Central   DISTRICT.

I, J. B. Tims, on oath state that I am 48 years of age, and a citizen by Blood of the Choctaw Nation; that my postoffice address is Fort Towson, Ind. Ter.; that I was personally acquainted with Wilson Tims who was a citizen, by Blood, of the Choctaw Nation; and that said Wilson Tims died on the 30 day of July, 1904

J.B. Tims

Witnesses To Mark:

Subscribed and sworn to before me this 16 day of Dec, 1905.

Thomas Fennell
Notary Public.

DEPARTMENT OF THE INTERIOR,
COMMISSIONER TO THE FIVE CIVILIZED TRIBES.
CHOCTAW-CHICKASAW DIVISION.

ooooOOoooo

Muskogee, Indian Territory, March 30, 1906.

In the matter of the enrollment of Wilson Tims, Choctaw New Born, Card Number 1424, Roll Number 1101.

Testimony taken ten miles east of Fort Towson, Indian Territory, March 21, 1906.

WILLIE TIMS, being first duly sworn, testified as follows:

BY THE COMMISSIONER:

Q What is your name? A Willie Tims.
Q What is your age? A 30.
Q What is your post office? A Fort Towson, I. T.
Q Are you a Choctaw? A Yes.
Q What is your wife's name?
A Mary Tims.

Applications for Enrollment of Choctaw Newborn
Act of 1905   Volume XIX

Q How old is she?
A I could not tell, I guess about 27.
Q Have you a little son named Roberson?
A Yes.
Q Are you the father of Wilson Tims?
A Yes.
Q When was Wilson Tims born?
A May 11, 1904.
Q When did Wilson Tims die?
A July 30, 1904.
Q Have you a record of Wilson Tim's[sic] death?
A Yes.
   The Church Register of the Methodist Episcopal Church South, Clear Creek, Indian Territory, is here exhibited, showing Wilson Tim's death on July 30, 1904.
Q Are you the Secretary of the Methodist Curch[sic] of Clear Creek?
A Yes.
Q The records of the Commission to the Five Civilized Tribes show that on the 16th of December 1905 you affirmed that your son, Wilson Tims, died on the 30th of July, 1904: Do you reaffirm said affidavit?
A Yes.

Witness Excused.

Testimony taken ten miles east of Fort Towsin[sic], Indian Territory, March 21, 1906.

MARY TIMS, being first duly sworn, testified as follows:

BY THE COMMISSIONER:

Through Interpreter, Jacob Homer.

Q What is your name? A Mary Tims.
Q What is your age? A About 27.
Q What is your post office address? A Fort Towson, I. T.
Q Are you a citizen by blood of the Choctaw Nation?
A Yes, sir.
Q Are you the wife of Willie Tims?
A Yes, sir.
Q Did you have a child named Wilson Tims?
A Yes, sir.
Q When was he born?
A I have forgot it.
Q When did Wilson Tims die?
A He died in July.
Q What year.[sic]
A Year before last.

Applications for Enrollment of Choctaw Newborn
Act of 1905   Volume XIX

Q   Have you given birth to a child since the death of Wilson Tims?
A   Yes.
Q   What is the name of your child born since the death of Wilson Tims?
A   Adeline Tims.
Q   When was she born?
A   July 6, 1905.
Q   Did Wilson Tims die in July the year before the birth of Adeline Tims?
A   I do not think it was quite a year after that child died until this one was born.
Q   The records of the Commission to the Five Civilized Tribes show that on the 29th of April, 1905, and again on the 21st of May 1905, you affirmed that Wilson Tims was born on the 11th of May 1904 and was living March 4, 1905: When you signed said affidavits did you know you were affirming that the child was living March 4, 1905?
A   The Notary Public never asked me anything about whether that child was living or dead, but I know that child was dead; I asked him whether that dead child would be enrolled or not, and he told me it did not make any difference whether it was dead or not it would be enrolled just the same.

Witness Excused.

Testimony taken ten miles east of Fort Towson, Indian Territory, March 21, 1906.

<u>NANCY LEWIS</u>, being first duly sworn, testified as follows:

<u>BY THE COMMISSIONER</u>:
Through Interpreter Jacob Homer.

Q   What is your name?   A   Nancy Lewis.
Q   What is your age?   A   I do not know, I guess about 80.
Q   What is your post office address?   A   Fort Towson, I. T.
Q   How old are you?
A   I do not know, I guess about 80.
Q   Are you a Choctaw or Chickasaw?
A   Choctaw.
Q   Did you attend Mary Tims, wife of Willie Tims, at the time their son, Wilson Tims, was born?
A   Yes.
Q   When did Wilson Tims die?
A   In July 1904.
Q   When you appeared before a Notary Public the 21st of June 1905 and made affidavit that Wilson Tims was born the 11th of May 1904, did you know that you were affirming that the child was living March 4, 1905?
A   The Notary Public did not ask me anything about whether that child was living or not.

Witness Excused

Applications for Enrollment of Choctaw Newborn
Act of 1905 Volume XIX

W. P Covington, being first duly sworn, states that the above and foregoing is a full, true and correct transcript of his stenographic notes taken in said case on said date.

W. P. Covington

Subscribed and sworn to before me, this 30" day of   March   1906.

(Name Illegible)
Notary Public.

7--NB--1424

Muskogee, Indian Territory, June 3, 1905.

Willie Tims,
    Fort Towson, Indian Territory.

Dear Sir:

There is enclosed you herewith for execution application for the enrollment of your infant child, Wilson Tims.

In the affidavit of the mother of this application executed April 29, 1905, the date of the applicant's birth is given as May 11, 1904, while in the affidavit of the attending physician executed on same date the date of the birth of the applicant is given as May 11, 1905. In the enclosed application the date of birth has been lef[sic] blank. Please insert the correct date and when the affidavits have been properly executed return to this office.

Respectfully,

[sic]

---

7 NB 1424

Muskogee, Indian Territory, June 24, 1905.

Willie Tims,
    Fort Towson, Indian Territory.

Dear Sir:

Receipt is hereby acknowledged of the affidavits of Mary Tims and Nancy Lewis to the birth of Wilson Tims, son of Willie and Mary Tims, May 11, 1904, and the same have been filed with our records in the matter of the enrollment of said child.

Applications for Enrollment of Choctaw Newborn
Act of 1905 Volume XIX

Respectfully,

Chairman.

7 N B 1424

Kinta, Ind. Ter., Sept. 25, 1905.

Honorable Tams Bixby, Commissioner,
    Muskogee, Indian Territory.

Sir:--

    I am in receipt of a letter from Willie Tims, a Choctaw by blood whose post office address is Ft. Towsen[sic], I. T., stating that he had made an affidavit to the effect that Wilson Tims, a new born, was living on the 4th day of March, 1905, when in truth and in fact said child Wilson Tims, was at that time deceased, and that he made this mistake in the affidavit ignorantly, and wants to make the proper correction in order that the childs[sic] name may be stricken from the rolls that has been duly approved by the Department. Please forward him blank affidavit with proper instructions or forward same to this office and I will take occasion to have him make affidavit to that effect.

    Yours truly,
    Green McCurtain
    Prin. Chief C. N.

7-NB-1424

Muskogee, Indian Territory, December 20, 1905.

Willie Tims,
    Fort Towson, Indian Territory.

Dear Sir:

    Receipt is hereby acknowledged of your affidavit and the affidavit of J. B. Tims to the death of your child Wilson Tims a citizen by blood of the Choctaw Nation which occurred July 30, 1904, and the same has been filed with the records as evidence of the death of said child.

    Respectfully,

    Commissioner.

Applications for Enrollment of Choctaw Newborn
Act of 1905   Volume XIX

Muskogee, Indian Territory, April 7, 1906.

The Honorable,
   The Secretary of the Interior.

Sir:

June 26, 1905, the Commission to the Five Civilized Tribes had the honor to transmit for Departmental approval a schedule of children of citizens by blood of the Choctaw Nation constituting part of the final roll of citizens by blood of the Choctaw Nation under the Act of Congress approved March 3, 1905 (33 Stat. 1060) Nos. 905 to 1110 inclusive, copies of which have been heretofore returned approved by the Secretary of the Interior, July 12, 1905.

Referring to the name of Wilson Tims, which appears thereon opposite No. 1101, I have the honor to report that the enrollment of this citizen is erroneous and should be cancelled.

This office was in receipt of a letter from Honorable Green McCurtain, Principal Chief of the Choctaw Nation, under date of September 25, 1905, to the effect that he had been informed by Willie Tims, father of Wilson Tims, that he had ignorantly made affidavits to the fact that his son Wilson Tims, a new born Choctaw, was living March 4, 1905, when in fact said child was at that time deceased, and that he desired to make the proper correction in order that the child's name might be stricken from the rolls as duly approved by the Department.

In accordance with this information an investigation was directed by this office and on March 21, 1906, the testimony of Willie Tims, Mary Tims and Nancy Lewis was secured near Fort Towson, Indian Territory, from which it developed that Wilson Tims was born May 11, 1904 and died July 20, 1904.

For the information of the Department a copy of this testimony is inclosed herewith.

I have further to report that no selection of allotment has been made in the name of Wilson Tims, deceased, and inasmuch as the act of Congress approved March 3, 1905, provided for the enrollment of children born to citizens of the Choctaw and Chickasaw Nations subsequent to September 25, 1902, and prior to March 4, 1905, and living on the latter date, I have the honor to recomend[sic] that the enrollment of Wilson Tims at No. 1101 upon the approved roll of citizens by blood of the Choctaw Nation under the act of Congress approved March 3, 1905, be cancelled upon the schedules and letter of transmittal in the Department and the Indian Office and that this office be authorized to make like cancellation upon the schedules and letter of transmittal in its possession.

Applications for Enrollment of Choctaw Newborn
Act of 1905   Volume XIX

Respectfully,

Through the Commissioner
of Indian Affairs.   Commissioner.

Choctaw New Born 1424

7-NB-1424

Muskogee, Indian Territory, April 18, 1906.

Chief Clerk,
   Choctaw Land Office,
      Atoka, Indian Territory.

Dear Sir:

There is inclosed herewith for the information of your office copy of letter of April 7, 1906, addressed to the Secretary of the Interior recommending the cancellation for the enrollment of Wilson Tims at No. 1101 upon the approved roll of new born citizens of the Choctaw Nation.

You are therefore directed to withhold the issuance of citizenship certificate and the making of allotment to this citizen until otherwise further directed.

When this office is advised of Departmental action on this recommendation you will be notified.

Respectfully,

EB 5-18   Acting Commissioner.

Applications for Enrollment of Choctaw Newborn
Act of 1905   Volume XIX

COPY

DEPARTMENT OF THE INTERIOR,

OFFICE OF INDIAN AFFAIRS,

LAND
31876-1906.

WASHINGTON.

May 19, 1906.

The Honorable,
    The Secretary of the Interior.
Sir:

    There is enclosed a report from the Commissioner to the Five Civilized Tribes, dated April 7, 1906, saying that the enrollment of Wilson Tims, No. 1101 approved roll of Choctaws by blood, should be canceled.

    Mr. Bixby reports that he is in receipt of a communication from the Principal Chief of the Choctaw Nation, dated September 25, 1905, to the effect that he had been informed by Willis[sic] Tims, father of Wilson Tims, that he had ignorantly made affidavits to the effect that his son, Wilson Tims, a newborn Choctaw, was living on March 4, 1905, when in fact said child was not living at that time, and that he desired to make the proper correction in order that the child's name might be striken[sic] from the approved rolls.

    In accordance with this information Mr. Bixby caused an investigation to be held, on March 21, 1906, and he forwarded the testimony of Willie Tims, Mary Tims, and Nancy Lewis, which shows that Wilson Tims was born May 11, 1904, and died on June[sic] 30, 1904.

    He recommends that the name of Wilson Tims be striken[sic] from the approved rolls of Choctaws by blood, newborn children.

    As it is shown that Wilson Tims was not living on March 4, 1905, he is not entitled to enrollment, and the recommendation of the Commissioner to the Five Civilized Tribes is concurred in.

                  Very respectfully,

                        C. F. Larrabee,

                                Acting Commissioner.

GAW-GH

Applications for Enrollment of Choctaw Newborn
Act of 1905   Volume XIX

J.S.J.

W.H.M.

DEPARTMENT OF THE INTERIOR,
WASHINGTON.

D.C. 21519
I.T.D. 9208-1906.

May 25, 1906.

L.R.S.

The Commissioner to the Five Civilized Tribes,
Muskogee, Indian Territory.

Sir:

On April 7, 1906, you forwarded a report relative to the erroneous enrollment of Wilson Tims, whose name appears opposite No. 1101 upon the approved roll of children of citizens by blood of the Choctaw Nation, being a part of the final roll of citizens by blood of the Choctaw Nation under the Act of Congress approved March 3, 1905 (33 Stat., 1060).

It appears that Willis[sic] Tims, the father of Wilson Tims, ignorantly made affidavit to the fact that his son, Wilson Tims, a new born Choctaw, was living March 4, 1905, when, in fact said child died July 30, 1904.

You state that no selection of allotment has been made in the name of Wilson Tims, deceased, and you request authority to cancel said name from the Choctaw rolls in your possession.

Reporting May 19, 1906, the Indian Office concurs in your recommendation. A copy of its letter is enclosed.

It being evident that Wilson Tims was not living on March 4, 1905, you are authorized to cancel the name of Wilson Tims, opposite No. 1101 upon the roll of children of citizens by blood of the Choctaw Nation.

The Department has cancelled said name upon the part of the roll in its possession, and has requested the Indian Office to do the same.

Respectfully,

Jesse E. Wilson,

Assistant Secretary

1 inclosure.

Applications for Enrollment of Choctaw Newborn
Act of 1905 Volume XIX

7-NB-1424

Muskogee, Indian Territory, June 30, 1906.

Chief Clerk,
    Choctaw Land Office,
        Atoka, Indian Territory.

Dear Sir:-

For your information there is enclosed herewith copy of Departmental letter of May 25, 1906, (I.T.D. 9208-1906), authorizing the cancellation of the enrollment of Wilson Tims at No. 1101 upon the approved roll of new born citizens of the Choctaw Nation under the Act of Congress approved March 3, 1905.

You are, therefore, directed to cancel the enrollment of this citizen at No. 1101 upon the copies of schedules of such new born citizens of the Choctaw Nation in the possession of your office, and also upon the letters transmitting said schedules.

                Respectfully,

WLM. 30/3   Commissioner.

7-NB-1424

Muskogee, Indian Territory, July 2, 1906.

Chief Clerk,
    Choctaw Land Office,
        Atoka, Indian Territory.

Dear Sir:-

You are hereby advised that a red line has this day been drawn through the name of Wilson Tims at No. 1 on Choctaw roll card NB-1424, and the following notation in red ink has been placed upon said card:

"No. 1 died July 30, 1904. Enrollment cancelled under Departmental authority of May 25, 1906, (I.T.D. 9208-1906) D. C. 21519-1906."

You are, therefore, directed to make like changes upon Choctaw roll card NB-1424 in the possession of your office.

                Respectfully,

                                            Commissioner.

Applications for Enrollment of Choctaw Newborn
Act of 1905 Volume XIX

7-NB-1424

Muskogee, Indian Territory, October 12, 1906.

Willie Tims,
    Fort Towson, Indian Territory.

Dear Sir:

    Receipt is hereby acknowledged of your letter of October 3, 1906, in which you ask if your child Willie Tims has been approved.

    In reply to your letter you are advised that it appears from the records of this office that your child Wilson Tims died prior to March 3, 1905, and his enrollment as a new born citizen of the Choctaw Nation under the Act of Congress approved March 3, 1905 was cancelled by the Department May 25, 1906. No selection of allotment can therefore be made for said child.

                                      Respectfully,

                                                      Commissioner.

<u>Choc. New Born 1425</u>
    Benjamin Nelson
    (Born Feb. 17, 1905)

DEPARTMENT OF THE INTERIOR,
COMMISSION TO THE FIVE CIVILIZED TRIBES.
SOUTH McALESTER, I. T.   APRIL 29, 1905.

    In the matter of the application for the enrollment of Benjamin Nelson as a citizen by blood of the Choctaw Nation.

Jackson F. Nelson being first duly sworn testifies as follows:

EXAMINATION BY THE COMMISSION:

Q What is your name? A Jackson F. Nelson.
Q What is your age? A Thirty-seven.
Q What is your post office address? A Coleman, I. T.

Applications for Enrollment of Choctaw Newborn
Act of 1905   Volume XIX

Q You have this day made application for the enrollment of your child Benjamin Nelson; when was he born? A 17th of February 1905.
Q Was he living on March 4, 1905? A Yes, sir.
Q Who is the mother of Benjamin Nelson.[sic] A Emma C. Nelson.
Q Who attended your wife when Benjamin Nelson was born? A Nobody but myself.
Q You have no other witness here today who knows of the birth of this child?
A No, sir.

Witness excused.

Chas. T. Difendafer being first duly sworn states that the above and foregoing is a full, true and correct transcript of the stenographic notes taken in said cause on said date.

Chas. T. Difendafer

Subscribed and sworn to before me this 29th day of April 1905.

OL Johnson
Notary Public.

7- 9385
BIRTH AFFIDAVIT.

DEPARTMENT OF THE INTERIOR.
COMMISSION TO THE FIVE CIVILIZED TRIBES.

IN RE APPLICATION FOR ENROLLMENT, as a citizen of the   Choctaw   Nation, of Benjamin Nelson   , born on the 17   day of February   , 1905

Name of Father: Jackson F. Nelson   a citizen of the   Choc   Nation.
Name of Mother: Emma C. Nelson   a citizen of the   Choc   Nation.

Postoffice   Coleman I.T.

AFFIDAVIT OF MOTHER.

UNITED STATES OF AMERICA, Indian Territory,
Central   DISTRICT.

I, Emma C Nelson   , on oath state that I am 25   years of age and a citizen by   blood   , of the   Choc   Nation; that I am the lawful wife of   Jackson F Nelson   , who is a citizen, by blood of the   Choc   Nation; that a   male child was born to me on   17   day of   February   , 1905; that said child has been named   Benjamin Nelson   , and was living March 4, 1905.

Emma C Nelson

Applications for Enrollment of Choctaw Newborn
Act of 1905   Volume XIX

Witnesses To Mark:

Subscribed and sworn to before me this 1st day of May, 1905

David A. Bailey
Notary Public.
My commission expires Jan 11-1909

AFFIDAVIT OF ATTENDING PHYSICIAN OR MID-WIFE.

UNITED STATES OF AMERICA, Indian Territory,
DISTRICT.

I, , a , on oath state that I attended on Mrs. , wife of on the day of , 190; that there was born to her on said date a male child; that said child was living March 4, 1905, *See Testimony* ave been named

Witnesses To Mark:

Subscribed and sworn to before me this day of , 1905

Notary Public.

Affidavit

June 10 - 1905

State of Indian Territory,   Central Dist. I.T.
Co. or = Dist. 15 -

Jackson F. Nelson of Coleman, I.T. In the County or Dist. aforesaid Being Duly Sworn Says - That a male child was Born to Emma C. Nelson his wife on Feby. 17 - 1905 and that he was named Benjamin Nelson, and was Living on the 4th day of March 1905 - and is now Living.

Jackson F Nelson
Coleman, I.T.

Witness   WD Phillips M.D.
Siney Thompson

Applications for Enrollment of Choctaw Newborn
Act of 1905   Volume XIX

Being Duly Sworn Declares that the foregoing Statements are facts and True to the best of their knowledge

WD Phillips M.D.
Siney Thompson

Subscribed and sworn to before me this Sworn to Before me a Notary Public - Central District, I.T.

David A. Bailey
My Commission Expires Jan 11- 1909

JUN 10 1905

7-3252

Muskogee, Indian Territory, May 8, 1905.

Jackson F. Nelson,
    Coleman, Indian Territory.

Dear Sir:

    Receipt is hereby acknowledged of the affidavit of Emma C. Nelson to the birth of Benjamin Nelson, son of Jackson F. and Emma C. Nelson, February 17, 1905, and the same have been filed with our records as an application for the enrollment of said child.

Respectfully,

Commissioner in Charge.

7--NB--1425

Muskogee, Indian Territory, June 2, 1905.

Jackson F. Nelson,
    Coleman, Indian Territory.

Dear Sir:

    Referring to the application for the enrollment of your infant child, Benjamin Nelson, born February 17, 1905, it is noted from the affidavits heretofore filed in this office that you were the only one in attendance upon your wife at the time of the birth of the applicant.

Applications for Enrollment of Choctaw Newborn
Act of 1905 Volume XIX

In this event it will be necessary that the affidavits of two persons, who are disinterested and not related to the applicant, who have actual knowledge of the facts that the child was born, the date of his birth; that he was living on March 4, 1905, and that Emma C. Nelson is his mother be filed in this office.

This matter should receive your immediate attention as no further action can be taken relative to the enrollment of your child until the Commission has been furnished these affidavits.

Respectfully,

[sic]

7 NB 1425

Muskogee, Indian Territory, June 14, 1905.

Jackson F. Nelson,
    Coleman, Indian Territory.

Dear Sir:

Receipt is hereby acknowledged of your affidavit and the joint affidavit of W. D. Phillips and Siney Thompson to the birth of Benjamin Nelson, son of Jackson F. and Emma C. Nelson, February 17, 1905, and the same have been filed in the matter of the enrollment of said child.

Respectfully,

Chairman.

<u>Choc. New Born 1426</u>
    Sim Bohanan[sic]
    (Born March 3, 1905)

Applications for Enrollment of Choctaw Newborn
Act of 1905 Volume XIX

BIRTH AFFIDAVIT.

DEPARTMENT OF THE INTERIOR.
COMMISSION TO THE FIVE CIVILIZED TRIBES.

IN RE APPLICATION FOR ENROLLMENT, as a citizen of the　　Choctaw　　Nation, of Sim Bohanon　　, born on the 3rd　day of　March　, 1905

Name of Father: Joe Bohanon　　　　　a citizen of the　Choctaw　Nation.
Name of Mother: Mary Bohanon　　　　a citizen of the　Choctaw　Nation.

　　　　　　　　　　　　　Postoffice　　Kinta I.T.

AFFIDAVIT OF MOTHER.

UNITED STATES OF AMERICA, Indian Territory, ⎫
　　Western　　　　　　DISTRICT. ⎭

　　I,　Mary Bohanon　, on oath state that I am　20　years of age and a citizen by　blood　, of the　Choctaw　Nation; that I am the lawful wife of　Joe Bohanon　, who is a citizen, by blood　of the　Choctaw　Nation; that a male　child was born to me on　3rd　day of　March　, 1905; that said child has been named　Sim Bohanon　, and was living March 4, 1905.

　　　　　　　　　　　　　　　　　　her
　　　　　　　　　　　　　　　　Mary x Bohanon
Witnesses To Mark:　　　　　　　　mark
　⎰ Green McCurtain
　⎱ *(Name Illegible)*

　　Subscribed and sworn to before me this　20th　day of　April　, 1905

My commission expires　　　　　*(Name Illegible)*
March 4th 1907　　　　　　　　　　　　Notary Public.

AFFIDAVIT OF ATTENDING PHYSICIAN OR MID-WIFE.

UNITED STATES OF AMERICA, Indian Territory, ⎫
　　Western　　　　　　DISTRICT. ⎭

　　I,　Dora Drake　, a　midwife　, on oath state that I attended on Mrs. Mary Bohanon　, wife of　Joe Bohanon　on the 3rd day of March　, 1905; that there was born to her on said date a　male　child; that said child was living March 4, 1905, and is said to have been named Sim Bohanon

　　　　　　　　　　　　　　　　　　her
　　　　　　　　　　　　　　　　Dora x Drake
　　　　　　　　　　　　　　　　　mark

Applications for Enrollment of Choctaw Newborn
Act of 1905   Volume XIX

Witnesses To Mark:
{ Green McCurtain
{ *(Name Illegible)*

Subscribed and sworn to before me this 20th day of April , 1905

My commission expires *(Name Illegible)*
March 4th 1907 Notary Public.

Choctaw 2730.

Muskogee, Indian Territory, April 29, 1905.

Houston Terrell,
    Kinta, Indian Territory.

Dear Sir:

    Receipt is hereby acknowledged of your letter of April 20, inclosing affidavits of Louisa Terrell (James) and Mary Bohannon[sic] to the birth of Jesse James Terrell, son of Houston and Louisa Terrell, October 9, 1904, and the same have been filed as an application for the enrollment of said child.

    Receipt is also acknowledged of the affidavits of Mary Bohanon and Susan[sic] Drake to the birth of Sim Bohanon, son of Joe and Mary Bohanon, March 3, 1905.

    It is stated in the affidavit of the mother that she is a citizen by blood of the Choctaw Nation you are requested to state the name under which she was enrolled, the names of her parents, and if she has selected an allotment of the lands of the Choctaw or Chickasaw Nation please give her roll number as the same appears upon her allotment certificate.

                      Respectfully,

                              Chairman.

Applications for Enrollment of Choctaw Newborn
Act of 1905   Volume XIX

7-5398

Muskogee, Indian Territory, May 12, 1905.

Joe Bohanon,
    Kinta, Indian Territory.

Dear Sir:

    Receipt is hereby acknowledged of your letter of May 8, 1905, giving the maiden name of your wife Mary Bohanon and her roll number.

    In reply to your letter you are advised that this information has enabled the Commission to identify her upon its records as an enrolled citizen by blood of the Choctaw Nation, and the affidavits heretofore forwarded to the birth of your child Sim Bohanon have been filed with our records as an application for the enrollment of said child.

Respectfully,

Chairman.

(The letter below does not belong with the current applicant.)

7-NB-1496

Muskogee, Indian Territory, August 25, 1905.

Simon Taylor,
    Attorney at Law.
        Garvin, Indian Territory.

Dear Sir:

    Receipt is hereby acknowledged of your letter of August 18, 1905, giving the names of the parents of Lizzie Hickman and her roll number in the matter of the application for the enrollment of her child Patsy Takubbe as a citizen by blood of the Choctaw Nation.

    This information has enabled this office to identify Lizzie Hickman as an enrolled citizen by blood of the Choctaw Nation and the affidavits heretofore forwarded to the birth of Patsy Takubbe have been filed as an application for the enrollment of said child.

Respectfully,

Commissioner.

Applications for Enrollment of Choctaw Newborn
Act of 1905 Volume XIX

Choc. New Born 1427
    Josephine Hardy
    (Born July 28, 1904)[sic]

NEW-BORN AFFIDAVIT.

Number..................

...Choctaw Enrolling Commission...

IN THE MATTER OF THE APPLICATION FOR ENROLLMENT, as a citizen of the Choctaw Nation, of Josephine Hardy

born on the 14 day of January 190 5

Name of father Thomas Hardy   a citizen of Choctaw
Nation final enrollment No. 5538
Name of mother Emily Hardy   a citizen of Choctaw
Nation final enrollment No. 5539

Postoffice Nashoba, I.T.

AFFIDAVIT OF MOTHER.

UNITED STATES OF AMERICA
INDIAN TERRITORY
    Central   DISTRICT

I Emily Hardy, on oath state that I am 28 years of age and a citizen by Blood of the Choctaw Nation, and as such have been placed upon the final roll of the Choctaw Nation, by the Honorable Secretary of the Interior my final enrollment number being 5539 ; that I am the lawful wife of Thomas Hardy, who is a citizen of the Choctaw Nation, and as such been placed upon the final roll of said Nation by the Honorable Secretary of the Interior, his final enrollment number being 5538 and that a Female child was born to me on the 14 day of January 190 5; that said child has been named Josephine Hardy, and is now living.

                                            her
                                      Emily x Hardy
Witnesseth.   mark

Must be two Witnesses who are Citizens.
    Hodgen Baker
    Charlie Colbert

Applications for Enrollment of Choctaw Newborn
Act of 1905   Volume XIX

Subscribed and sworn to before me this   15   day of   Mar   190 5

P.W. Hudson
Notary Public.

My commission expires: Feby 24 - 1906

AFFIDAVIT OF ATTENDING PHYSICIAN OR MIDWIFE

UNITED STATES OF AMERICA
INDIAN TERRITORY
  Central   DISTRICT

I,   Jane Cooper   a   Midwife on oath state that I attended on Mrs.   Emily Hardy   wife of   Thomas Hardy on the   14   day of January , 190 5, that there was born to her on said date a   Female   child, that said child is now living, and is said to have been named   Josephine Hardy

her
Jane x Cooper   ~~M.D.~~
mark

WITNESSETH:
Must be two witnesses who are citizens and know the child.
{ Hodgen Baker
  Charlie Colbert

Subscribed and sworn to before me this, the   15   day of   March   190 5
My Commission Expires Feb. 24, 1906.

P.W. Hudson   Notary Public.

We hereby certify that we are well acquainted with   Jane Cooper a   Midwife   and know   her   to be reputable and of good standing in the community.

{ Hodgen baker
  Charlie Colbert

7 - 5538 - 5539
BIRTH AFFIDAVIT.

DEPARTMENT OF THE INTERIOR.
COMMISSION TO THE FIVE CIVILIZED TRIBES.

IN RE APPLICATION FOR ENROLLMENT, as a citizen of the   Choctaw   Nation, of Josephine Hardy , born on the   14   day of   January , 1905

Name of Father: Thomas Hardy   a citizen of the   Choc   Nation.
Name of Mother: Emily Hardy   a citizen of the   Choc   Nation.

Applications for Enrollment of Choctaw Newborn
Act of 1905   Volume XIX

Postoffice   Nashoba I.T.

AFFIDAVIT OF MOTHER.

UNITED STATES OF AMERICA, Indian Territory, }
   Central   DISTRICT.

I,   Emily Hardy   , on oath state that I am   25   years of age and a citizen by blood   , of the   Choctaw   Nation; that I am the lawful wife of   Thomas Hardy , who is a citizen, by blood   of the   Choctaw   Nation; that a   female   child was born to me on   14   day of   January   , 1905; that said child has been named Josephine Hardy   , and was living March 4, 1905.

                                          her
                                   Emily x Hardy

Witnesses To Mark: mark
  { Frank L. Loman
    (Name Illegible)

Subscribed and sworn to before me this   14   day of   April   , 1905

                                 F. M. Fuller
                                      Notary Public.

AFFIDAVIT OF ATTENDING PHYSICIAN OR MID-WIFE.

UNITED STATES OF AMERICA, Indian Territory, }
   Central   DISTRICT.

I,   Jane Cooper   , a   midwife   , on oath state that I attended on Mrs.   Emily Hardy   , wife of   Thomas Hardy   on the   14   day of   January , 1905; that there was born to her on said date a   female   child; that said child was living March 4, 1905, and is said to have been named   Josephine Hardy

                                     her
                                Jane x Cooper

Witnesses To Mark: mark
  { Frank L. Loman
    (Name Illegible)

Subscribed and sworn to before me this   14   day of   April   , 1905

                                 F. M. Fuller
                                      Notary Public.

My commission expires April 18th 1908

Applications for Enrollment of Choctaw Newborn
Act of 1905   Volume XIX

7-1936

Muskogee, Indian Territory, May 9, 1905.

Thomas Hardy,
    Nashoba, Indian Territory.

Dear Sir:

    Receipt is hereby acknowledged of the affidavits of Emily Hardy and Jane Cooper to the birth of Josephine Hardy, daughter of Thomas and Emily Hardy, January 14, 1905, and the same have been filed with our records as an application for the enrollment of said child.

                  Respectfully,

                  Commissioner in Charge.

<u>Choc. New Born 1428</u>
      Edward A. Harris
      (Born Sep. 4, 1904)

7-_____

BIRTH AFFIDAVIT.

DEPARTMENT OF THE INTERIOR.
COMMISSION TO THE FIVE CIVILIZED TRIBES.

    IN RE APPLICATION FOR ENROLLMENT, as a citizen of the   Choctaw   Nation, of Edward A Harris   , born on the 4 day of September , 1904

Name of Father: Henry Harris   a citizen of the Choc   Nation.
Name of Mother: Frances Harris   a citizen of the U States   Nation.

                  Postoffice   Monroe I.T.

AFFIDAVIT OF MOTHER.

UNITED STATES OF AMERICA, Indian Territory,
    Central   **DISTRICT.**

    I, Frances Harris   , on oath state that I am 24 years of age and a citizen by _____ , of the United States Nation; that I am the lawful wife of Henry

Applications for Enrollment of Choctaw Newborn
Act of 1905 Volume XIX

Harris, who is a citizen, by blood of the Choctaw Nation; that a male child was born to me on 4th day of September , 1904; that said child has been named Edward A Harris , and was living March 4, 1905.

Frances Harris

Witnesses To Mark:
{ Chas. T. Difendafer
{ OL Johnson

Subscribed and sworn to before me this 18 day of April , 1905

OL Johnson
Notary Public.

AFFIDAVIT OF ATTENDING PHYSICIAN OR MID-WIFE.

UNITED STATES OF AMERICA, Indian Territory, }
Central DISTRICT. }

I, C.E. Riggins[sic] , a physician , on oath state that I attended on Mrs. Frances Harris , wife of Henry Harris on the 4 day of September , 1904; that there was born to her on said date a male child; that said child was living March 4, 1905, and is said to have been named Edward A. Harris

C.E. Riggan M.D.

Witnesses To Mark:
{

Subscribed and sworn to before me this 9 day of May , 1905

(Name Illegible)
Notary Public.

7-2292

Muskogee, Indian Territory, May 12, 1905.

Henry Harris,
    Monroe, Indian Territory.

Dear Sir:

Receipt is hereby acknowledged of the affidavits of Francis Harris and C. E. Riggan to the birth of Edward A. Harris son of Henry and Francis Harris, September 4,

Applications for Enrollment of Choctaw Newborn
Act of 1905 Volume XIX

1904, and the same have been filed with our records as an application for the enrollment of said child.

                         Respectfully,

                                               Chairman.

Choc. New Born 1429
       Anna Wilson
       (Born Nov. 10, 1904)

NEW-BORN AFFIDAVIT.

               Number..................

           ...Choctaw Enrolling Commission...

      IN THE MATTER OF THE APPLICATION FOR ENROLLMENT, as a citizen of the Choctaw   Nation, of   Anna Wilson

born on the   10th day of   November   190 4

Name of father   Ed Wilson   a citizen of   Choctaw
Nation final enrollment No.   2220
Name of mother   Sarah Wilson   *nee Shield*   a citizen of   Choctaw
Nation final enrollment No.   11937

                                     Postoffice   Atoka I.T.

                     AFFIDAVIT OF MOTHER.

UNITED STATES OF AMERICA
INDIAN TERRITORY
    Central   DISTRICT

             I   Sarah Wilson *nee Shields*   , on oath state that I am   27   years of age and a citizen by   blood   of the   Choctaw   Nation, and as such have been placed upon the final roll of the   Choctaw   Nation, by the Honorable Secretary of the Interior my final enrollment number being   11937   ; that I am the lawful wife of   Ed Wilson   , who is a citizen of the   Choctaw   Nation, and as such has been placed upon the final roll of said Nation by the Honorable Secretary of the Interior, his final enrollment number being   2220   and that a   Female   child was born to me on the   10th day of   November   190 4; that said child has been named   Anna Wilson nee Shield[sic]   , and is now living.

Applications for Enrollment of Choctaw Newborn
Act of 1905 Volume XIX

                     her
             Anna x Wilson nee Shield

Witnesseth.   mark

    Must be two   Ben Moses
    Witnesses who
    are Citizens.   Robert Boyd

Subscribed and sworn to before me this 2^d day of March 1905

                     AE Folsom
                                    Notary Public.

My commission expires:
Jan 9 - 1909

AFFIDAVIT OF ATTENDING PHYSICIAN OR MIDWIFE

UNITED STATES OF AMERICA
INDIAN TERRITORY
    Central   DISTRICT

    I, Nancy Shield a mid wife on oath state that I attended on Mrs. Sarah Wilson nee Shield wife of Ed Wilson on the 10th day of November, 1904, that there was born to her on said date a Female child, that said child is now living, and is said to have been named Anna Wilson

                     her
             Nancy x Shield   M.D.
WITNESSETH: mark

    Must be two witnesses   Ben Moses
    who are citizens and
    know the child.   Robert Boyd

Subscribed and sworn to before me this, the 2^d day of March 1905

                   AE Folsom   Notary Public.

    We hereby certify that we are well acquainted with Nancy Shield a mid wife and know her to be reputable and of good standing in the community.

                           Ben Moses

                           Robert Boyd

Applications for Enrollment of Choctaw Newborn
Act of 1905   Volume XIX

BIRTH AFFIDAVIT.

DEPARTMENT OF THE INTERIOR.
COMMISSION TO THE FIVE CIVILIZED TRIBES.

IN RE APPLICATION FOR ENROLLMENT, as a citizen of the Choctaw Nation, of Anna Wilson, born on the 10th day of November, 1904

Name of Father: Ed Wilson   *Roll 2220*   a citizen of the Choctaw Nation.
Name of Mother: Sarah Wilson *nee Shields*   a citizen of the Choctaw Nation.
Roll 11937

Postoffice   Atoka I.T.

AFFIDAVIT OF MOTHER.

UNITED STATES OF AMERICA, Indian Territory, } DISTRICT.

I, Sarah Wilson, on oath state that I am 19 years of age and a citizen by blood, of the Choctaw Nation; that I am the lawful wife of Ed Wilson, who is a citizen, by blood of the Choctaw Nation; that a female child was born to me on 10th day of November, 1904; that said child has been named Anna Wilson, and was living March 4, 1905.

Her
Sarah x Wilson
mark

Witnesses To Mark:
{ Ben Moses
{ *(Name Illegible)*

Subscribed and sworn to before me this 21 day of August, 1905

WA McBride
Notary Public.

AFFIDAVIT OF ATTENDING PHYSICIAN OR MID-WIFE.

UNITED STATES OF AMERICA, Indian Territory, } DISTRICT.

I, Nancy Shield, a midwife, on oath state that I attended on Mrs. Sarah Wilson, wife of Ed Wilson on the 10th day of November, 1904; that there was born to her on said date a female child; that said child was living March 4, 1905, and is said to have been named Anna Wilson

her
Nancy x Shield
mark

Applications for Enrollment of Choctaw Newborn
Act of 1905   Volume XIX

Witnesses To Mark:
{ Ben Moses
{ Sim Moses

Subscribed and sworn to before me this 21st day of   August   , 1905

WA McBride
Notary Public.

My Com expires Aug 30th 1908

BIRTH AFFIDAVIT.

DEPARTMENT OF THE INTERIOR,
COMMISSIONER TO THE FIVE CIVILIZED TRIBES.

ENROLLMENT OF MINORS.   ACT OF CONGRESS, APPROVED APRIL 26, 1906.

IN RE APPLICATION FOR ENROLLMENT, as a citizen of the   Choctaw   Nation, of   Anna Wilson   , born on the   10   day of   November   , 1904

Name of Father: Ed Wilson   a citizen of the   Choctaw   Nation.
Name of Mother: Sarah Wilson   a citizen of the   Choctaw   Nation.

Tribal enrollment of father   Freedman   Tribal enrollment of mother   Choctaw

Postoffice   Atoka, Indian Territory

AFFIDAVIT OF MOTHER.

UNITED STATES OF AMERICA, Indian Territory, }
   Central   District.   }

I,   Sarah Wilson   , on oath state that I am................years of age and a citizen by .... , of the   Choctaw   Nation; that I am the lawful wife of   Ed Wilson   , who is a citizen, by   Blood   of the   Choctaw   Nation; that a   female   child was born to me on   10th day of   November   , 1904, that said child has been named   Anna Wilson   , and was living March *16*, 190*5*.

her
Sarah x Wilson
mark

WITNESSES TO MARK:
{ W.L. Thomas
{ *(Name Illegible)*

Applications for Enrollment of Choctaw Newborn
Act of 1905   Volume XIX

Subscribed and sworn to before me this 28th day of November , 1906.

> *(Name Illegible)*
> Notary Public.
> My commission expires
> Dec 5, 1909

AFFIDAVIT OF ATTENDING PHYSICIAN OR MID-WIFE.

UNITED STATES OF AMERICA, Indian Territory,
Central District.

    I, Nancy Shields[sic] , a .... , on oath state that I attended on Sarah Wilson , wife of Ed Wilson on the 10 day of November , 1904 ; that there was born to her on said date a female child; that said child was living ~~March 4, 1906~~, and is said to have been named Anna Wilson
March 16, 1905

WITNESSES TO MARK:
    { W.L. Thomas
      (Name Illegible)

her
Nancy x Shield
mark

Subscribed and sworn to before me this 28th day of November , 1906.

> *(Name Illegible)*
> Notary Public.
> My commission expires
> Dec 5, 1909

7--NB--1429

Muskogee, Indian Territory, June 1, 1905.

Ed Wilson,
    Atoka, Indian Territory.

Dear Sir:

    There is enclosed you herewith for execution application for the enrollment of your infant child, Anna Wilson, born November 10, 1904.

    The affidavits heretofore filed with the Commission show the child was living on March, 1905. It is necessary, for the child to be enrolled, that she was living on March 4, 1905.

    In having these affidavits executed care should be exercised to see that all names are written in full, as they appear in the body of the affidavit, and in the event that either

Applications for Enrollment of Choctaw Newborn
Act of 1905   Volume XIX

of the persons signing the affidavit are unable to write, signatures by mark must be attested by two witnesses. Each affidavit must be executed before a Notary Public and the notarial seal and signature of the officer must be attached to each separate affidavit.

>Respectfully,
>
>Chairman.

FVK-14

7-NB-1429

>Muskogee, Indian Territory, July 28, 1905.

Ed Wilson,
    Atoka, Indian Territory.

Dear Sir:

    Your attention is called to a communication addressed to you by the Commission to the Five Civilized Tribes, under date of June 1, 1905, with which there was inclosed application to be executed for the enrollment of your infant child, Anna Wilson, born November 10, 1904.

    In said letter you were advised that the affidavits heretofore filed in this office show that the child was living March 2, 1905, that it would be necessary for the child to be enrolled that she was living on March 4, 1905. No reply to this letter has been received.

    You are requested to have the application executed in due form and return to this office immediately, as no further action can be taken relative to the enrollment of your said child, until the evidence requested is supplied.

>Respectfully,
>
>Commissioner.

Applications for Enrollment of Choctaw Newborn
Act of 1905   Volume XIX

7-NB-1429

Muskogee, Indian Territory, August 25, 1905.

Sarah Wilson,
    Atoka, Indian Territory.

Dear Madam:

    Receipt is hereby acknowledged of your letter of August 22, 1905, transmitting your affidavit and the affidavit of Nancy Shield to the birth of Anna Wilson, daughter of Ed and Sarah Wilson, November 10, 1904, and the same have been filed in the matter of the enrollment of said child.

                      Respectfully,

                                  Commissioner.

---

7 NB 1429

Muskogee, Indian Territory, December 17, 1906.

George F. Robertson,
    Atoka, Indian Territory.

Dear Sir:

    Receipt is hereby acknowledged of your letter of December 8, 1906, inclosing affidavits to the birth of Anna Wilson, child of Ed and Sarah Wilson November 10, 1904 in response to office letter of July 28, 1905.

    In reply to your letter you are advised that Anna Wilson was enrolled as a new born citizen of the Choctaw Nation under the act of Congress approved March 3, 1905 and her enrollment as such was approved by the Secretary of the Interior March 14, 1906.

                      Respectfully,

                                  Commissioner.

Applications for Enrollment of Choctaw Newborn
Act of 1905   Volume XIX

Choc. New Born 1430
     Bertsworth Martin
     (Born Apr. 23, 1904)

NEW-BORN AFFIDAVIT.

        Number..................

...Choctaw Enrolling Commission...

     IN THE MATTER OF THE APPLICATION FOR ENROLLMENT, as a citizen of the Choctaw Nation, of Bertsworth Martin

born on the 23 day of __April__ 190 4

Name of father   William Martin Jr   a citizen of   Choctaw
Nation final enrollment No.   ~~8002~~ 7376
Name of mother   Charlotte Martin   a citizen of   Choctaw
Nation final enrollment No.   8002

                                    Postoffice   Stigler, I.T.

AFFIDAVIT OF MOTHER.

UNITED STATES OF AMERICA
INDIAN TERRITORY
   Central   DISTRICT

       I   Charlotte Martin   , on oath state that I am 21 years of age and a citizen by   blood   of the   Choctaw   Nation, and as such have been placed upon the final roll of the   Choctaw   Nation, by the Honorable Secretary of the Interior my final enrollment number being   8002 ; that I am the lawful wife of   William Martin Jr   , who is a citizen of the   Choctaw   Nation, and as such has been placed upon the final roll of said Nation by the Honorable Secretary of the Interior, his final enrollment number being   7376   and that a   Male   child was born to me on the 23 day of   April   190 4; that said child has been named   Bertsworth Martin   , and is now living.

                                    Charlotte Martin

Witnesseth.
   Must be two
   Witnesses who   Ben Jackson
   are Citizens.   James Cooper

Applications for Enrollment of Choctaw Newborn
Act of 1905   Volume XIX

Subscribed and sworn to before me this 3 day of Jan 190 5

James Bower
Notary Public.

My commission expires:
Sept 23 1907

AFFIDAVIT OF ATTENDING PHYSICIAN OR MIDWIFE

UNITED STATES OF AMERICA
INDIAN TERRITORY
   Central   DISTRICT

I, R.F. Terrell a Practicing Physician on oath state that I attended on Mrs. Charlotte Martin wife of William Martin Jr on the 23^d day of April , 190 4, that there was born to her on said date a male child, that said child is now living, and is said to have been named Bertsworth Martin

R.F. Terrell

Subscribed and sworn to before me this, the 3 day of January 190 5

James Bower   Notary Public.

WITNESSETH:
Must be two witnesses who are citizens
   { Emeline Scott
     Anna Martin

We hereby certify that we are well acquainted with _____ a_____ and know _____ to be reputable and of good standing in the community.

   James Cooper   _____

   Ben Jackson   _____

BIRTH AFFIDAVIT.
DEPARTMENT OF THE INTERIOR.
COMMISSION TO THE FIVE CIVILIZED TRIBES.

IN RE APPLICATION FOR ENROLLMENT, as a citizen of the Choctaw Nation, of Bertsworth Martin , born on the 23d day of April , 1904

Name of Father: William Martin   a citizen of the Choctaw Nation.
Name of Mother: Charlotte Martin   a citizen of the Choctaw Nation.

Postoffice   Stigler, I.T.

Applications for Enrollment of Choctaw Newborn
Act of 1905 Volume XIX

AFFIDAVIT OF MOTHER.

UNITED STATES OF AMERICA, Indian Territory, }
Central DISTRICT. }

I, Charlotte Martin, on oath state that I am 22 years of age and a citizen by blood, of the Choctaw Nation; that I am the lawful wife of William Martin, who is a citizen, by blood of the Choctaw Nation; that a male child was born to me on 23 day of April, 1904; that said child has been named Bertsworth Martin, and was living March 4, 1905.

Charlotte Martin

Witnesses To Mark:
{

Subscribed and sworn to before me this 3 day of April, 1905

E.M. Dalton
Notary Public.
My commission expires Oct 20, 1908

AFFIDAVIT OF ATTENDING PHYSICIAN OR MID-WIFE.

UNITED STATES OF AMERICA, Indian Territory, }
Central DISTRICT. }

I, R.F. Terrell, a Physician, on oath state that I attended on Mrs. Charlotte Martin, wife of William Martin on the 23rd day of April, 1904; that there was born to her on said date a male child; that said child was living March 4, 1905, and is said to have been named Bertsworth Martin

R.F. Terrell, M.D.

Witnesses To Mark:
{

Subscribed and sworn to before me this 5th day of April, 1905

E.M. Dalton
Notary Public.
My commission expires Oct 20, 1908

Applications for Enrollment of Choctaw Newborn
Act of 1905   Volume XIX

Choctaw 2628.

Muskogee, Indian Territory, April 18, 1905.

Foster & Dalton,
    Attorneys at Law,
        Stigler, Indian Territory.

Gentlemen:

    Receipt is hereby acknowledged of your letter of April 4, transmitting the affidavits of Charlotte Martin and R. F. Terrell to the birth of Bertsworth Martin, son of William and Charlotte Martin, April 23, 1904. It is stated in the affidavit of the mother that she is a citizen by blood of the Choctaw Nation, and if this is correct you are requested to state under what name she was enrolled, the names of her parents, and if she has selected an allotment of the lands of the Choctaw and Chickasaw Nations, please give her roll number as the same appears upon her allotment certificate.

Respectfully,

Chairman.

Choc. New Born 1431
    Roxy Henson
    (Born Feb. 19, 1903)

BIRTH AFFIDAVIT.

DEPARTMENT OF THE INTERIOR.
COMMISSION TO THE FIVE CIVILIZED TRIBES.

IN RE APPLICATION FOR ENROLLMENT, as a citizen of the Choctaw Nation, of Roxy Henson, born on the 19th day of February, 1903

Name of Father: Andrew Henson   a citizen of the --------- Nation.
Name of Mother: Alice Henson, nee Wheat   a citizen of the Choctaw Nation.

Postoffice   Quinton, Indian Territory.

Applications for Enrollment of Choctaw Newborn
Act of 1905   Volume XIX

AFFIDAVIT OF MOTHER.

UNITED STATES OF AMERICA, Indian Territory,
Western   DISTRICT.

I,   Alice Henson, nee Wheat   , on oath state that I am   23   years of age and a citizen by   blood   , of the   Choctaw   Nation; that I am the lawful wife of Andrew Henson   , who is a citizen, by   -----------   of the   --------------------   Nation; that a   Female   child was born to me on   19th   day of   February   , 1903; that said child has been named   Roxy Henson   , and was living March 4, 1905.

her
Alice x Henson
mark

Witnesses To Mark:
{ (Name Illegible) Quinton I.T.
{ (Name Illegible) Quinton I.T.

Subscribed and sworn to before me this 1st day of   May   , 1905

Guy A Curry
Notary Public.

AFFIDAVIT OF ATTENDING PHYSICIAN OR MID-WIFE.

UNITED STATES OF AMERICA, Indian Territory,
Western   DISTRICT.

I,   Lena Henson   , a   mid-wife   , on oath state that I attended on Mrs.   Alice Henson   , wife of   Andrew Henson   on the   19th   day of February, 1903; that there was born to her on said date a   Female   child; that said child was living March 4, 1905, and is said to have been named   Roxy Henson

Lena Henson

Witnesses To Mark:
{

Subscribed and sworn to before me this 1st day of   May   , 1905

Guy A Curry
Notary Public.

Applications for Enrollment of Choctaw Newborn
Act of 1905 Volume XIX

7--4523.

Muskogee, Indian Territory, May 9, 1905.

Andrew Henson,
    Quinton, Indian Territory.

Dear Sir:

    Receipt is hereby acknowledged of the affidavits of Alice Henson and Lena Henson to the birth of Roxy Henson, daughter of Andrew and Alice Henson, February 19, 1903, and the same have been filed with our records as an application for the enrollment of said child.

                    Respectfully,

                                    Commissioner in Charge.

Choc. New Born 1432
    Phoebe Coleman
    (Born Feb. 23, 1905)

BIRTH AFFIDAVIT.

DEPARTMENT OF THE INTERIOR.
COMMISSION TO THE FIVE CIVILIZED TRIBES.

    IN RE APPLICATION FOR ENROLLMENT, as a citizen of the Choctaw Nation, of Phoebe Coleman, born on the 23rd day of Feby, 1905

Name of Father: Norman Coleman   a citizen of the Choctaw Nation.
Name of Mother: Elie Coleman *(nee Moore)*   a citizen of the Choctaw Nation.

                    Postoffice   Caney, IT

AFFIDAVIT OF MOTHER.

UNITED STATES OF AMERICA, Indian Territory, }
    Central   DISTRICT.

    I, Elie Coleman *(nee Elie Moore)*, on oath state that I am 20 years of age and a citizen by blood, of the Choctaw Nation; that I am the lawful wife of

Applications for Enrollment of Choctaw Newborn
Act of 1905   Volume XIX

Norman Coleman, who is a citizen, by blood of the Choctaw Nation; that a female child was born to me on 23rd day of February, 1905; that said child has been named Phoebe Coleman, and was living March 4, 1905.

                                            Elie Coleman

Witnesses To Mark:
{

    Subscribed and sworn to before me this 2nd day of May, 1905.

                                          W.H. Angell
                                          Notary Public.

AFFIDAVIT OF ATTENDING PHYSICIAN OR MID-WIFE.

UNITED STATES OF AMERICA, Indian Territory, }
    Central   DISTRICT.}

    I, Louisa Jones, a Mid wife, on oath state that I attended on Mrs. Elie Coleman *(nee Moore)*, wife of Norman Coleman on the 23rd day of February, 1905; that there was born to her on said date a female child; that said child was living March 4, 1905, and is said to have been named Phoebe Coleman

                                       Her
                                Louisa x Jones
Witnesses To Mark: mark
{ *(Name Illegible)*
  James Culberson

    Subscribed and sworn to before me this 2nd day of May, 1905.

                                          W.H. Angell
                                          Notary Public.

Choc. New Born 1433
        Minnie Holloway
        (Born Sep. 3, 1903)

Applications for Enrollment of Choctaw Newborn
Act of 1905   Volume XIX

NEW-BORN AFFIDAVIT.

Number..............

...Choctaw Enrolling Commission...

IN THE MATTER OF THE APPLICATION FOR ENROLLMENT, as a citizen of the Choctaw Nation, of   Minnie Holloway

born on the 3 day of __September__   190 3

Name of father   John Holloway   a citizen of   Choctaw
Nation final enrollment No. 8738   (*Sissie John*)
Name of mother   Sissie Holloway   a citizen of   Choctaw
Nation final enrollment No. 8921

Postoffice   LeFlore I.T.

AFFIDAVIT OF MOTHER.

UNITED STATES OF AMERICA
INDIAN TERRITORY
    Central   DISTRICT

I   Sissie Holloway   (*Sissie John*)   , on oath state that I am 22 years of age and a citizen by blood of the Choctaw Nation, and as such have been placed upon the final roll of the Choctaw Nation, by the Honorable Secretary of the Interior my final enrollment number being 8921 ; that I am the lawful wife of   John Holloway   , who is a citizen of the   Choctaw   Nation, and as such has been placed upon the final roll of said Nation by the Honorable Secretary of the Interior, his final enrollment number being   8738   and that a   female   child was born to me on the   22[sic]   day of   September   190 3; that said child has been named   Minnie Holloway   , and is now living.

                                Sissie Holloway

Witnesseth.
 Must be two ⎫   Willie Isaac
 Witnesses who ⎬
 are Citizens. ⎭   Morris Sam

Subscribed and sworn to before me this   28 day of   Feb   190 5

                                Robert E Lee
                                     Notary Public.

My commission expires: Jany 11 1906

Applications for Enrollment of Choctaw Newborn
Act of 1905   Volume XIX

AFFIDAVIT OF ATTENDING PHYSICIAN OR MIDWIFE

UNITED STATES OF AMERICA
INDIAN TERRITORY
   Central   DISTRICT

I,   Mertha Collin   a   Midwife   on oath state that I attended on Mrs. Sissie Holloway *(Sissie John)* wife of   John Holloway   on the   22[sic]   day of   September , 190 3 , that there was born to her on said date a female   child, that said child is now living, and is said to have been named   Minnie Holloway

                                      Mertha Collin   *M.D.*

        Subscribed and sworn to before me this, the   28   day of February   190 5

                          Robert E Lee   Notary Public.

WITNESSETH: { Willie Isaac
Must be two witnesses
who are citizens   Morris Sam

    We hereby certify that we are well acquainted with   Mertha Collin   a   Midwife   and know   her   to be reputable and of good standing in the community.

                                      Willie Isaac

                                      Morris Sam

BIRTH AFFIDAVIT.

DEPARTMENT OF THE INTERIOR.
COMMISSION TO THE FIVE CIVILIZED TRIBES.

IN RE APPLICATION FOR ENROLLMENT, as a citizen of the   Choctaw   Nation, of   Minnie Holloway , born on the   3rd   day of   Sept , 1903

Name of Father: John Holloway   a citizen of the   Choctaw   Nation.
                      (nee Sissie John)
Name of Mother: Sissie Holloway   a citizen of the   Choctaw   Nation.

                      Postoffice   Leflore, I.T.

Applications for Enrollment of Choctaw Newborn
Act of 1905 Volume XIX

AFFIDAVIT OF MOTHER.

UNITED STATES OF AMERICA, Indian Territory,
Central DISTRICT.

I, Sissie Holloway *(nee Sissie John)*, on oath state that I am 22 years of age and a citizen by blood, of the Choctaw Nation; that I am the lawful wife of John Holloway, who is a citizen, by blood of the Choctaw Nation; that a female child was born to me on 3rd day of Sept, 1903; that said child has been named Minnie Holloway, and was living March 4, 1905.

Sissie Holloway (nee John)

Witnesses To Mark:

Subscribed and sworn to before me this 18 day of April, 1905.

Robert E Lee
Notary Public.

My com expires Jan 11-1906

AFFIDAVIT OF ATTENDING PHYSICIAN OR MID-WIFE.

UNITED STATES OF AMERICA, Indian Territory,
Central DISTRICT.

I, Mertha Collin, a midwife, on oath state that I attended on Mrs. Sissie Holloway (nee John), wife of John Holloway on the 3rd day of September, 1903; that there was born to her on said date a female child; that said child was living March 4, 1905, and is said to have been named Minnie Holloway

Mertha x Collin
mark

Witnesses To Mark:
  W H Hawkins
  Jesse Collin

Subscribed and sworn to before me this 18 day of April, 1905.

Robert E Lee
Notary Public.

My com expires Jan 11-1906

Final enrollment No. of John Holloway being No   8738
Final enrollment No. of Sissie Holloway nee[sic] *being No.* 8921

Applications for Enrollment of Choctaw Newborn
Act of 1905 Volume XIX

BIRTH AFFIDAVIT.

DEPARTMENT OF THE INTERIOR.
COMMISSION TO THE FIVE CIVILIZED TRIBES.

IN RE APPLICATION FOR ENROLLMENT, as a citizen of the Choctaw Nation, of Minnie Holloway, born on the 3 day of Sept, 1903

Name of Father: John Holloway Roll 8738 a citizen of the Choctaw Nation.
Name of Mother: Sissie Holloway " 8921 a citizen of the Choctaw Nation.
nee John

Postoffice   LeFlore I.T.

AFFIDAVIT OF MOTHER.

UNITED STATES OF AMERICA, Indian Territory, } DISTRICT.

I, Sissie Holloway, nee John, on oath state that I am 22 years of age and a citizen by blood, of the Choctaw Nation; that I am the lawful wife of John Holloway, who is a citizen, by blood of the Choctaw Nation; that a female child was born to me on 3 day of Sept, 1903; that said child has been named Minnie Holloway, and was living March 4, 1905.

Sissie Holloway nee John

Witnesses To Mark:
{

Subscribed and sworn to before me this 16 day of June, 1905

My Com Exp 7/8/08   W.L. Harris
                           Notary Public.

AFFIDAVIT OF ATTENDING PHYSICIAN OR MID-WIFE.

UNITED STATES OF AMERICA, Indian Territory, } Central DISTRICT.

I, Mertha Collin, a midwife, on oath state that I attended on Mrs. Sissie Holloway, wife of John Holloway on the 3 day of Sept, 1903; that there was born to her on said date a female child; that said child was living March 4, 1905, and is said to have been named Minnie Holloway

                    her
            Mertha x Collin
                    mark

Applications for Enrollment of Choctaw Newborn
Act of 1905   Volume XIX

Witnesses To Mark:
{ Morris Sam
{ *(Name Illegible)*

    Subscribed and sworn to before me this   16 day of   June   , 1905

My Com Exp 7/8/08   W.L. Harris
                                    Notary Public.

                                                    7--NB--1433

                          Muskogee, Indian Territory, June 2, 1905.

John Holloway,
    LeFlore, Indian Territory.

Dear Sir:

    There is enclosed you herewith for execution application for the enrollment of your infant child, Minnie Holloway.

    In the affidavits of February 28, 1905, the date of the applicant's birth is given as September 22, 1903, while in the affidavits of April 18, 1905, this date is given as September 3, 1903. In the enclosed application the date of birth is left blank. Please insert the correct date and when the affidavits are properly executed return them to this office.

    In having these affidavits executed care should be exercised to see that all names are written in full, as they appear in the body of the affidavit, and in the event that either of the persons signing the affidavit are unable to write, signatures by mark must be attested by two witnesses. Each affidavit must be executed before a Notary Public and the notarial seal and signature of the officer must be attached to each separate affidavit.

    This matter should receive your immediate attention as no further action can be taken relative to the enrollment of said child until the Commission has been furnished these affidavits.

                          Respectfully,

Enc-FVK-6   [sic]

Applications for Enrollment of Choctaw Newborn
Act of 1905 Volume XIX

7 NB 1433

Muskogee, Indian Territory, June 20, 1905.

John Holloway,
    Leflore, Indian Territory.

Dear Sir:

    Receipt is hereby acknowledged of the affidavits of Sissie Holloway nee John and Mertha Collin to the birth of Minnie Holloway daughter of John and Sissie Holloway, September 3, 1903, and the same have been filed with our records in the matter of the enrollment of said child.

                  Respectfully,

                              Chairman.

Choc. New Born 1434
    Thompson McKinney
    (Born Feb. 16, 1905)

NEW BORN AFFIDAVIT

No

CHOCTAW ENROLLING COMMISSION

IN THE MATTER OF THE APPLICATION FOR ENROLLMENT as a citizen of the Choctaw Nation, of Thompson McKinney born on the 16th day of Feb 190 5

Name of father Swinney McKinney   a citizen of Choctaw Nation, final enrollment No. 5990

Name of mother Bisey McKinney   a citizen of Choctaw Nation, final enrollment No. 8310

                          Sans Bois   Postoffice.

Applications for Enrollment of Choctaw Newborn
Act of 1905 Volume XIX

AFFIDAVIT OF MOTHER

UNITED STATES OF AMERICA }
INDIAN TERRITORY }
DISTRICT   Western }

I   Bisey McKinney   , on oath state that I am 23   years of age and a citizen by   blood   of the   Choctaw   Nation, and as such have been placed upon the final roll of the   Choctaw   Nation, by the Honorable Secretary of the Interior my final enrollment number being   8310   ; that I am the lawful wife of   Swinney McKinney   , who is a citizen of the   Choctaw   Nation, and as such has been placed upon the final roll of said Nation by the Honorable Secretary of the Interior, his final enrollment number being   5990   and that a   Male   child was born to me on the   16th day of   February   190 5; that said child has been named   Thompson McKinney   , and is now living.

                                            her
                                  Bisey x McKinney

WITNESSETH: mark

Must be two witnesses { Isom Thompson
who are citizens   { William Thompson

Subscribed and sworn to before me this, the   31 day of   March   , 190 5

                                  HW Mason
                                      Notary Public.

My Commission Expires:

Affidavit of Attending Physician or Midwife

UNITED STATES OF AMERICA, }
INDIAN TERRITORY, }
Western   DISTRICT }

I,   A.C. Foyil   a   physician on oath state that I attended on Mrs. Bisey McKinney   wife of Swinney McKinney on the   16th day of   February , 190 5, that there was born to her on said date a   male child, that said child is now living, and is said to have been named   Thompson McKinney

                                A.C. Foyil   M. D.

Subscribed and sworn to before me this the   30   day of   March   1905

                                H W Mason
                                Notary Public.

WITNESSETH:

Must be two witnesses { Isom Thompson
who are citizens and   {
know the child.   { William Thompson

Applications for Enrollment of Choctaw Newborn
Act of 1905   Volume XIX

We hereby certify that we are well acquainted with A. C. Foyil a physician and know him to be reputable and of good standing in the community.

Must be two citizen witnesses. { Isom Thompson / William Thompson }

BIRTH AFFIDAVIT.

DEPARTMENT OF THE INTERIOR.
COMMISSION TO THE FIVE CIVILIZED TRIBES.

IN RE APPLICATION FOR ENROLLMENT, as a citizen of the Choctaw Nation, of Thompson McKinney, born on the 16th day of February, 1905

Name of Father: Swinney McKinney   a citizen of the Choctaw Nation.
Name of Mother: Bisey Thompson   a citizen of the Choctaw Nation.

Postoffice   San Bois, Ind Ter

AFFIDAVIT OF MOTHER.

UNITED STATES OF AMERICA, Indian Territory,
Western DISTRICT.

I, Bisey Thompson, on oath state that I am 23 years of age and a citizen by Blood, of the Choctaw Nation; that I am the lawful wife of Swinney McKinney, who is a citizen, by Blood of the Choctaw Nation; that a male child was born to me on 16th day of February, 1905; that said child has been named Thompson McKinney, and was living March 4, 1905.

Bisey Thompson

Witnesses To Mark:
{ Jimpson Thompson / (Name Illegible) }

Subscribed and sworn to before me this 25th day of April, 1905

My commission expires Dec. 19, 1908

H W Mason
Notary Public.

Applications for Enrollment of Choctaw Newborn
Act of 1905   Volume XIX

AFFIDAVIT OF ATTENDING PHYSICIAN OR MID-WIFE.

UNITED STATES OF AMERICA, Indian Territory, }
.... DISTRICT. }

    I,   A. C. Foyil   , a   Physician   , on oath state that I attended on Mrs.   Bisey Thompson   , wife of   Swinney McKinney   on the 16   day of Feby , 1905; that there was born to her on said date a   male   child; that said child was living March 4, 1905, and is said to have been named Thompson McKinney

                                      A.C. Foyil a regular practicing physician

Witnesses To Mark:
  { HW Mason
  { Jimpson Thompson

    Subscribed and sworn to before me this 25th day of   April   , 1905

My commission expires Dec. 19, 1908   H W Mason
                                                    Notary Public.

                                                                ~~7-2826~~

                          Muskogee, Indian Territory, May 9, 1905.

Swinney McKinney,
    Sans Bois, Indian Territory.

Dear Sir:

    Receipt is hereby acknowledged of the affidavits of Bisey Thompson, and A. C. Foyil to the birth of Thompson McKinney, son of Swinney McKinney and Bisey Thompson, February 16, 1905, and the same have been filed with our records as an application for the enrollment of said child.

                                    Respectfully,

                                            Commissioner in Charge.

Applications for Enrollment of Choctaw Newborn
Act of 1905   Volume XIX

Choc. New Born 1435
    Louisa Bacon
    (Born May 15, 1903)
    Mattie Bacon
    (Born Feb. 1, 1904)

BIRTH AFFIDAVIT.

DEPARTMENT OF THE INTERIOR.
COMMISSION TO THE FIVE CIVILIZED TRIBES.

IN RE APPLICATION FOR ENROLLMENT, as a citizen of the Choctaw Nation, of Mattie Bacon, born on the 1st day of February, 1905[sic]

Name of Father: Daniel Bacon   a citizen of the Choctaw Nation.
Name of Mother: Epsie Bacon   a citizen of the Chickasaw Nation.

        Postoffice   Blanco, Ind. Ter.

AFFIDAVIT OF MOTHER.

UNITED STATES OF AMERICA, Indian Territory,
    Central   DISTRICT.

I, Epsie Bacon, on oath state that I am 40 years of age and a citizen by blood, of the Chickasaw Nation; that I am the lawful wife of Daniel Bacon, who is a citizen, by blood of the Choctaw Nation; that a female child was born to me on 1st day of February, 1905; that said child has been named Mattie Bacon, and was living March 4, 1905.

                               her
                          Epsie x Bacon
Witnesses To Mark: mark
    OL Johnson
    Chas. T. Difendafer

    Subscribed and sworn to before me this 28th day of April, 1905

                          OL Johnson
                              Notary Public.

Applications for Enrollment of Choctaw Newborn
Act of 1905   Volume XIX

AFFIDAVIT OF ATTENDING PHYSICIAN OR MID-WIFE.

UNITED STATES OF AMERICA, Indian Territory, }
   Central   DISTRICT.

    I,   Martha E. Dailey   , a   midwife , on oath state that I attended on Mrs. Epsie Bacon , wife of Daniel Bacon   on the 1st day of February , 1905; that there was born to her on said date a   female   child; that said child was living March 4, 1905, and is said to have been named Mattie Bacon

                               Martha E Dailey

Witnesses To Mark:
{

    Subscribed and sworn to before me this 28th day of   April   , 1905

                               OL Johnson
                               Notary Public.

BIRTH AFFIDAVIT.

DEPARTMENT OF THE INTERIOR.
COMMISSION TO THE FIVE CIVILIZED TRIBES.

    IN RE APPLICATION FOR ENROLLMENT, as a citizen of the   Choctaw   Nation, of Louisa Bacon , born on the   15 day of May , 1903

Name of Father: Daniel Bacon   a citizen of the Choctaw Nation.
Name of Mother: Epsie Bacon   a citizen of the Chickasaw Nation.

                    Postoffice   Blanco, Ind. Ter.

AFFIDAVIT OF MOTHER.

UNITED STATES OF AMERICA, Indian Territory, }
   Central   DISTRICT.

    I, Epsie Bacon , on oath state that I am 40 years of age and a citizen by blood , of the Chickasaw Nation; that I am the lawful wife of Daniel Bacon , who is a citizen, by blood of the Choctaw Nation; that a female child was born to me on 15 day of May , 1903; that said child has been named Louisa Bacon , and was living March 4, 1905.

                                her
                          Epsie x Bacon
                             mark

Applications for Enrollment of Choctaw Newborn
Act of 1905   Volume XIX

Witnesses To Mark:
  { Alfred Worcester
  { OL Johnson

   Subscribed and sworn to before me this 28 day of   April   , 1905

                                        OL Johnson
                                        Notary Public.

AFFIDAVIT OF ATTENDING PHYSICIAN OR MID-WIFE.

UNITED STATES OF AMERICA, Indian Territory, }
   Central   DISTRICT.   }

   I,   Martha E. Dailey   , a midwife , on oath state that I attended on Mrs. Epsie Bacon , wife of Daniel Bacon   on the 15 day of   May   ,1903; that there was born to her on said date a   female   child; that said child was living March 4, 1905, and is said to have been named Louisa Bacon

                                        Martha E Dailey

Witnesses To Mark:
  {
  {

   Subscribed and sworn to before me this 28 day of   April   , 1905

                                        OL Johnson
                                        Notary Public.

DEPARTMENT OF THE INTERIOR,
COMMISSION TO THE FIVE CIVILIZED TRIBES.
SOUTH McALESTER, IND. TER. APRIL 28, 1905.

   In the matter of the application for the enrollment of Mattie Bacon as a citizen by blood of the Chickasaw Nation.

Daniel Bacon being first duly sworn and examined through interpreter Henry Dailey testifies as follows:

EXAMINATION BY THE COMMISSION:

Q What is your name? A Daniel Bacon.
Q What is your age? A About forty.
Q What is your post office address? A Blanco.
Q You have this day made application for the enrollment of your child Mattie Bacon; when was she born? A February 1, 1904.

Applications for Enrollment of Choctaw Newborn
Act of 1905   Volume XIX

Q Was that baby living on March 4, 1905? A Yes, sir.
Q Who is the mother of that baby? A Epsie Bacon.
Q Of what nation is your wife a citizen? A Chickasaw.
Q Of what nation are you a citizen? A Choctaw.
Q Do you wish to elect in which nation this child should be enrolled? A Yes, sir.
Q In which nation do you desire to have your child enrolled? A Chickasaw.

Witness excused.

Chas. T. Difendafer being first duly sworn states that the above and foregoing is a full, true and correct transcript of his stenographic notes taken in said cause on said date.

Chas.T. Difendafer

Subscribed and sworn to before me this 28th day of April 1905.

OL Johnson
Notary Public.

DEPARTMENT OF THE INTERIOR,
COMMISSION TO THE FIVE CIVILIZED TRIBES.
SOUTH McALESTER, IND. TER. APRIL 28, 1905.

In the matter of the application for the enrollment of Louisa Bacon as a citizen by blood of the Chickasaw Nation.

Daniel bacon[sic] being first duly sworn and examined through interpreter Henry Dailey testifies as follows:

EXAMINATION BY THE COMMISSION:

Q What is your name? A Daniel Bacon.
Q What is your age? A About forty.
Q What is your post office address? A Blanco.
Q You have this day made application for the enrollment of your child Louisa Bacon; when was she born? A May 15, 1903.
Q Was Louisa living on March 4, 1905? A Yes, sir.
Q What is the name of your wife? A Epsie Bacon.
Q Of what nation is she a citizen? A Chickasaw.
Q Of what nation are you a citizen? A Choctaw.
Q Do you desire to elect in which nation Louisa shall be enrolled? A Yes, sir.
Q In which nation do you desire to have Louisa Bacon enrolled and receive her allotment of lands and distribution of money? A Chickasaw.

Witness excused.

Applications for Enrollment of Choctaw Newborn
Act of 1905   Volume XIX

Chas. T. Difendafer being first duly sworn states that the above and foregoing is a full, true and correct transcript of his stenographic notes taken in said cause on said date.

Chas.T. Difendafer

Subscribed and sworn to before me this 28th day of April 1905.

OL Johnson
Notary Public.

Choc. New Born 1436
    Sampson Noah
    (Born Dec. 5, 1903)

BIRTH AFFIDAVIT.

DEPARTMENT OF THE INTERIOR.
COMMISSION TO THE FIVE CIVILIZED TRIBES.

IN RE APPLICATION FOR ENROLLMENT, as a citizen of the Choctaw Nation, of Sampson Noah, born on the 5th day of December, 1903

Name of Father: Alfered[sic] Noah   a citizen of the Choctaw Nation.
Name of Mother: _____ a citizen of the Choctaw Nation.

Postoffice   Cairo, Ind. Ter.

AFFIDAVIT OF MOTHER.

UNITED STATES OF AMERICA, Indian Territory,
    Central   **DISTRICT.**

I, Alfered Noah, Father of Sampson Noah, on oath state that I am 31 years of age and a citizen by blood, of the Choctaw Nation; that I am the lawful ~~wife~~ husband *that Silindy Noah my wife is now dead; she died January 20" 1905* who is a citizen, by blood of the Choctaw Nation; that a male child was born to ~~me~~ his wife on 5th day of December, 1903; that said child has been named Sampson Noah, and was living March 4, 1905.

his
Alfered x Noah
mark

174

Applications for Enrollment of Choctaw Newborn
Act of 1905   Volume XIX

Witnesses To Mark:
{ N.P. McMillan
  Eli Perry

    Subscribed and sworn to before me this   4th day of   April   , 1905

Geo A Fooshee
Notary Public.

AFFIDAVIT OF ATTENDING PHYSICIAN OR MID-WIFE.

UNITED STATES OF AMERICA, Indian Territory,
   Central   DISTRICT.

    I,   Tennessee Anderson , a mid-wife , on oath state that I attended on Mrs. Sibindy Noah *now dead* , wife of Alfred Noah   on the 5th day of December , 1903; that there was born to her on said date a   male   child; that said child was living March 4, 1905, and is said to have been named Sampson Noah

her
Tennessee x Anderson
mark

Witnesses To Mark:
{ N.P. McMillan
  Eli Perry

    Subscribed and sworn to before me this 8" day of   April   , 1905

D.D. Brunson
Notary Public.

United States of America
  Indian Territory
  Central District.

Be it remembered, that on this   9   *day of*   June   *personally appeared before me*   Henry Brock   *at*   Cairo I.T.   *and after being duly sworn, on his oath stated that he was personally acquainted with*   Sibindy Noah, wife of Alfred Noah, *and that on December the fifth (5) 1903 her child Sampson Noah was born and that he was living on March the fourth (4) 1905.*

Henry Brock

Subscribed and sworn to before me this 9   *day of* June   *A.D. 1905*

W.B. Harl
Notary Public

My commission expires May *19* 07

Applications for Enrollment of Choctaw Newborn
Act of 1905   Volume XIX

United States of America
   Indian Territory
   Central District.

Be it remembered, that on this   9   *day of*   June   *personally appeared before me* J I Hayhurst   *at*   Cairo I.T.   *and after being duly sworn, on his oath stated that he was personally acquainted with Sibindy Noah, wife of Alfred Noah, and that on December the fifth (5) 1903 her child Sampson Noah was born and that he was living on March the fourth (4) 1905.*

J I Hayhurst

Subscribed and sworn to before me this   9   *day of*   June   *A.D. 1905*

W.B. Harl
Notary Public

My commission expires   May   *19* 07

Sub   7-NB-1436.

Muskogee, Indian Territory, June 3, 1905.

Alfred Noah,
   Cairo, Indian Territory.

Dear Sir:

   Referring to the application for the enrollment of your infant child, Sampson Noah, Indian Territory born December 5, 1903, it is noted from the affidavits heretofore filed in this office that the mother of the applicant is dead.

   In this event it will be necessary that you file in this office the affidavits of two persons, who are disinterested and not related to the applicant, who have actual knowledge of the facts that the child was born, the date of his birth; that he was living on Mrch 4, 1905, and that Sibindy Noah was his mother.

Respectfully,

Commissioner in Charge.

Applications for Enrollment of Choctaw Newborn
Act of 1905 Volume XIX

7 NB 1436

Muskogee, Indian Territory, June 13, 1905.

Alfred Noah,
    Cairo, Indian Territory.

Dear Sir:

Receipt is hereby acknowledged of the affidavits of Henry Brock and J. I. Hayhurst to the birth of Sampson Noah, son of Alfred and Sibindy Noah, December 5, 1903, and the same have been filed in the matter of the enrollment of said child.

    Respectfully,

    Chairman.

Choc. New Born 1437
    Lena Bell Crowder
    (Born Oct. 23, 1902)
    Maud May Crowder
    (Born Dec. 9, 1904)

This certify that Mrs Julia Crowder and Mr. Elie[sic] Crowder were united by me in the bonds of matrimony on the 4th day of January A.D. 1902

    R. C. Gardner
    County and Probate Judge
    Jackson County Choctaw Nation

Recorded this the 4th day of March A.D. 1902

    Ausbon N. Jones
    County and Probate Clerk
    Jackson County
    Choctaw Nation

Applications for Enrollment of Choctaw Newborn
Act of 1905 Volume XIX

I here by certify that the fore going is a true and correct copy of the original as on file in my office.

R. C. Gardner
County and Probate Clerk[sic]
Jackson County
Choctaw Nation
June 5th 1905

BIRTH AFFIDAVIT

Department of the Interior,
COMMISSION TO THE FIVE CIVILIZED TRIBES.

IN RE APPLICATION FOR ENROLLMENT, as a citizen of the Choctaw Nation, of Lena Crowder, born on the 23 day of October, 190 2

Name of Father: Eli Crowder   a citizen of the Choctaw Nation.
Name of Mother: Julia A. Crowder   a citizen of the Choctaw Nation.

Post-Office: Crowder, Ind. Ter

AFFIDAVIT OF MOTHER.

UNITED STATES OF AMERICA,
INDIAN TERRITORY,
Central District.

I, Julia A. Crowder, on oath state that I am 36 years of age and a citizen by adoption, of the Choctaw Nation; that I am the lawful wife of Eli Crowder, who is a citizen, by blood of the Choctaw Nation; that a female child was born to me on 23 day of October, 190 2, that said child has been named Lena Crowder, and is now living.

Julia A Crowder

WITNESSES TO MARK:

Subscribed and sworn to before me this 5 day of December, 190 2

H.C. Risteen
Notary Public.

Applications for Enrollment of Choctaw Newborn
Act of 1905   Volume XIX

NEW-BORN AFFIDAVIT.

Number..........

Choctaw Enrolling Commission.

IN THE MATTER OF THE APPLICATION FOR ENROLLMENT, as a citizen of the Choctaw Nation, of Maud May Crowder

born on the 9 day of Dec 190 4

Name of father   Eli Crowder   a citizen of   Choctaw
Nation final enrollment No   4447
Name of mother   Julia Crowder   a citizen of   ————
Nation final enrollment No   ————

Postoffice   Boswell I T

AFFIDAVIT OF MOTHER.

UNITED STATES OF AMERICA,
   INDIAN TERRITORY,
   Cent   DISTRICT

I   Julia Crowder   on oath state that I am 38 years of age and a citizen by —— of the ....Nation, and as such have been placed upon the final roll of the................Nation, by the Honorable Secretary of the Interior my final enrollment number being —— ; that I am the lawful wife of   Eli Crowder   , who is a citizen of the   Choctaw   Nation, and as such has been placed upon the final roll of said Nation by the Honorable Secretary of the Interior, his final enrollment number being   4447   and that a   Female   child was born to me on the   9th   day of   Dec   190 4 ; that said child has been named   Maud May Crowder , and is now living.

Julia Crowder

WITNESSETH:
   Must be two
   Witnesses who   G D Duncan
   are Citizens.   John T Brown

Subscribed and sworn to before me this   22   day of   Jan   190 5

Perry M Clark
Notary Public.

My commission expires   2/5/05

Applications for Enrollment of Choctaw Newborn
Act of 1905   Volume XIX

Affidavit of Attending Physician or Midwife

UNITED STATES OF AMERICA,
   INDIAN TERRITORY,
Cent   DISTRICT

I, Fannie Wallace a Midwife on oath state that I attended on Mrs. Julia Crowder wife of Eli Crowder on the 9th day of Dec, 190 4, that there was born to her on said date a Female child, that said child is now living, and is said to have been named Maud May Crowder

          Fannie Wallace   M. D.

Subscribed and sworn to before me this the 22 day of Jan 1905

          Perry M Clark
                Notary Public.

WITNESSETH:

Must be two witnesses who are citizens and know the child.
- G D Duncan
- John T Brown

We hereby certify that we are well acquainted with Fannie Wallace a Midwife and know her to be reputable and of good standing in the community.

Must be two citizen witnesses.
- G D Duncan
- John T Brown

BIRTH AFFIDAVIT.

DEPARTMENT OF THE INTERIOR.
COMMISSION TO THE FIVE CIVILIZED TRIBES.

IN RE APPLICATION FOR ENROLLMENT, as a citizen of the Choctaw Nation, of Maud May Crowder, born on the 9 day of December, 1904

Name of Father: Eli Crowder   *Roll 4447*   a citizen of the Choctaw Nation.
Name of Mother: Julia Crowder   a citizen of the non citizen Nation.

          Postoffice   Boswell IT

Applications for Enrollment of Choctaw Newborn
Act of 1905   Volume XIX

AFFIDAVIT OF MOTHER.

UNITED STATES OF AMERICA, Indian Territory,　}
　　Central　　　　　　　DISTRICT.

　　　I,　Julia Crowder　, on oath state that I am　38　years of age and a citizen by — , of the　United States　Nation; that I am the lawful wife of　Eli Crowder , who is a citizen, by blood　of the　Choctaw　Nation; that a　female　child was born to me on　9th　day of　December　, 1904; that said child has been named Maud May Crowder　, and was living March 4, 1905.

　　　　　　　　　　　　　　　　　　　　Julia Crowder

Witnesses To Mark:
{

　　　Subscribed and sworn to before me this　6th　day of　June　, 1905

　　　　　　　　　　　　　　　　　　　　Perry M Clark
　　　　　　　　　　　　　　　　　　　　　　Notary Public.

AFFIDAVIT OF ATTENDING PHYSICIAN OR MID-WIFE.

UNITED STATES OF AMERICA, Indian Territory,　}
　　Central　　　　　　　DISTRICT.

　　　I,　Fannie Wallace　　, a midwife　　, on oath state that I attended on Mrs.　Julia Crowder　, wife of　Eli Crowder　on the　9th　day of　December , 1904; that there was born to her on said date a　female　child; that said child was living March 4, 1905, and is said to have been named　Maud May Crowder

　　　　　　　　　　　　　　　　　　　　Fannie Wallace

Witnesses To Mark:
{

　　　Subscribed and sworn to before me this　6th　day of　June　, 1905

　　　　　　　　　　　　　　　　　　　　Perry M Clark
　　　　　　　　　　　　　　　　　　　　　　Notary Public.

My commission exp 2/27/09

Applications for Enrollment of Choctaw Newborn
Act of 1905   Volume XIX

NEW-BORN AFFIDAVIT.

Number..........

Choctaw Enrolling Commission.

IN THE MATTER OF THE APPLICATION FOR ENROLLMENT, as a citizen of the Choctaw   Nation, of   Lena Bell Crowder

born on the   23   day of   Oct   190 2

Name of father   Eli Crowder   a citizen of   Choctaw
Nation final enrollment No   4447
Name of mother   Julia Crowder   a citizen of   ————
Nation final enrollment No   ————

Postoffice   Boswell I T

AFFIDAVIT OF MOTHER.

UNITED STATES OF AMERICA,
INDIAN TERRITORY,
Cent   DISTRICT

I   Julia Crowder   on oath state that I am 38 years of age and a citizen by ———— of the .... Nation, and as such have been placed upon the final roll of the..........................Nation, by the Honorable Secretary of the Interior my final enrollment number being   ———— ; that I am the lawful wife of   Eli Crowder   , who is a citizen of the   Choctaw   Nation, and as such has been placed upon the final roll of said Nation by the Honorable Secretary of the Interior, his final enrollment number being   4447   and that a   Female   child was born to me on the   23   day of   Oct   190 2 ; that said child has been named   Lena Bell Crowder , and is now living.

Julia Crowder

WITNESSETH:
Must be two
Witnesses who
are Citizens.   G D Duncan

John T Brown

Subscribed and sworn to before me this   22   day of   Jan   190 5

Perry M Clark
Notary Public.

My commission expires   2/5/05

Applications for Enrollment of Choctaw Newborn
Act of 1905 Volume XIX

Affidavit of Attending Physician or Midwife

UNITED STATES OF AMERICA,
    INDIAN TERRITORY,
Cent   DISTRICT

I, Francis Brown a midwife on oath state that I attended on Mrs. Julia Crowder wife of Eli Crowder on the 23 day of Oct , 190 5[sic], that there was born to her on said date a Female child, that said child is now living, and is said to have been named Lena Bell Crowder

                                       Francis Brown   M. D.

Subscribed and sworn to before me this the 22 day of Jan 1905

                                       Perry M Clark
                                                   Notary Public.

WITNESSETH:
Must be two witnesses who are citizens and know the child. { G D Duncan
                              John T Brown

We hereby certify that we are well acquainted with Francis Brown a midwife and know her to be reputable and of good standing in the community.

                         Must be two citizen witnesses. { G D Duncan
                                                    John T Brown

BIRTH AFFIDAVIT.

DEPARTMENT OF THE INTERIOR.
COMMISSION TO THE FIVE CIVILIZED TRIBES.

IN RE APPLICATION FOR ENROLLMENT, as a citizen of the Choctaw Nation, of Lena Bell Crowder , born on the 23^d day of October , 1902

Name of Father: Eli Crowder   a citizen of the Choctaw Nation.
Name of Mother: Julia Crowder   a citizen of the non citizen Nation.

                                 Postoffice   Boswell I.T.

Applications for Enrollment of Choctaw Newborn
Act of 1905   Volume XIX

AFFIDAVIT OF MOTHER.

UNITED STATES OF AMERICA, Indian Territory, }
Central   DISTRICT.

I, Julia Crowder, on oath state that I am 38 years of age and a citizen by ———, of the United States Nation; that I am the lawful wife of Eli Crowder, who is a citizen, by blood of the Choctaw Nation; that a female child was born to me on 23^d day of October, 1902; that said child has been named Lena Bell Crowder, and was living March 4, 1905.

Julia Crowder

Witnesses To Mark:
{

Subscribed and sworn to before me this 6th day of June, 1905

Perry M Clark
Notary Public.

AFFIDAVIT OF ATTENDING PHYSICIAN OR MID-WIFE.

UNITED STATES OF AMERICA, Indian Territory, }
Central   DISTRICT.

I, Francis Brown, a midwife, on oath state that I attended on Mrs. Julia Crowder, wife of Eli Crowder on the 23^d day of October, 1902; that there was born to her on said date a female child; that said child was living March 4, 1905, and is said to have been named Lena Bell Crowder

Francis Brown

Witnesses To Mark:
{

Subscribed and sworn to before me this 6th day of June, 1905

Perry M Clark
Notary Public.

My commission exp 2/27/09

Applications for Enrollment of Choctaw Newborn
Act of 1905   Volume XIX

7-N.B. 1437.

Muskogee, Indian Territory, May 25, 1905.

Eli Crowder,
    Boswell, Indian Territory.

Dear Sir:

    Receipt is hereby acknowledged of your letter of May 20, stating that sometime ago you wrote in regard to the applications for the enrollment of your two children, Lena Bell and Maude[sic] May Crowder, and you wish to be advised what has been done with them.

    In reply to your letter you are advised that the affidavits heretofore forwarded to the birth of your children, Lena Bell and Maude May Crowder, have been filed as applications for the enrollment of said children, and in the event further evidence is necessary to enable us to determine their right to enrollment you will be duly notified.

Respectfully,

Chairman.

7--NB--1437

Muskogee, Indian Territory, June 1, 1905.

Eli Crowder,
    Boswell, Indian Territory.

Dear Sir:

    There is enclosed you herewith for execution applications for the enrollment of your infant children, Lena Bell Crowder, born October 23, 1902 and Maud May Crowder, born December 9, 1904.

    The affidavits heretofore filed with the Commission show these children were living on January 22, 1905. It is necessary, for the children to be enrolled, that they were living on March 4, 1905.

    In having these affidavits executed care should be exercised to see that all names are written in full, as they appear in the body of the affidavit, and in the event that either of the persons signing the affidavit are unable to write, signatures by mark must be attested by two witnesses. Each affidavit must be executed before a Notary Public and the notarial seal and signature of the officer must be attached to each separate affidavit.

Applications for Enrollment of Choctaw Newborn
Act of 1905   Volume XIX

It is also noted from the applications heretofore filed for the enrollment of these infant children that the applicants claim through you.

In this event it will be necessary for you to file in this office, either the original, or a certified copy of the license and certificate of your marriage to the applicants[sic] mother, Julia Crowder.

Respectfully,

Chairman.

Enc. FVK-13

Choctaw N B 1437

Muskogee, Indian Territory, June 8, 1905.

Eli Crowder,
    Boswell, Indian Territory.

Dear Sir:

Receipt is hereby acknowledged of your letter of May 25, asking what disposition has been made of the application for the enrollment of your daughter, Lena Bell Crowder.

In reply to your letter you are advised that on June 1, 1905, a letter was addressed you advising fully what further information was necessary in the matter of the enrollment of your children, Lena Bell and Maud May Crowder. Upon receipt of the information requested the matter of the enrollment of your two children will receive further consideration.

Respectfully,

Chairman.

7-NB-1437.

Muskogee, Indian Territory, June 10, 1905.

Eli Crowder,
    Boswell, Indian Territory.

Dear Sir:

Receipt is hereby acknowledged of the affidavits of Julia Crowder and Francis Brown to the birth of Lena Bell Crowder; also the affidavits of Julia Crowder and Fannie Wallace to the birth of Maud May Crowder, children of Eli and Julia Crowder, October 23, 1902, and December 9, 1904, respectively, and also a certified copy of the marriage

Applications for Enrollment of Choctaw Newborn
Act of 1905   Volume XIX

certificate between Eli Crowder and Julia Crowder, and the same have been filed with our records in the matter of the enrollment of these children.

        Respectfully,

                                Chairman.

Choc. New Born 1438
    Mary Pickens
    (Born Jan. 29, 1903)

    Cancelled record transferred
        to Choc. New Born No. 727
    Act of Congress approved Apr. 26, 1906.
    July 13, 1906.

1438

CHOCTAW
NEW BORN
ACT OF CONGRESS APPROVED MARCH 30, 1905.

Mary Pickens
(Born Jan. 29, 1903)

CANCELLED
Record transferred to
CHOCTAW NEW BORN *No.* 727
ACT OF CONGRESS APPROVED APRIL 25, 1906.

JUL 13 1906

Applications for Enrollment of Choctaw Newborn
Act of 1905   Volume XIX

Choc. New Born 1439
    Earl Dude Wyatt
    (Born July 16, 1903)
    Bonnie Pearl Wyatt
    (Born Jan. 11, 1905)

BIRTH AFFIDAVIT.

DEPARTMENT OF THE INTERIOR.
COMMISSION TO THE FIVE CIVILIZED TRIBES.

IN RE APPLICATION FOR ENROLLMENT, as a citizen of the   Choctaw   Nation, of Earl Dude Wyatt   , born on the   16   day of   July   , 1903

Name of Father: E. L. Wyatt   a citizen of the   U S   Nation.
Name of Mother: Celie Wyatt   a citizen of the   Choctaw   Nation.

    Postoffice   Center IT

AFFIDAVIT OF MOTHER.

UNITED STATES OF AMERICA, Indian Territory, }
    Suthrn[sic]   DISTRICT. }

    I,   Celie Wyatt   , on oath state that I am   26   years of age and a citizen by blood   , of the   Choctaw   Nation; that I am the lawful wife of   E L Wyatt   , who is a citizen, by .... of the   U S   Nation; that a   male   child was born to me on   16   day of   July   , 1903, that said child has been named   Earl Dude Wyatt   , and is now living.

                            Celie Wyatt
Witnesses To Mark:

    Subscribed and sworn to before me this   21   day of   Apr   , 1905.

                            J J Copeland
                            Notary Public.

Applications for Enrollment of Choctaw Newborn
Act of 1905   Volume XIX

AFFIDAVIT OF ATTENDING PHYSICIAN OR MID-WIFE.

UNITED STATES OF AMERICA, Indian Territory,
  Suthrn   DISTRICT.

I,   J R Craig   , a physician   , on oath state that I attended on Mrs.   Celie Wyatt   , wife of   E L Wyatt   on the .... day of ...., 1......; that there was born to her on said date a   male   child; that said child is now living and is said to have been named   Earl Dude Wyatt

J R Craig M.D.

Witnesses To Mark:
{

Subscribed and sworn to before me this 21 day of   Apr   , 1905.

J J Copeland
Notary Public.

BIRTH AFFIDAVIT.

DEPARTMENT OF THE INTERIOR.
COMMISSION TO THE FIVE CIVILIZED TRIBES.

IN RE APPLICATION FOR ENROLLMENT, as a citizen of the   Choctaw   Nation, of   Earl Dude Wyatt , born on the   16   day of   July   , 1903

Name of Father: E. L. Wyatt   a citizen of the   U S   Nation.
Name of Mother: Celie[sic] Wyatt   a citizen of the   Choctaw   Nation.

Postoffice   Center IT

AFFIDAVIT OF MOTHER.

UNITED STATES OF AMERICA, Indian Territory,
  Suthrn[sic]   DISTRICT.

I,   Celie Wyatt   , on oath state that I am   26   years of age and a citizen by blood   , of the   Choctaw   Nation; that I am the lawful wife of   E L Wyatt   , who is a citizen, by .... of the   U S   Nation; that a   male   child was born to me on   16   day of   July   , 1903, that said child has been named   Earl Dude Wyatt   , and is now living.

Celie Wyatt

Witnesses To Mark:
{

189

Applications for Enrollment of Choctaw Newborn
Act of 1905   Volume XIX

Subscribed and sworn to before me this 21 day of   Apr , 1905.

                          J J Copeland
                          Notary Public.

AFFIDAVIT OF ATTENDING PHYSICIAN OR MID-WIFE.

UNITED STATES OF AMERICA, Indian Territory,
   Suthrn   DISTRICT.

    I,   J R Craig   , a physician   , on oath state that I attended on Mrs. Celia Wyatt   , wife of   E L Wyatt   on the   16   day of   July , 1903; that there was born to her on said date a   male   child; that said child is now living and is said to have been named   Earl Dude Wyatt

                          J R Craig M.D.

Witnesses To Mark:

Subscribed and sworn to before me this 21 day of   Apr , 1905.

                          J J Copeland
                          Notary Public.

BIRTH AFFIDAVIT.

    IN RE-APPLICATION FOR ENROLLMENT, as a citizen of the   Choctaw   Nation, of Bunnie[sic] Pearl Wyatt   , born on the   11   day of   Jan. , 190 5

Name of Father: E L Wyatt   a citizen of the   U S   Nation.
Name of Mother: Celia Wyatt   a citizen of the   Choctaw   Nation.

                  Postoffice   Center IT

AFFIDAVIT OF MOTHER.

UNITED STATES OF AMERICA, INDIAN TERRITORY,
   Suthrn[sic]   District.

    I,   Celia Wyatt   , on oath state that I am   26   years of age and a citizen by blood , of the   Choctaw   Nation; that I am the lawful wife of   E L Wyatt , who is a citizen, by .... of the   U S   ~~Nation~~; that a   Female   child was born to me on 11   day of   Jan , 1905 , that said child has been named   Bunnie Pearl Wyatt   , and is now living.

                         Celia Wyatt

Applications for Enrollment of Choctaw Newborn
Act of 1905   Volume XIX

Witnesses To Mark:

{

Subscribed and sworn to before me this 22   day of   Apr   , 1905.

J J Copeland
Notary Public.

AFFIDAVIT OF ATTENDING PHYSICIAN OR MID-WIFE.

UNITED STATES OF AMERICA, INDIAN TERRITORY, }
  Suthrn   District.

I,   J R Craig   , a   Physician   , on oath state that I attended on Mrs. Celie Wyatt , wife of E L Wyatt   on the 11 day of Jan , 190 5; that there was born to her on said date a Female child; that said child is now living and is said to have been named Bunnie Pearl Wyatt

J R Craig MD

Witnesses To Mark:

{

Subscribed and sworn to before me this 22   day of   Apr   , 1905.

J J Copeland
Notary Public.

BIRTH AFFIDAVIT.

DEPARTMENT OF THE INTERIOR.
COMMISSION TO THE FIVE CIVILIZED TRIBES.

IN RE APPLICATION FOR ENROLLMENT, as a citizen of the   Chocktaw[sic]   Nation, of   Earl Dude Wyatt   , born on the 16 day of July , 1903

Name of Father: Elijah L Wyatt   a citizen of the .... Nation.
Name of Mother: Celie Wyatt   a citizen of the   Chocktaw   Nation.

Postoffice   Center I.T.

AFFIDAVIT OF MOTHER.

UNITED STATES OF AMERICA, Indian Territory, }
  Southern   DISTRICT.

I, Celie Wyatt   , on oath state that I am 26 years of age and a citizen by blood , of the   Chocktaw   Nation; that I am the lawful wife of Elijah L Wyatt ,

Applications for Enrollment of Choctaw Newborn
Act of 1905   Volume XIX

who is a citizen, by _____ of the _____ Nation; that a male child was born to me on 16 day of July, 1903; that said child has been named Earl Dude Wyatt, and was living March 4, 1905.

                              Celie Wyatt

Witnesses To Mark:
{

    Subscribed and sworn to before me this 2 day of May, 1905

                              JE Williams
                              Notary Public.

AFFIDAVIT OF ATTENDING PHYSICIAN OR MID-WIFE.

UNITED STATES OF AMERICA, Indian Territory, }
   Southern   DISTRICT.

    I, J R Craig, a _____, on oath state that I attended on Mrs. Celie Wyatt, wife of E L Wyatt on the 16 day of July, 1903; that there was born to her on said date a male child; that said child was living March 4, 1905, and is said to have been named Earl Dude Wyatt

                            J R Craig M.D.

Witnesses To Mark:
{

    Subscribed and sworn to before me this 2 day of May, 1905

                              JE Williams
                              Notary Public.

BIRTH AFFIDAVIT.

DEPARTMENT OF THE INTERIOR.
COMMISSION TO THE FIVE CIVILIZED TRIBES.

    IN RE APPLICATION FOR ENROLLMENT, as a citizen of the Chocktaw[sic] Nation, of Bonnie Pearl Wyatt, born on the 11 day of January, 1905

Name of Father: Elijah L Wyatt   a citizen of the _____ Nation.
Name of Mother: Celie Wyatt   a citizen of the Chocktaw Nation.

                    Postoffice   Center

Applications for Enrollment of Choctaw Newborn
Act of 1905   Volume XIX

AFFIDAVIT OF MOTHER.

UNITED STATES OF AMERICA, Indian Territory, }
Southern   DISTRICT.

I,   Celie Wyatt   , on oath state that I am   26   years of age and a citizen by blood   , of the   Chocktaw   Nation; that I am the lawful wife of   Elijah L Wyatt   , who is a citizen, by .... of the .... Nation; that a   male[sic] child was born to me on   11   day of   January   , 1905; that said child has been named   Bonnie Pearl Wyatt   , and was living March 4, 1905.

Celie Wyatt

Witnesses To Mark:
{

Subscribed and sworn to before me this   2   day of   May   , 1905

JE Williams
Notary Public.

AFFIDAVIT OF ATTENDING PHYSICIAN OR MID-WIFE.

UNITED STATES OF AMERICA, Indian Territory, }
Southern   DISTRICT.

I,   J R Craig   , a ...., on oath state that I attended on Mrs.   Celie Wyatt   , wife of   E L Wyatt   on the   11   day of   January   , 1905; that there was born to her on said date a   Female   child; that said child was living March 4, 1905, and is said to have been named   Bonnie Pearl Wyatt

J R Craig M.D.

Witnesses To Mark:
{

Subscribed and sworn to before me this   2   day of   May   , 1905

JE Williams
Notary Public.

Applications for Enrollment of Choctaw Newborn
Act of 1905   Volume XIX

Choctaw D-589.

Muskogee, Indian Territory, April 28, 1905.

E. L. Wyatt,
    Center, Indian Territory.

Dear Sir:

    Receipt is hereby acknowledged of the affidavits of Celie Wyatt and J. R. Craig to the birth of Earl Dude Wyatt and Bonnie Pearl Wyatt, July 16, 1903, and January 11, 1905, respectively.

    It appears from you[sic] records that you are a noncitizen and that the application for the enrollment of your wife, Seely Wyatt, has not yet been passed upon. As the act of Congress approved March 3, 1905, authorizes the Commission for a period of sixty days from that date to receive applications for the enrollment of children born to citizens by blood of the Choctaw and Chickasaw Nations, whose enrollment had prior to that time been approved by the Secretary of the Interior, you will see that the Commission is without authority to enroll your child.

        Respectfully,

                Chairman.

Choc. New Born 1440
    Jewel Simmons
    (Born Jan. 9, 1903)

7- _____ ?.W.

BIRTH AFFIDAVIT.   739

DEPARTMENT OF THE INTERIOR.
COMMISSION TO THE FIVE CIVILIZED TRIBES.

IN RE APPLICATION FOR ENROLLMENT, as a citizen of the   Choctaw   Nation, of Jewel Simmons   , born on the   9   day of   January   , 1903

Name of Father: John Simmons   a citizen of the   Choc   Nation.
Name of Mother: Mamie Simmons   a citizen of the   Choc   Nation.

        Postoffice   Guertie I.T.

Applications for Enrollment of Choctaw Newborn
Act of 1905 Volume XIX

AFFIDAVIT OF MOTHER.

UNITED STATES OF AMERICA, Indian Territory,
Central DISTRICT.

I, Mamie Simmons, on oath state that I am 31 years of age and a citizen by intermarriage, of the Choctaw Nation; that I am the lawful wife of John Simmons, who is a citizen, by blood of the Choctaw Nation; that a female child was born to me on 9 day of January, 1903; that said child has been named Jewel Simmons, and was living March 4, 1905.

Mamie Simmons

Witnesses To Mark:

Subscribed and sworn to before me this 26 day of April, 1905

OL Johnson
Notary Public.

AFFIDAVIT OF ATTENDING PHYSICIAN OR MID-WIFE.

UNITED STATES OF AMERICA, Indian Territory,
Southern DISTRICT.

I, Jane Glisson, a midwife, on oath state that I attended on Mrs. Mamie Simmons, wife of John Simmons on the 9 day of January, 1903; that there was born to her on said date a female child; that said child was living March 4, 1905, and is said to have been named Jewel Simmons

Witnesses To Mark:

Subscribed and sworn to before me this ...... day of ...., 1905.

Notary Public.

Applications for Enrollment of Choctaw Newborn
Act of 1905   Volume XIX

(The affidavit below typed as given.)

I Matilda A Harrison a nurse on oath state that I attend and nusrd Mrs Mammie Simmons after confinement she having gave birth to a female child on or about the 9 of Jan 1903 said child was alive March 4 1905 and was named Jewel Simmons

Matilda A Harrison

Subscribed and sworn to before me this first day of May 1905

My com exp 3-28-1906

Virgil M Wallace
Notary Public

I Albert S Harrison on oath state that I lived with Mr & Mrs Simmons after the 4 day after Mrs Mammie Simmons was confined that a female child was born to her said Mammie Simmons on or about the 9 of January 1903 said child was named Jewel Simmons said child was alive March 4, 1905

Albert S Harrison
~~Virgil M Wallace~~ Notry Public

My commission exp 3-28-06

Sworn to and subscribed before me this first day May 1905

Virgil M Wallace
N.P.

Applications for Enrollment of Choctaw Newborn
Act of 1905 Volume XIX

7--3114.

Muskogee, Indian Territory, May 10, 1905.

John Simmons,
    Guertie, Indian Territory.

Dear Sir:

    Receipt is hereby acknowledged of your letter of April 30, enclosing the affidavits of Mamie Simmons, Matilda A. Harrison and Albert S. Harrison to the birth of Jewel Simmons, daughter of John and Mamie Simmons, January 9, 1903, and the same have been filed with our records as an application for the enrollment of said child.

Respectfully,

Commissioner in Charge.

Choc. New Born 1441
    Johny Carr
    (Born June 12, 1903)

7-9199.

DEPARTMENT OF THE INTERIOR,
COMMISSION TO THE FIVE CIVILIZED TRIBES.
SOUTH McALESTER, I. T.   APRIL 24, 1905.

    In the matter of the application for the enrollment of Johny Carr as a citizen by blood of the Choctaw Nation.

Osborne Carr being first duly sworn testifies as follows:

    EXAMINATION BY THE COMMISSION:

Q What is your name? A Osborne Carr.
Q How old are you? A Twenty-five.
Q What is your post office address? A Higgins.
Q Are you a citizen by blood of the Choctaw Nation? A Yes, sir.
Q You have this day made application for the enrollment of your child Johny Carr as a citizen of the Choctaw Nation; when was this child born? A 12th day June 1903.
Q Who is the mother of this child? A Silen Carr.
Q When were you married to her? A 5th day January 1904.

Applications for Enrollment of Choctaw Newborn
Act of 1905 Volume XIX

Q What was your wife's name before you married her? [sic] Silen Murphy.
Q What was her maiden name? A Silen Seely.
Q Is she a citizen of either the Choctaw or Chickasaw Nation?
A Yes, sir, part Choctaw and part Chickasaw.
Q Has she made application to the Commission for enrollment as a citizen of either the Choctaw or Chickasaw Nation? A No, sir, I reckon not.
Q Who was her father? A Bond Seely.
Q Who was her mother? A Susie Seely.
Q Of what nation was her father a citizen? A Her father was part Chickasaw.
Q Where was he enrolled? A I don't know about that.
Q Where did he live during his lifetime? A Close to Wilburton born and raised there.
Q Of what nation was her mother a citizen? A Choctaw.
Q In case it should be determined that this child has rights in both the Choctaw and Chickasaw Nations in which nation do you desire to have this child enrolled?
A Choctaw.
Q Did your wife draw the 1893 leased district payment money? A Yes, sir, in the Chickasaw Nation.
Q What was her name in 1893 at the time she drew the money? A Silen Willis.
Q With whom was she living? A With Mose Willis.

Witness excused.

Silen Carr being first duly sworn testifies as follows:

EXAMINATION BY THE COMMISSION:

Q What is your name? A Silen Carr.
Q How old are you? A Twenty-eight.
Q What is your post office address? A Higgins.
Q You have this day made application for your child Johny Carr as a citizen of the Choctaw Nation; when was this child born? A 12th June 1903.
Q Who is the father of this child? A Osborne Carr.
Q When were you married to Osborne Carr? A 5th day January 1904.

Witness excused.

Chas. T. Difendafer being first duly sworn states that the above and foregoing is a full, true and correct transcript of his stenographic notes taken in said cause on said date.

Chas.T. Difendafer

Subscribed and sworn to before me this 2nd day of May 1905.

OL Johnson
Notary Public.

Applications for Enrollment of Choctaw Newborn
Act of 1905   Volume XIX

7- 9199

BIRTH AFFIDAVIT.

DEPARTMENT OF THE INTERIOR.
COMMISSION TO THE FIVE CIVILIZED TRIBES.

IN RE APPLICATION FOR ENROLLMENT, as a citizen of the Choctaw Nation, of Johny Carr, born on the 12 day of June, 1903

Name of Father: Osborn Carr   a citizen of the Choc Nation.
Name of Mother: Silen Carr nee Murphy   a citizen of the Choc-Chick Nation.

Postoffice   Higgins I.T.

AFFIDAVIT OF MOTHER.

UNITED STATES OF AMERICA, Indian Territory, } Central DISTRICT.

I, Silen Carr, on oath state that I am 28 years of age and a citizen by blood, of the Choc - Chick Nation; that I am the lawful wife of Osborn Carr, who is a citizen, by blood of the Choctaw Nation; that a male child was born to me on 12 day of June, 1903; that said child has been named Johny Carr, and was living March 4, 1905.

                         her
                    Silen x Carr
Witnesses To Mark: mark
{ Chas.T. Difendafer
  OL Johnson

Subscribed and sworn to before me this 24 day of April, 1905

                         OL Johnson
                         Notary Public.

AFFIDAVIT OF ATTENDING PHYSICIAN OR MID-WIFE.

UNITED STATES OF AMERICA, Indian Territory, } Central DISTRICT.

I, Lucinda King, a midwife, on oath state that I attended on Mrs. Silen carr, wife of Osborn Carr on the 12 day of June, 1903; that there was born to her on said date a male child; that said child was living March 4, 1905, and is said to have been named Johny Carr

Applications for Enrollment of Choctaw Newborn
Act of 1905   Volume XIX

Witnesses To Mark:
{ Jas. S. Ingram
{ S.E. Rogus

                     her
Lucinda x King
                    mark

Subscribed and sworn to before me this 29th day of April, 1905

My Com Ex in 1908.

Wm J Hulsey
Notary Public.

Choc. New Born 1442

    Act May 3, 1905

    Sam Miller

    Transferred to 23-1279
    Jan. 8, 1907

1442

Choctaw NEW BORN
Act May 3 1905

Sam Miller

Transferred to 23-1279

Jan. 8 1907

Applications for Enrollment of Choctaw Newborn
Act of 1905 Volume XIX

Choc. New Born 1443
    Annie Frances Sorrells
    (Born Oct. 9, 1902)
    Nancy Elizabeth Sorrells
    (Born Feb. 17, 1904)

BIRTH AFFIDAVIT.

DEPARTMENT OF THE INTERIOR.
COMMISSION TO THE FIVE CIVILIZED TRIBES.

IN RE APPLICATION FOR ENROLLMENT, as a citizen of the Choctaw Nation, of Nancy Elizabeth Sorrells, born on the 17th day of February, 1904

Name of Father: Thomas Jefferson Sorrells   a citizen of the Choctaw Nation.
Name of Mother: Mary Frances Sorrells   a citizen of the Choctaw Nation.

          Postoffice   Courtney Ind. Ter.

AFFIDAVIT OF MOTHER.

UNITED STATES OF AMERICA, Indian Territory,
    Southern   **DISTRICT.**

    I, Mary Frances Sorrells, on oath state that I am 24 years of age and a citizen by Blood, of the Choctaw Nation; that I am the lawful wife of Thomas Jefferson Sorrells, who is a citizen, by marriage of the Choctaw Nation; that a Female child was born to me on 17th day of February, 1904; that said child has been named Nancy Elizabeth Sorrells, and was living March 4, 1905.

                                    Mary Frances Sorrells

Witnesses To Mark:
    W.J. Fike

    Subscribed and sworn to before me this 31st day of March, 1905

                              L. L. Lee
                                      Notary Public.
                              Sou Dist

Applications for Enrollment of Choctaw Newborn
Act of 1905   Volume XIX

AFFIDAVIT OF ATTENDING PHYSICIAN OR MID-WIFE.

UNITED STATES OF AMERICA, Indian Territory,
   Southern   DISTRICT.

    I, W. J. Fike , a Physician , on oath state that I attended on Mrs. Mary Frances Sorrells , wife of Thomas Jefferson Sorrells on the 17th day of February , 1904; that there was born to her on said date a Female child; that said child was living March 4, 1905, and is said to have been named Nancy Elizabeth Sorrells

                                      W. J. Fike M.D.

Witnesses To Mark:
   { E.T. Stuart

       Subscribed and sworn to before me this 31st day of March , 1905

                            L. L. Lee
                                     Notary Public.
                            Sou Dist

BIRTH AFFIDAVIT.

DEPARTMENT OF THE INTERIOR.
COMMISSION TO THE FIVE CIVILIZED TRIBES.

    IN RE APPLICATION FOR ENROLLMENT, as a citizen of the Choctaw Nation, of Annie Frances Sorrells , born on the 9th day of Oct , 1902

Name of Father: Thomas Jefferson Sorrells   a citizen of the Choctaw Nation.
Name of Mother: Mary Frances Sorrells   a citizen of the Choctaw Nation.

                         Postoffice   Courtney Ind. Ter.

AFFIDAVIT OF MOTHER.

UNITED STATES OF AMERICA, Indian Territory,
   Southern   DISTRICT.

    I, Mary Frances Sorrells , on oath state that I am 24 years of age and a citizen by Blood , of the Choctaw Nation; that I am the lawful wife of Thomas Jefferson Sorrells , who is a citizen, by marriage of the Choctaw Nation; that a Female child was born to me on the 9th day of October , 1902; that said child has been named Annie Frances Sorrells , and was living March 4, 1905.

                                Mary Frances Sorrells

Applications for Enrollment of Choctaw Newborn
Act of 1905   Volume XIX

Witnesses To Mark:
{ W.J. Fike

Subscribed and sworn to before me this 31st day of   March   , 1905

L. L. Lee
Notary Public.
Sou Dist

AFFIDAVIT OF ATTENDING PHYSICIAN OR MID-WIFE.

UNITED STATES OF AMERICA, Indian Territory, }
Central   DISTRICT.

I,   Mary Ann Gordon   , a mid wife   , on oath state that I attended on Mrs. Mary Frances Sorrells   , wife of   Thomas Jefferson Sorrells   on the 9 day of October   , 1902; that there was born to her on said date a   Female   child; that said child was living March 4, 1905, and is said to have been named Aney[sic] Frances Sorrells

Mary Ann Gordon

Witnesses To Mark:
{ E.T. Stuart

Subscribed and sworn to before me this 10   day of   April   , 1905

(Name Illegible)
Notary Public.

Muskogee, Indian Territory, April 25, 1905.

Thomas Jefferson Sorrells,
    Courtney, Indian Territory.

Dear Sir:

Receipt is hereby acknowledged of the affidavits of Mary Francis Sorrells and W. J. Fike to the birth of Nancy Elizabeth Sorrells, daughter of Thomas Jefferson Sorrells and Mary Frances Sorrells, February 17, 1904; also affidavits of Mary Frances Sorrells and Mary Ann Gordon, October 9, 1902.

It is stated in the affidavit of the mother that she is a citizen by blood of the Choctaw Nation. If this is correct you are requested to state the name under which she was enrolled, the names of her parents, and if she has selected an allotment of the lands

Applications for Enrollment of Choctaw Newborn
Act of 1905   Volume XIX

of the Choctaw or Chickasaw Nation please give her roll number as it appears upon her allotment certificate.

       Respectfully,

                Chairman.

Choc. New Born 1444
   (Annie Doneghey)
   (Born May 22, 1904)

BIRTH AFFIDAVIT.

        DEPARTMENT OF THE INTERIOR.
     COMMISSION TO THE FIVE CIVILIZED TRIBES.

   IN RE APPLICATION FOR ENROLLMENT, as a citizen of the   Choctaw   Nation, of Annie Doneghey , born on the 22 day of May , 1904

Name of Father: Cornelious Doneghey   a citizen of the Choctaw Nation.
Name of Mother: Agnas[sic] Doneghey   a citizen of the Choctaw Nation.

        Postoffice   Lula I.T.

      AFFIDAVIT OF MOTHER.

UNITED STATES OF AMERICA, Indian Territory,
   Central   **DISTRICT.**

  I, Agnas Doneghey , on oath state that I am 23 years of age and a citizen by Blood , of the Choctaw Nation; that I am the lawful wife of Cornelious Doneghey , who is a citizen, by Blood of the Choctaw Nation; that a Female child was born to me on 22 day of May , 1904; that said child has been named Annie Doneghey , and was living March 4, 1905.

            her
         Agnas x Doneghey
Witnesses To Mark: mark
 { *(Name Illegible)*
  G. W. Hudlow

Applications for Enrollment of Choctaw Newborn
Act of 1905   Volume XIX

Subscribed and sworn to before me this 4 day of   April   , 1905

                                      W.H. Hudlow
                                            Notary Public.

AFFIDAVIT OF ATTENDING PHYSICIAN OR MID-WIFE.

UNITED STATES OF AMERICA, Indian Territory, }
    Central   DISTRICT. }

    I,   Francis Burris   , a Mid wife   , on oath state that I attended on Mrs.   Agnas Doneghey   , wife of   Cornelious Doneghey   on the 22 day of May , 1904; that there was born to her on said date a .... child; that said child was living March 4, 1905, and is said to have been named Annie Doneghey

                                      Francis Buris[sic]
Witnesses To Mark:
  { J.D. Lucas

Subscribed and sworn to before me this 4 day of   April   , 1905

                                        W.H. Hudlow
                                            Notary Public.
My com exp March 14/ 1907

BIRTH AFFIDAVIT.
DEPARTMENT OF THE INTERIOR.
COMMISSION TO THE FIVE CIVILIZED TRIBES.

    IN RE APPLICATION FOR ENROLLMENT, as a citizen of the   Choctaw   Nation, of Annie Donegay[sic]   , born on the 22 day of May , 1904

Name of Father: Cornelius Donegay   a citizen of the   Choctaw   Nation.
Name of Mother: Agnes Donegay   a citizen of the   Choctaw   Nation.

                            Postoffice   Lula Ind. Ter.

AFFIDAVIT OF MOTHER.

UNITED STATES OF AMERICA, Indian Territory, }
    Central   DISTRICT. }

    I,   Agnes Donegay, on oath state that I am 23   years of age and a citizen by blood , of the   Choctaw   Nation; that I am the lawful wife of Cornelius Donegay ,

Applications for Enrollment of Choctaw Newborn
Act of 1905   Volume XIX

who is a ~~citizen, by~~ freedman of the Choctaw Nation; that a female child was born to me on 22 day of May , 1904; that said child has been named Annie Donegay, and was living March 4, 1905.

                                      her
                                Agnes x Donegay

Witnesses To Mark: mark
  { A. J. Payte
    S.B. McCray

    Subscribed and sworn to before me this 8 day of   July   , 1905

                                D. Allen
                                Notary Public.

AFFIDAVIT OF ATTENDING PHYSICIAN OR MID-WIFE.

UNITED STATES OF AMERICA, Indian Territory, }
    Central   **DISTRICT.**

    I, Flora Brown , a Midwife , on oath state that I attended on Mrs. Agnes Donegay, wife of Cornelius Donegay on the 22 day of   May , 1904; that there was born to her on said date a female child; that said child was living March 4, 1905, and is said to have been named Annie Donegay

                                    her
                              Flora x Brown
Witnesses To Mark: mark
  { A. J. Payte
    S.B. McCray

    Subscribed and sworn to before me this 8 day of   July   , 1905

                                D. Allen
                                Notary Public.

Applications for Enrollment of Choctaw Newborn
Act of 1905   Volume XIX

$W^m O.B.$

COMMISSIONERS:
TAMS BIXBY,
THOMAS B. NEEDLES,
C.R. BRECKINBRIDGE.

DEPARTMENT OF THE INTERIOR,
COMMISSIONER TO THE FIVE CIVILIZED TRIBES.

REFER IN REPLY TO THE FOLLOWING:

WM. O. BEALL
Secretary

ADDRESS ONLY THE
COMMISSION TO THE FIVE CIVILIZED TRIBES.

Muskogee, Indian Territory, April 24, 1905.

Cornelius Doneghey,
    Lula, Indian Territory.

Dear Sir:

    Receipt is hereby acknowledged of the affidavits of Agnas[sic] Doneghey and Francis Burris to the birth of Annie Doneghey daughter of Cornelius and Agnas Doneghey, May 22, 1904.

    It is stated in the affidavit of the mother that she is a citizen by blood of the Choctaw Nation. If this is correct you are requested to state the name under which she was enrolled, the names of her parents, and if she has selected an allotment of the lands of the Choctaw or Chickasaw Nation please give her roll number as it appears upon her allotment certificate.

                    Respectfully,
                      Tams Bixby
                          Chairman.

Roll No 13257
certificate No 8729

(The letter below typed as given.)

(COPY)

                      Lula, I. T.
                      5/2/1905.

Chairman,
    Muskogee, I. T.

Dear Sir: I will send you the naims of my Parants Mr. Elis Gibson & Siliney Gibson her in Roll No. 13257 and her certificate no. is 8729.

                    Yours truly
                    Cornelius Doneghey
                          Lula I. T.

Applications for Enrollment of Choctaw Newborn
Act of 1905 Volume XIX

Wm O.B.

COMMISSIONERS:
TAMS BIXBY,
THOMAS B. NEEDLES,
C.R. BRECKINRIDGE.

WM. O. BEALL
Secretary

DEPARTMENT OF THE INTERIOR,
COMMISSIONER TO THE FIVE CIVILIZED TRIBES.

REFER IN REPLY TO THE FOLLOWING:

7--NB--1444.

ADDRESS ONLY THE
COMMISSION TO THE FIVE CIVILIZED TRIBES.

Muskogee, Indian Territory, June 15, 1905.

Cornelius Doneghey,
    Lula, Indian Territory.

Dear Sir:

    Referring to the application for the enrollment of your infant child, Annie Doneghey, born May 22, 1904, it is noted in the affidavits heretofore filed in this office the you claim to be a citizen by blood of the Choctaw Nation.

    If this is correct you are requested to state when, where and under what name you were listed for enrollment, the names of your parents and other members of your family for whom application was made at the same time, and if you have selected an allotment of land, please give your roll number as the same appears upon your allotment certificate.

                        Respectfully,
                        Tams Bixby
                            Chairman.

(COPY)   9-NB-1444.

                            Lula, I. T.
                            June 26, 1905.

Hon. Daws[sic] Commission,
    Muskogee, I. T.

    Gentlemen: In answer to your letter which I inclose herewith, I will state that I am the father of the child, Annie Doneghey, and that I am an enrolled freedman, enrolled under my present name. My wife, and the mother of the child, is a citizen of the Choctaw Nation by blood. She enrolled under the name of Agnes Stone. Her maiden name was Agnes Gipson.

    My roll number is 4281. as it appears upon my allotment certificate which is 4218.

    If this is not satisfactory, please advise me at your earliest convenience.

Applications for Enrollment of Choctaw Newborn
Act of 1905   Volume XIX

Respectfully yours,
Cornelius Doneghey.

---

7 NB 1444

Muskogee, Indian Territory, July 1, 1905.

Cornelius Doneghey,
    Lula, Indian Territory.

Dear Sir:

    Receipt is hereby acknowledged of your letter of June 26, 1905, in the matter of the application for the enrollment of your child Annie Doneghey in which you state that you are enrolled as a Choctaw freedman under your present name and that your roll number is 4281.

    In reply to your letter you are advised that this information has enabled us to identify you upon our records as an enrolled Choctaw freedman and has been made a matter of record in the application for the enrollment of your child Annie Doneghey.

Respectfully,

Commissioner.

(The above letter given again, this time with date July 3, 1905.)

<u>Choc. New Born 1445</u>
    Milburn Cisney Ingram
    (Born Apr. 25, 1903)
    Nancy Jane Ingram
    (Born Feb. 24, 1905)

Applications for Enrollment of Choctaw Newborn
Act of 1905   Volume XIX

BIRTH AFFIDAVIT.

DEPARTMENT OF THE INTERIOR.
COMMISSION TO THE FIVE CIVILIZED TRIBES.

IN RE APPLICATION FOR ENROLLMENT, as a citizen of the Choctaw Nation, of Nancy Jane Ingram, born on the 24 day of Feb, 1905

Name of Father: John R. Ingram   a citizen of the   U.S.   Nation.
Name of Mother: Mary A. Ingram   a citizen of the   Choctaw   Nation.

Postoffice   Stonewall, Ind. Ter.

AFFIDAVIT OF MOTHER.

UNITED STATES OF AMERICA, Indian Territory, }
    16th DISTRICT.   }

I, Mary A. Ingram, on oath state that I am Twenty Three years of age and a citizen by blood, of the Choctaw Nation; that I am the lawful wife of John R. Ingram, who is a citizen, by blood of the U.S. Nation; that a Female child was born to me on 24 day of Feb, 1905; that said child has been named Nancy Jane Ingram, and was living March 4, 1905.

                                        Mary A Ingram
Witnesses To Mark:
{

Subscribed and sworn to before me this 14 day of April, 1905

                                        Minnie Lillard
                                        Notary Public.

AFFIDAVIT OF ATTENDING PHYSICIAN OR MID-WIFE.

UNITED STATES OF AMERICA, Indian Territory, }
    16 Dist   DISTRICT.   }

I, B. F. Sullivan, a Physician, on oath state that I attended on Mrs. Mary A. Ingram, wife of John R. Ingram on the 24 day of Feb., 1905; that there was born to her on said date a Female child; that said child was living March 4, 1905, and is said to have been named Nancy Jane Ingram

                                        B. F. Sullivan
Witnesses To Mark:
{

Applications for Enrollment of Choctaw Newborn
Act of 1905   Volume XIX

Subscribed and sworn to before me this   14   day of   April   , 1905

          Minnie Lillard
          Notary Public.

BIRTH AFFIDAVIT.

DEPARTMENT OF THE INTERIOR.
COMMISSION TO THE FIVE CIVILIZED TRIBES.

IN RE APPLICATION FOR ENROLLMENT, as a citizen of the   Choctaw   Nation, of   Milburn Cisney Ingram   , born on the   25   day of   April   , 1903

Name of Father: John R. Ingram   a citizen of the   U.S.   Nation.
Name of Mother: Mary A. Ingram   a citizen of the   Choctaw   Nation.

      Postoffice   Stonewall, Ind. Ter.

AFFIDAVIT OF MOTHER.

UNITED STATES OF AMERICA, Indian Territory, }
  16th DISTRICT.

I,   Mary A. Ingram   , on oath state that I am   Twenty Three   years of age and a citizen by   blood   , of the   Choctaw   Nation; that I am the lawful wife of   John R. Ingram   , who is a citizen, by   blood   of the   U.S.   Nation; that a   male   child was born to me on   25   day of   April   , 1903; that said child has been named   Milburn Cisney Ingram   , and was living March 4, 1905.

         Mary A Ingram

Witnesses To Mark:
{

Subscribed and sworn to before me this   14   day of   April   , 1905

         Minnie Lillard
         Notary Public.

AFFIDAVIT OF ATTENDING PHYSICIAN OR MID-WIFE.

UNITED STATES OF AMERICA, Indian Territory, }
.... DISTRICT.

I,   E. L. Collins   , a   Physician   , on oath state that I attended on Mrs.   Mary A. Ingram   , wife of   John R. Ingram   on the   25   day of   April   ,

Applications for Enrollment of Choctaw Newborn
Act of 1905   Volume XIX

1903; that there was born to her on said date a   Male   child; that said child was living March 4, 1905, and is said to have been named Milburn Cisney Ingram

E.L. Collins MD

Witnesses To Mark:

{ Subscribed and sworn to before me this   18 day of   April   , 1905

John H Goodnight
Notary Public.
My commission expires Jan 19th 1908

Muskogee, Indian Territory, April 28, 1905.

John R. Ingram,
    Stonewall, Indian Territory.

Dear Sir:

    Receipt is hereby acknowledged of the affidavits of Mary A. Ingram and E. L. Collins to the birth of Milburn Cisney Ingram; also the affidavits of Mary A. Ingram and B. F. Sullivan to the birth of Nancy Jane Ingram, children of John R. and Mary A. Ingram, April 25, 1903 and February 24, 1905, respectively.

    It appears from the affidavit of the mother that she is a citizen by blood of the Choctaw Nation, and if this is correct, you are requested to state under what name she was enrolled, the names of her parents, and if she has selected an allotment of the lands of the Choctaw and Chickasaw Nations, give her roll number as it appears upon her allotment certificate.

Respectfully,

Chairman.

7--2561.

Muskogee, Indian Territory, May 15, 1905.

Mary A. Ingram,
    Stonewall, Indian Territory.

Dear Madam:

    Receipt is hereby acknowledged of your letter of May 8, giving information relative to your enrollment and you have been identified upon our records as an enrolled citizen by blood of the Choctaw Nation, and the affidavits heretofore forwarded to the

Applications for Enrollment of Choctaw Newborn
Act of 1905   Volume XIX

birth of Nancy J. Ingram have been filed with our records as an application for the enrollment of said child.

Respectfully,

Chairman.

7-N.B. 1445.

Muskogee, Indian Territory, May 26, 1905.

Mary A. Ingram,
    Stonewall, Indian Territory.

Dear Madam:

    Receipt is hereby acknowledged of your letter of May 22, asking why the application for the enrollment of only one of your children has been filed.

    In reply to your letter you are advised that it appears from our records that the affidavits heretofore forwarded to the birth of Milburn Cisney Ingram and Nancy Jane Ingram, children of John R. and Mary A. Ingram, have been filed as applications for the enrollment of said children, and you will be notified if further evidence is necessary to enable us to determine their right to enrollment.

Respectfully,

Chairman.

<u>Choc. New Born 1446</u>
    Evinie Boling
    (Born Aug. 9, 1904)

BIRTH AFFIDAVIT.

DEPARTMENT OF THE INTERIOR.
COMMISSION TO THE FIVE CIVILIZED TRIBES.

IN RE APPLICATION FOR ENROLLMENT, as a citizen of the Choctaw Nation, of Evinie Boling, born on the 9th day of August, 1904.

Name of Father: Billy Boling   a citizen of the Choctaw Nation.
Name of Mother: Seanis Boling   a citizen of the Choctaw Nation.

Applications for Enrollment of Choctaw Newborn
Act of 1905   Volume XIX

Postoffice   Lukfata, I. T.

_____

AFFIDAVIT OF ~~MOTHER~~ *Father*

UNITED STATES OF AMERICA, Indian Territory,   } *The Mother is dead*
Central   DISTRICT.

I,   Billy Boling   , on oath state that I am   31   years of age and a citizen by Blood   , of the   Choctaw   Nation; that I am the lawful ~~wife~~ *Husband* of   Seanis Boling Deceased   , who ~~is~~ *was* a citizen, by Blood   of the   Choctaw Nation; that a   Female   child was born to me on   9th   day of August   , 1904; that said child has been named   Evinie Boling   , and was living March 4, 1905. *The Mother of this child Died November 24 1904*

Billy Boling

Witnesses To Mark:
{

Subscribed and sworn to before me this 25th   day of   April   , 1905

J.W. Castilow
Notary Public.

_____

AFFIDAVIT OF ATTENDING PHYSICIAN OR MID-WIFE.

UNITED STATES OF AMERICA, Indian Territory, }
Central   DISTRICT.

I,   Sophin Wilson   , a   midwife   , on oath state that I attended on Mrs.   Seanis Boling   , wife of   Billy Boling   on the 9th   day of   August   , 1904; that there was born to her on said date a   Female   child; that said child was living March 4, 1905, and is said to have been named   Evinie Boling

her
Sophin x Wilson
mark

Witnesses To Mark:
{ W.A. Julian

Subscribed and sworn to before me this 25 day of   April   , 1905

J.W. Castilow
Notary Public.

Applications for Enrollment of Choctaw Newborn
Act of 1905   Volume XIX

United States of America
Indian Territory
Central District

I, Charlie Hliohtambi, being duly sworn, states that he is forty nine years of age and a citizen of the Choctaw Nation by blood.

That he is personally acquainted with Billy Boling and his deceased wife, Seanis Boling (nee) Crosby.

That he is in no way interested or related to Billy Boling: That there was born to the said Billy Boling on the 9th of Aug. 1904 a female child and is said to have been named Evinie Boling and was living March 4th 1905

That Seanis Boling, deceased was her mother.

His
Charles x Hliohtambi
Mark

Witnesses to Mark
    (Name Illegible)
    WJ Johnson

Subscribed and sworn to before me this the 10th day of June 1905

J.W. Castilow
Notary Public

My commission expires Feb 24th 1908

United States of America
Indian Territory
Central District

I, A.H. Clay, being duly sworn, states that he is thirty three years of age and a citizen of the Choctaw Nation by blood. That he is personally acquainted with Billy Boling and his deceased wife, Seanis Boling (nee) Crosby. That he is in no way interested or related to Billy Boling: That there was born to the said Billy Boling on the 9th of Aug. 1904 a female child and is said to have been named Evinie Boling: That the mother of Evinie Boling was Seanis Boling, (nee) Crosby, now deceased.

A H Clay

Applications for Enrollment of Choctaw Newborn
Act of 1905   Volume XIX

Subscribed and sworn to before me this 10th day of June 1905

J. W. Castilow
Notary Public

My commission expires Feb 24th 1908

Muskogee, Indian Territory, May 2, 1905.

Billy Boling,
    Lukfata, Indian Territory.

Dear Sir:

    Receipt is hereby acknowledged of the affidavits of Billy Boling and Sophin Wilson to the birth of Evinie Boling, daughter of Billy and Seanis Boling, August 9, 1904.

    It is stated in the affidavit of the mother that she is a citizen by blood of the Choctaw Nation. If this is correct you are requested to state the name under which she was enrolled, the names of her parents, and if she has selected an allotment of the lands of the Choctaw or Chickasaw Nation please give her roll number as it appears upon her allotment certificate.

                  Respectfully,

                                          Chairman.

                (COPY)

                                        Lukfata, I. T.
                                        May 8, 1905.

Commission to the Five Civilized Tribes,
    Muskogee, I. T.

Sir:

    Your letter of May 2nd received. In reply will say that my deceased wife, the mother of Evinie Boling was a Choctaw by blood, her maiden name was Seanis Crosby, daughter of Josiah Crosby.
    Her Roll Number if[sic] 2352.

                    Yours truly,
                                      Billy Boling.

Applications for Enrollment of Choctaw Newborn
Act of 1905 Volume XIX

7--NB--1446

Muskogee, Indian Territory, June 2, 1905.

Billy Boling,
    Lukfata, Indian Territory.

Dear Sir:

Referring to the application for the enrollment of your infant child, Evinie Boling, born August 9, 1904, it is noted from the affidavits heretofore filed in this office that the mother of the child is dead.

In this event it will be necessary that the affidavits of two persons, who are disinterested and not related to the applicant, who have actual knowledge that the child was born, the date of her birth; that she was living on March 4, 1905, and that Seanis Boling was her mother be filed with the Commission.

This matter should receive your immediate attention as no further action can be taken relative to the enrollment of said child until the Commission has been furnished these affidavits.

    Respectfully,

[sic]

---

7 NB 1446

Muskogee, Indian Territory, June 16, 1905.

Billy Boling,
    Lukfata, Indian Territory.

Dear Sir:

Receipt is hereby acknowledged of the affidavits of Charlie Hlichtambi and A. H. Clay to the birth of Evinie Boling, daughter of Billy Boling and Seanis Boling (nee) Crosby, August 9, 1904, and the same have been filed with our records in the matter of the enrollment of said child.

    Respectfully,

    Chairman.

Applications for Enrollment of Choctaw Newborn
Act of 1905   Volume XIX

Choc. New Born 1447
    Rena Cunnish
    (Born Jan. 18, 1904)

BIRTH AFFIDAVIT.

DEPARTMENT OF THE INTERIOR.
COMMISSION TO THE FIVE CIVILIZED TRIBES.

IN RE APPLICATION FOR ENROLLMENT, as a citizen of the Choctaw Nation, of Rena Cornish[sic]   , born on the 18   day of Jan   , 1904

Name of Father: Webster Cornish   a citizen of the Choctaw Nation.
Name of Mother: Martha Cornish   a citizen of the Choctaw Nation.

                Postoffice   McGee, I.T.

AFFIDAVIT OF MOTHER.

UNITED STATES OF AMERICA, Indian Territory,
    Southern   **DISTRICT.**

    I,   Martha Cornish   , on oath state that I am   25   years of age and a citizen by   Blood   , of the   Choctaw   Nation; that I am the lawful wife of   Webster Cornish (Deceased.)   , who is a citizen, by Blood   of the   Choctaw   Nation; that a   Female   child was born to me on   18 day of   Jan   , 1904; that said child has been named   Rena Cornish   , and was living March 4, 1905.

                                   her
                          Martha x Cornish
Witnesses To Mark: mark
   { S.E. Lewis
   { *(Name Illegible)*

    Subscribed and sworn to before me this   25   day of   March   , 1905

                          Jos A Edwards
                            Notary Public.

Applications for Enrollment of Choctaw Newborn
Act of 1905   Volume XIX

AFFIDAVIT OF ATTENDING PHYSICIAN OR MID-WIFE.

UNITED STATES OF AMERICA, Indian Territory,
Central   DISTRICT.

    I, Emma King, a mid-wife, on oath state that I attended on Mrs. Martha Cornish, wife of Webster Cornish on the 18 day of Jan, 1904; that there was born to her on said date a Female child; that said child was living March 4, 1905, and is said to have been named Rena Cornish

                                               her
                                     Emma King x
Witnesses To Mark: mark
   { H M Byford
     Mitchell King

    Subscribed and sworn to before me this 3 day of April, 1905

                                    Richard E Kemp
                                      Notary Public.

                            Muskogee, Indian Territory, April 27, 1905.

Martha Cornish,
      McGee, Indian Territory.

Dear Madam:

    Receipt is hereby acknowledged of the application for the enrollment as a citizen of the Choctaw Nation of Rena Cornish, infant daughter of Webster Cornish, deceased, and Martha Cornish, born January 18, 1904.

    You are informed that we are unable to locate your name or the name of Webster Cornish upon our records as applicants to this Commission for citizenship in the Choctaw Nation, and it is requested that you inform this office of the time and place you and your husband made application, the name under which you made such application, whether you applied as a Choctaw by blood or a Mississippi Choctaw, and such other information as you may possess that will enable us to identify your name or the name of Webster Cornish upon our records.

                            Respectfully,

                                                  Chairman.

Applications for Enrollment of Choctaw Newborn
Act of 1905 Volume XIX

7- N.B. 1447.

Muskogee, Indian Territory, May 26, 1905.

Martha Cunnish,
    McGee, Indian Territory.

Dear Madam:

    Receipt is hereby acknowledged of your letter of May 18, stating that your name was spelled wrong and should have been Cunnish instead of Cornish; you then give the roll number of yourself and your husband, Webster Cunnish.

    In reply to your letter you are advised that you and your husband have been identified upon our records as enrolled citizens by blood of the Choctaw Nation, and the affidavits heretofore forwarded to the birth of your child, Rena Cornish, have been filed with our records as an application for the enrollment of said child.

        Respectfully,

                Chairman.

---

7 NB 1444[sic]

Muskogee, Indian Territory, June 12, 1905.

H. M. Byford,
    McGee, Indian Territory.

Dear Sir:

    Receipt is hereby acknowledged of your letter of June 6, 1905, asking if Renner[sic] Cunnish has been enrolled and approved by the Secretary of the Interior so that land can be selected for her; you also ask if Martha Cunnish can file on land for her deceased child.

    In reply to your letter you are advised that the affidavits heretofore forwarded to the birth of Rena Cunnish has been filed with our records as an application for the enrollment of said child, but her name has not yet been placed upon a schedule of citizens by blood of the Choctaw Nation prepared for forwarding to the Secretary of the Interior and pending the approval of her enrollment by him no selection of allotment can be made in her behalf.

    You are further advised that as you do not state the name of the deceased child to whom you refer it is impracticable to give you any information as to its right to enrollment and allotment.

Applications for Enrollment of Choctaw Newborn
Act of 1905 Volume XIX

Respectfully,

Chairman.

7-NB-1447

Muskogee, Indian Territory, August 10, 1905.

H. M. Byford,
    McGee, Indian Territory.

Dear Sir:

    Receipt is hereby acknowledged of your letter of August 4, 1905, transmitting affidavits to the death of Renner Cunnish which occurred March 19, 1905, and the same have been filed as evidence of the death of the above named child.

    You ask if her mother Martha Cunnish may file for her without being appointed administrator; you also inquire why the townsite money has not been paid to her.

    In reply to your letter you are advised that selection of allotment for deceased persons must be made by an administrator appointed by the United States Court in Indian Territory.

    Replying to that portion of your letter in which you ask why the townsite money has not been paid to Rena Cunnish, you are advised that the payment of townsite moneys to citizens of the Choctaw and Chickasaw Nations is within the jurisdiction of the United States Indian Agent and for information relative thereto you should address him at Muskogee, Indian Territory.

    You are further advised that on August 2, 1905, the Secretary of the Interior approved the enrollment of Rena Cunnish as a citizen by blood of the Choctaw Nation.

Respectfully,

Acting Commissioner.

Applications for Enrollment of Choctaw Newborn
Act of 1905   Volume XIX

Choc. New Born 1448
    (Mary Ann Stallaby)
    (Born March 24, 1904)

Choctaw card 5616
BIRTH AFFIDAVIT.

DEPARTMENT OF THE INTERIOR.
COMMISSION TO THE FIVE CIVILIZED TRIBES.

IN RE APPLICATION FOR ENROLLMENT, as a citizen of the Choctaw Nation, of Mary Ann Stallaby, born on the 24 day of March, 1904

Name of Father: Thomas Stallaby   a citizen of the Choctaw Nation.
Name of Mother: Sallie Stallaby   a citizen of the Choctaw Nation.

             Postoffice   Ironbridge Ind Ter

AFFIDAVIT OF MOTHER.

UNITED STATES OF AMERICA, Indian Territory,
    Central   DISTRICT.

    I, Sallie Stallaby, on oath state that I am 20 years of age and a citizen by blood, of the Choctaw Nation; that I am the lawful wife of Thomas Stallaby, who is a citizen, by blood of the Choctaw Nation; that a female child was born to me on 24 day of March, 1904; that said child has been named Mary Ann Stallaby, and was living March 4, 1905.

                                          her
                                  Sallie x Stallaby
Witnesses To Mark: mark
    { Cephus Scott
      James Hunt

    Subscribed and sworn to before me this 3 day of April, 1905

                                OL Johnson
                                    Notary Public.

Applications for Enrollment of Choctaw Newborn
Act of 1905   Volume XIX

AFFIDAVIT OF ATTENDING PHYSICIAN OR MID-WIFE.

UNITED STATES OF AMERICA, Indian Territory, }
   Central   DISTRICT.

    I, Nancy Gage, a midwife, on oath state that I attended on Mrs. Sallie Stallaby, wife of Thomas Stallaby on the 24 day of March, 1904; that there was born to her on said date a female child; that said child was living March 4, 1905, and is said to have been named Mary Ann Stallaby

                                  her
                            Nancy x Gage
Witnesses To Mark: mark
  { Cephus Scott
    James Hunt

    Subscribed and sworn to before me this 3 day of April, 1905

                              OL Johnson
                                  Notary Public.

                    Muskogee, Indian Territory, April 11, 1905.

Thomas Stallaby,
    Ironbridge, Indian Territory.

Dear Sir:

    Receipt is hereby acknowledged of the affidavits of Sallie Stallaby and Nancy Gage to the birth of Mary Ann Stallaby daughter of Thomas and Sallie Stallaby, March 24, 1904.

    It is stated in the affidavit of the mother that she is a citizen by blood of the Choctaw Nation and if this is correct you are requested to state the name under which she was enrolled, the names of her parents, and if she has secured an allotment of the lands of the Choctaw and Chickasaw Nations please give her roll number as it appears upon the allotment certificate.

                      Respectfully,

                                  Commissioner in Charge.

Applications for Enrollment of Choctaw Newborn
Act of 1905   Volume XIX

C. T. Mitchell,
Attorney at Law,

Iron Bridge, Ind. Ter   5/8 1905.

Commission To The Five Civilized Tribes,
        Muskogee,
              Ind. Ter.

Dear Gentlemen:-

    Replying to your letter of April the 11th, relative to the affidavits of Sallie Stallaby, and Nancy Gage, as to the birth of Mary Ann Stallaby, daughter of Thomas and Sallie Stallaby of March the 24th, will say, it is true as it appears in the affidavit that Sallie Stallaby is the Mother of Mary Ann Stallaby. Sallie Stallaby was formerly Sallie Gage, the name under which she was enrolled, her father being Harry Gage and her mother Nancy Gage.

Said Sallie Stallaby, formerly Sallie Gage, has selected her allotment and her roll number as it appears on her certificate 7564 .

                Respect,

                           (signed) Thos Staleby

Choc. New Born 1449
    John Lewis
    (Born March 1, 1905)

        Cancelled and record transferred
        to Chick. New Born Card #549

                March 9, 1906

Applications for Enrollment of Choctaw Newborn
Act of 1905 Volume XIX

CHOCTAW

NEW BORN

1449

John Lewis
(Born March 1, 1905.)

ACT OF CONGRESS APPROVED MARCH 30, 1905.

CANCELLED

And record transferred to:
CHICKASAW NEW BORN *card*
 # 549

MAR 9 1906

Choc. New Born 1450
    Opal Daggs
    (Born May 22, 1904)

BIRTH AFFIDAVIT.

DEPARTMENT OF THE INTERIOR.
COMMISSION TO THE FIVE CIVILIZED TRIBES.

    IN RE APPLICATION FOR ENROLLMENT, as a citizen of the Chockataw[sic] Nation, of Opal Daggs, born on the 22 day of May, 1904

Name of Father: William W Daggs   a citizen of the Chockataw Nation.
Name of Mother: Mollie Daggs   a citizen of the intermarriage Nation.

        Postoffice   Ada

Applications for Enrollment of Choctaw Newborn
Act of 1905   Volume XIX

AFFIDAVIT OF MOTHER.

UNITED STATES OF AMERICA, Indian Territory, }
   Southern   DISTRICT. }

    I, Mollie Daggs, on oath state that I am 26 years of age and a citizen by intermarriage, of the Chocketaw Nation; that I am the lawful wife of William W Daggs, who is a citizen, by blood of the Chocketaw Nation; that a Female child was born to me on 22 day of May, 1904; that said child has been named Opal Daggs, and was living March 4, 1905.

                                    Mollie Daggs

Witnesses To Mark:
{

    Subscribed and sworn to before me this 1 day of May, 1905

                                    JE Williams
                                         Notary Public.

AFFIDAVIT OF ATTENDING PHYSICIAN OR MID-WIFE.

UNITED STATES OF AMERICA, Indian Territory, }
   Southern   DISTRICT. }

    I, W.T. Nolen, a physician, on oath state that I attended on Mrs. Mollie Daggs, wife of William W Daggs on the 22 day of May, 1904; that there was born to her on said date a Female child; that said child was living March 4, 1905, and is said to have been named ....

                                    W T Nolen

Witnesses To Mark:
{

    Subscribed and sworn to before me this 1 day of May, 1905

                                      JE Williams
                                         Notary Public.

Applications for Enrollment of Choctaw Newborn
Act of 1905 Volume XIX

7-NB. 1450.

Muskogee, Indian Territory, June 15, 1905.

J. E. Williams,
    Chickasaw Land Office,
        Ardmore, Indian Territory

Dear Sir:

    There is enclosed herewith application for the enrollment of Opal Daggs, born May 22, 1904. The affidavits fail to show in what capacity W. T. Nolen attended upon Mollie Daggs at the time of the birth of the applicant.

    You will please make the proper correction in the affidavits and then return them to this office.

        Respectfully,

DeB--5/15.   Chairman.

7-NB-1450.

Muskogee, Indian Territory, June 17, 1905.

Commissioner in Charge,
    Chickasaw Land Office,
        Ardmore, Indian Territory.

Dear Sir:

    There is enclosed herewith application for the enrollment of Opal Daggs, born May 2nd[sic], 1904, which was executed before J. E. Williams, Notary Public, then an employe[sic] in your office. The affidavit of the attending physician or midwife fail to show in what capacity W. T. Nolen attended upon Mollie Daggs at the time of the birth of the applicant.

    You will please have this affidavit corrected and then return it to this office.

        Respectfully,

DeB--5/15   Chairman.

Applications for Enrollment of Choctaw Newborn
Act of 1905   Volume XIX

Choc. New Born 1451
    Elizabeth Eunice Woods
    (Born Oct. 30, 1903)

BIRTH AFFIDAVIT.

DEPARTMENT OF THE INTERIOR.
COMMISSION TO THE FIVE CIVILIZED TRIBES.

IN RE APPLICATION FOR ENROLLMENT, as a citizen of the Choctaw Nation, of Elizabeth Eunice Reynolds , born on the 30th day of October , 1903

Name of Father: David G. Reynolds   a citizen of the United States ~~Nation~~.
Name of Mother: Hattie Reynolds (nee Woods) a citizen of the Choctaw Nation.

Postoffice   Atlee, Indian Territory

AFFIDAVIT OF MOTHER.

UNITED STATES OF AMERICA, Indian Territory,
   Southern DISTRICT.

I, Hattie Reynolds , on oath state that I am 29 years of age and a citizen by blood , of the Choctaw Nation; that I am the lawful wife of David G Reynolds , who is a citizen, by ——— of the United States ~~Nation~~; that a female child was born to me on 30th day of October , 1903; that said child has been named Elizabeth Eunice Reynolds , and was living March 4, 1905.

                                                  her
                                      Hattie x Reynolds
Witnesses To Mark: mark
   { Sydney W Burton
     Willie *(Illegible)*
      P.O. Atlee I.T.

Subscribed and sworn to before me this 8th day of April A.D. , 1905

                                    (Name Illegible)
                                        Notary Public.

Applications for Enrollment of Choctaw Newborn
Act of 1905   Volume XIX

AFFIDAVIT OF ATTENDING PHYSICIAN OR MID-WIFE.

UNITED STATES OF AMERICA, Indian Territory, }
  Southern   DISTRICT.

    I, Victoria Lawrence , a midwife , on oath state that I attended on Mrs. Hattie Reynolds , wife of D. G. Reynolds on the 30th day of October , 1903; that there was born to her on said date a Female child; that said child was living March 4, 1905, and is said to have been named Elizabeth Eunice

                                      her
                            Victoria x Lawrence
Witnesses To Mark: mark
  { Ruth David
    W.O. Baylor

    Subscribed and sworn to before me this 20th day of April , 1905

                            W.A. Wilson
                            Notary Public.

(The letter below typed as given.)

                            Atlee I T
                            May 6th 1905

Commission to the Five Civilized Tribes,
            Muskogee, I T

  In reply to your of April 28 05 that I now enclose back to you in order to assist you in finding that I have not been denied in the citizenship Court I never was denied citizenship and have filed on my allotment. I am emrolled with the Dufords and my three minor children Mollie L. Willie M. and Edgar Woods, my roll number that appears on my land certificate is Choctaw by Blood 9344 you have our marriage license filed in that office and propely you have them filed with the rong Hattie Woods I wish you would look this up at once I was Married to David G. Reynolds on the 11th day of May 1902.

  I hope you havent got my affidavits misplaced that I sent down there to have my child enrolled and will see to it at once.

                        Yours Truly
                        (signed) Hattie Reynolds.

Applications for Enrollment of Choctaw Newborn
Act of 1905   Volume XIX

Choc. New Born 1452
    (Martha Emeyabbi)
    (Born November 6, 1903)

BIRTH AFFIDAVIT.

DEPARTMENT OF THE INTERIOR.
COMMISSION TO THE FIVE CIVILIZED TRIBES.

IN RE APPLICATION FOR ENROLLMENT, as a citizen of the Choctaw Nation, of Martha Emeyabbi, born on the 6 day of November, 1903

Name of Father: Forbis Emeyabbi   a citizen of the Choctaw Nation.
Name of Mother: Maneffie Edwards   a citizen of the Choctaw Nation.

           Postoffice   Noah Ind. Teritory[sic]

AFFIDAVIT OF MOTHER.

UNITED STATES OF AMERICA, Indian Territory, ⎫
....DISTRICT. ⎭

    I, Maneffie Edwards, on oath state that I am about 36 years of age and a citizen by Blood, of the Choctaw Nation; that I am the lawful wife of Forbis Emeyabbi, who is a citizen, by Blood of the Choctaw Nation; that a Female child was born to me on 6 day of November, 1903; that said child has been named Martha Emeyabbi, and was living March 4, 1905.

                                       Maneffie Edwards

Witnesses To Mark:
   ⎰ Paul Stephen Noah IT
   ⎱ Yyman Samis Noah IT

     Subscribed and sworn to before me this 8 day of April, 1905

                              J H Matthews Bethel IT
                                    Notary Public.

Applications for Enrollment of Choctaw Newborn
Act of 1905 Volume XIX

AFFIDAVIT OF ATTENDING PHYSICIAN OR MID-WIFE.

UNITED STATES OF AMERICA, Indian Territory, }
....DISTRICT. }

I, Forbis Emeyabbi , a........................., on oath state that I attended on Mrs. Maneffie Edwards , wife of Forbis Emeyabbi on the 6 day of November , 1903; that there was born to her on said date a Female child; that said child was living March 4, 1905, and is said to have been named Martha Emeyabbi

          Forbis + Emeyabbi
Witnesses To Mark: his mark
 { Isham Emeyabbi Noah I.T.
   Yyman Samis Noah IT

Subscribed and sworn to before me this 8 day of April , 1905

        J H Matthews Bethel IT
        Notary Public.

BIRTH AFFIDAVIT.

DEPARTMENT OF THE INTERIOR.
COMMISSION TO THE FIVE CIVILIZED TRIBES.

IN RE APPLICATION FOR ENROLLMENT, as a citizen of the Choctaw Nation, of Martha Emeyabbi , born on the 6 day of November , 1903

Name of Father: Forbis Emeyabbi a citizen of the Choctaw Nation.
Name of Mother: Maneffie Edwards a citizen of the Choctaw Nation.

      Postoffice Noah Ind. Ter.

AFFIDAVIT OF MOTHER.

UNITED STATES OF AMERICA, Indian Territory, }
  Central   DISTRICT. }

I, Maneffie Edwards , on oath state that I am 36 years of age and a citizen by blood , of the Choctaw Nation; that I am the lawful wife of Forbis Emeyabbi , who is a citizen, by blood of the Choctaw Nation; that a female child was born to me on 6th day of November , 1903; that said child has been named Martha Emeyabbi , and was living March 4, 1905.

        her
      Maneffie x Edwards
        mark

Applications for Enrollment of Choctaw Newborn
Act of 1905   Volume XIX

Witnesses To Mark:
- Sarah Matthews
- Tracy Matthews

Subscribed and sworn to before me this 3 day of July, 1905

J H Matthews
Notary Public.

AFFIDAVIT OF ATTENDING PHYSICIAN OR MID-WIFE.

UNITED STATES OF AMERICA, Indian Territory,
Central DISTRICT.

I, *John Noah* and *Smallwood Frazier*, on oath state that I ~~attended on~~ *are acquainted with* Mrs. Maneffie Edwards, wife of Forbis Emeyabbi on the 6th day of November, 1903; that there was born to her on said date a female child; that said child was living March 4, 1905, and is said to have been named Martha Emeyabbi

Witnesses To Mark:

John Noah
Smallwood Frazier
witnesses state that they are acquainted with party and are no relation to them

Subscribed and sworn to before me this 3 day of July, 1905

J H Matthews
Notary Public.

---

7 NB 1452

BIRTH AFFIDAVIT.

DEPARTMENT OF THE INTERIOR.
COMMISSION TO THE FIVE CIVILIZED TRIBES.

IN RE APPLICATION FOR ENROLLMENT, as a citizen of the Choctaw Nation, of Martha Emeyabbi, born on the 6 day of Nov, 1903.

Name of Father: Forbis Emeyabbi   a citizen of the Choctaw Nation.
Name of Mother: Maneffie Emeyabbi   a citizen of the Choctaw Nation.

Postoffice   Noah Ind Ter

Applications for Enrollment of Choctaw Newborn
Act of 1905   Volume XIX

AFFIDAVIT OF MOTHER.

UNITED STATES OF AMERICA, Indian Territory,
Central   DISTRICT.

I, Maneffie Emeyabbi, on oath state that I am about 36 years of age and a citizen by blood, of the Choctaw Nation; that I am the lawful wife of Forbis Emeyabbi, who is a citizen, by blood of the Choctaw Nation; that a female child was born to me on 6 day of November, 1903; that said child has been named Martha Emeyabbi, and was living March 4, 1905.

her
Maneffie x Emeyabbi
mark

Witnesses To Mark:
- E W Camey
- Johnson Noah

Subscribed and sworn to before me this 12th day of August, 1905.

W.H. McKinney
Notary Public.

AFFIDAVIT OF ATTENDING PHYSICIAN OR MID-WIFE.

UNITED STATES OF AMERICA, Indian Territory,
Central   DISTRICT.

We *John Noah* and *Smallwood Frazier*, on oath state that ~~I attended on~~ *we are acquainted with* Mrs. Maneffie Emeyabbi, wife of Forbis Emeyabbi on the 6 day of Nov, 1903; that there was born to her on said date a female child; that said child was living March 4, 1905, and is said to have been named Martha Emeyabbi

Witnesses To Mark:

John Noah
Smallwood Frazier

Subscribed and sworn to before me this 12th day of August, 1905.

W.H. McKinney
Notary Public.

My Commission expires
March 30, 1909.

Applications for Enrollment of Choctaw Newborn
Act of 1905   Volume XIX

7-3717

Muskogee, Indian Territory, May 5, 1905.

Forbis Emeyabbi,
    Noah, Indian Territory.

Dear Sir:

    Receipt is hereby acknowledged of the affidavits of Maneffie Edwards and Forbis Emeyabbi to the birth of Martha Emeyabbi, daughter of Forbis Emeyabbi and Maneffie Edwards November 6, 1903.

    The information contained in this application is not sufficient to enable us to identify the mother of this child. You give her name as Maneffie Edwards and her roll No. as 10523. It appears that the name of the citizen opposite No. 10523 upon the Choctaw roll is Elsie Wade and you are requested to state you wife's maiden name, the names of her parents, and her brothers and sisters names, and any other information you may possess which will enable us to identify her upon our records. This matter should receive immediate attention so that proper disposition may be made of the application for the enrollment of your child.

    Respectfully,

Commissioner in Charge.

(The letter above given again but with the date of May 6, 1905.)

(The letter below typed as given.)

(COPY)

Noah Ind Ter.

5/ 15   05.

Sir your letter May 6, 05 at hand Maneffie Edwards roll No. is 2307 her father name is Barnabas Edwards her mother name is Sallie Edwards her fatherhas been dead a long time Her brothers name is Moton Edwards and Isac[sic] Edwards her sister names is Silway Edwards Louisa Edwards Betsy Edwards Ebenezer Edwards
the notary mad a mistake on the roll nO.
    yours truly Forbis Emeyabbi

Paul Stephens
Noah, I.T.

Applications for Enrollment of Choctaw Newborn
Act of 1905   Volume XIX

7--879.

Muskogee, Indian Territory, May 24, 1905.

Forbis Emeyabbi,
    Noah, Indian Territory.

Dear Sir:

Receipt is hereby acknowledged of your letter of May 15, stating that the roll number of Maneffie Edwards is 2307 and her father and mother were named Barnabas and Sallie Edwards

This information has enabled us to identify Maneffie Edwards upon our records as an enrolled citizen by blood of the Choctaw Nation and the affidavits heretofore forwarded to the birth of your child, Martha Emeyabbi, have been filed with our records as an application for the enrollment of said child.

The communication of the Commission of May 6, 1905, enclosed with your letter is herewith returned.

    Respectfully,

                                Chairman.

DeB--6/24.

7-NB-1452.

Muskogee, Indian Territory, June 15, 1905.

Forbis Emeyabbi,
    Noah, Indian Territory.

Dear Sir:

There is enclosed herewith for execution application for the enrollment of your infant child, Martha Emeyabbi, born November 6, 1903.

It is noted in the application heretofore filed in this office that the Notary Public, before whom the mother's affidavit was executed, signed her name. If your wife can write you are requested to have her sign her name in her own hand, but if she cannot write she must sign by mark and her signature attested by two witnesses who can write.

It is also noted in the application above referred to that you attended upon your wife at the time of the birth of the applicant. If there was a physician or midwife in attendance besides yourself, you will please secure his or her affidavit, but if you were the only one in attendance it will be necessary for you to secure the affidavits of two

Applications for Enrollment of Choctaw Newborn
Act of 1905   Volume XIX

persons who are disinterested and not related to the applicant, who have actual knowledge of the facts; that the child was born, the date of her birth, that she was living on March 4, 190**5**, and that Maneffie Edwards Emeyabbi is her mother.

In having these affidavits executed care should be exercised to see that all names are written in full, as they appear in the body of the affidavits, and if either of the persons signing the affidavits are unable to write, signature by mark must be attested by two witnesses. Each affidavit must be executed before a Notary Public and the notarial seal and signature of the officer must be attached to each separate affidavit.

You are requested to give this matter your immediate [sic] as no further action can be taken relative to the enrollment of said child until these affidavits are filed with the Commission.

                Respectfully,

                                            Chairman.

DeB--7/15

7-NB-1452

                Muskogee, Indian Territory, July 28, 1905.

Forbis Emeyabbi,
    Noah, Indian Territory.

Dear Sir:

There is inclosed you herewith for execution application for the enrollment of your infant child, Martha Emeyabbi, born November 6, 1903.

In the affidavits of Maneffie Edwards, heretofore filed in this case, she alleges that she is your lawful wife, but signs the affiavit[sic] in her maiden name, Maneffie Edwards.

In the inclosed application her married name is given, and she should so sign the mother's affidavit, and also have the affidavits of John Noah and Norwood[sic] Frazier to the birth of said child, re-executed.   When the affidavits have been executed in accordance with directions herein, you will please forward to this office.

This matter should receive you immediate attention as no further action can be taken relative to the enrollment of the applicant until the inclosed application in due form is filed in this office.

                Respectfully,

LM 2/28   Commissioner.

Applications for Enrollment of Choctaw Newborn
Act of 1905   Volume XIX

7-NB-1452

Muskogee, Indian Territory, August 18, 1905.

Forbis Emeyabbi,
    Noah, Indian Territory.

Dear Sir:

    Receipt is hereby acknowledged of the affidavit of Maneffie Emeyabbi, and the joint affidavit f John Noah and Smallwood Frazier to the birth of Martha Emeyabbi, daughter of Forbis and Maneffie Emeyabbi, November 6, 1903, and the same have been filed in the matter of the enrollment of said child.

Respectfully,

Acting Commissioner.

Choc. New Born 1453
    Nicholas Bean
    (Born Sep. 3, 1904)

    Jacket empty.

Applications for Enrollment of Choctaw Newborn
Act of 1905 Volume XIX

1453

CANCELLED
NEW BORN
CHOCTAW
ENROLLMENT

NICHOLAS BEAN

(BORN SEPTEMBER 3, 1904)

As Citizen of the
CHOCTAW NATION
Act of Congress
Approved March 3, 1905
CANCELLED

TRANSFERRED TO CHICKASAW CARE N.B. 536
JULY 15, 1905

1453

Choc. New Born 1454
    Nelson McAlester
    (Born Jan. 1, 1904)

BIRTH AFFIDAVIT.

DEPARTMENT OF THE INTERIOR.
COMMISSION TO THE FIVE CIVILIZED TRIBES.

IN RE APPLICATION FOR ENROLLMENT, as a citizen of the Choctaw Nation, of Nelson McAlester, born on the 1st day of Jan., 1904

Name of Father: James McAlester   a citizen of the Choctaw Nation.
Name of Mother: Angline McAlester   a citizen of the Choctaw Nation.

                Postoffice   Alichi Ind Ter.

Applications for Enrollment of Choctaw Newborn
Act of 1905   Volume XIX

AFFIDAVIT OF MOTHER.

UNITED STATES OF AMERICA, Indian Territory, }
   Central   DISTRICT.

    I,   Angline McAlester   , on oath state that I am 22   years of age and a citizen by   Blood   , of the   Choctaw   Nation; that I am the lawful wife of   James McAlester   , who is a citizen, by Blood   of the   Choctaw   Nation; that a   male   child was born to me on   1st day of   January   , 1904; that said child has been named   Nelson McAlester   , and was living March 4, 1905.

                                            her
                                 Angline x McAlester
Witnesses To Mark: mark
{ *(Name Illegible)*
  Thos Fennell

    Subscribed and sworn to before me this   25th day of   March   , 1905

                                  Thomas Fennell
                                  Notary Public.

AFFIDAVIT OF ATTENDING PHYSICIAN OR MID-WIFE.

UNITED STATES OF AMERICA, Indian Territory, }
   Central   DISTRICT.

    I,   Sophia Home   , a   Midwife   , on oath state that I attended on Mrs.   Angline McAlester   , wife of   James McAlester   on the 1st day of January   , 1904; that there was born to her on said date a   male   child; that said child was living March 4, 1905, and is said to have been named   Nelson McAlester

                                  Sophia Home
Witnesses To Mark:

{

    Subscribed and sworn to before me this   25th day of   March   , 1905

                                  Thomas Fennell
                                  Notary Public.

Applications for Enrollment of Choctaw Newborn
Act of 1905   Volume XIX

Muskogee, Indian Territory, April 26, 1905.

James McAlester,
    Alichi, Indian Territory.

Dear Sir:

    Receipt is hereby acknowledged of the affidavits of Angline McAlester and Sophia Home, to the birth of Nelson McAlester, child of James and Angline McAlester, January 1, 1904.

    It appears from the affidavit of the mother, that she is a citizen by blood of the Choctaw Nation, if this [sic] correct, you are requested to state the name under which she was enrolled, the names of her parents, and if she has selected an allotment of land of the Choctaw or Chickasaw Nations[sic], give her Roll Number as the same appears upon her allotment certificate.

                    Respectfully,

                                  Chairman.

Alikchi Ind. T May 17, 1905.

Sirs. In answer to your inquiry of April 26 1905 will say that my wife's father's name is Lewis Noatabbe, mother's name is Selin Noatabbe. My wife was enrolled by the name of Antlin Noatabbe. She has taken her allotment of Chickasaw & Choctaw land her roll No. 5431 certificate Nos. 11515 - 9981.

                    Respt. Yours
                    James McAlester.

Choctaw 1899.

Muskogee, Indian Territory, May 25, 1905.

James McAlester,
    Alikchi, Indian Territory.

Dear Sir:

    Receipt is hereby acknowledged of your letter of May 17, giving the name under which your wife, Angline McAlester, was enrolled, her roll number, and the names of her parents, and this information has enabled us to identify her upon our records as an enrolled citizen by blood of the Choctaw Nation, and the affidavits heretofore forwarded to the birth of your child, Nelson McAlester, have been filed with our records as an application for his enrollment.

Applications for Enrollment of Choctaw Newborn
Act of 1905 Volume XIX

Respectfully,

Chairman.

Choc. New Born 1455
    Gertie Allie Carter
    (Born July 14, 1905)

BIRTH AFFIDAVIT.

DEPARTMENT OF THE INTERIOR.
COMMISSION TO THE FIVE CIVILIZED TRIBES.

    IN RE APPLICATION FOR ENROLLMENT, as a citizen of the Choctaw Nation, of Gertie Allie Carter, born on the 14th day of July, 1904

Name of Father: Jas. C. Carter   ~~a citizen of~~ the ———— Nation.
Name of Mother: Susie Carter   a citizen of the Choctaw Nation.

    Postoffice   Sulphur I.T.

AFFIDAVIT OF MOTHER.

UNITED STATES OF AMERICA, Indian Territory, ⎫
   Southern   DISTRICT. ⎭

    I, Susie Carter, on oath state that I am 25 years of age and a citizen by Blood, of the Choctaw Nation; that I am the lawful wife of Jas C. Carter, who is a citizen, by —— of the —— Nation; that a Female child was born to me on 14th day of July, 1904, that said child has been named Gertie Allie Carter, and is now living.

                                     Susie Carter

Witnesses To Mark:
   {

    Subscribed and sworn to before me this 28th day of April, 1905.

                                     T.F. Gafford
                                       Notary Public.

Applications for Enrollment of Choctaw Newborn
Act of 1905 Volume XIX

AFFIDAVIT OF ATTENDING PHYSICIAN OR MID-WIFE.

UNITED STATES OF AMERICA, Indian Territory,
~~Eastern~~ District   DISTRICT.
Western

I,   Caroline Brown   , a   Midwife   , on oath state that I attended on Mrs.   Susie Carter , wife of   J C Carter   on the   14th   day of   July , 1904; that there was born to her on said date a   Female   child; that said child is now living and is said to have been named   Gertie Allie Carter

                                                her
                                    Caroline x Brown

Witnesses To Mark: mark
   { James Choate
   { ? C. Tidwell

Subscribed and sworn to before me this   1st   day of   May , 1905.

                                    L.C. Tuey
                                          Notary Public.

                          Muskogee, Indian Territory, May 6, 1905.

James C. Carter,
    Sulphur, Indian Territory.

Dear Sir:

    Receipt is hereby acknowledged of the affidavits of Susie Carter and Caroline Brown to the birth of Gertie Allie Carter, daughter of James C. and Susie Carter, July 14, 1904.

    It is stated in the affidavit of the mother that she is a citizen by blood of the Choctaw Nation. If this is correct you are requested to state the name under which she was enrolled, the names of her parents, and if she has selected an allotment of the lands of the Choctaw or Chickasaw Nation please give her roll number as it appears upon her allotment certificate.

                          Respectfully,

                                            Commissioner in Charge.

Applications for Enrollment of Choctaw Newborn
Act of 1905 Volume XIX

7--2437.

Muskogee, Indian Territory, May 25, 1905.

T. J[sic]. Gafford,
    Sulphur, Indian Territory.

Dear Sir:

    Receipt is hereby acknowledged of your letter of May 16, giving information relative to the enrollment of Susie Carter in the matter of the application for the enrollment of her child, Gertie Allie Carter, and the same has enabled us to identify her upon our records as an enrolled citizen by blood of the Choctaw Nation, and the affidavits heretofore forwarded to the birth of Gertie Allie Carter have been filed with our records as an application for the enrollment of said child.

                      Respectfully,

                                          Chairman.

---

7 NB 1455

Muskogee, Indian Territory, June 16, 1905.

T. F. Gafford,
    Sulphur, Indian Territory.

Dear Sir:

    Receipt is hereby acknowledged of your letter of June 10, 1905, in which you state that J. C. Carter is anxious to file on land for his daughter Gertie Allie Carter for whom application was mad a short time ago.

    In reply to your letter you are advised that the name of Gertie Allie Carter is being placed upon a schedule of citizens by blood of the Choctaw Nation of the Choctaw Nation prepared for forwarding to the Secretary of the Interior but pending the approval of her enrollment by him no selection of allotment can be made in her behalf.

    Mr. Carter will be notified when the enrollment of his daughter is approved by the Secretary of the Interior.

                      Respectfully,

                                          Chairman.

Applications for Enrollment of Choctaw Newborn
Act of 1905   Volume XIX

Choc. New Born 1456
    Ella Jones
    (Born March 4, 1904)

NEW BORN AFFIDAVIT

No ....

CHOCTAW ENROLLING COMMISSION

IN THE MATTER OF THE APPLICATION FOR ENROLLMENT as a citizen of the Choctaw Nation, of   Ella Jones   born on the   4th day of   March   190 4

Name of father   Edmon Jones   a citizen of   Choctaw   Nation, final enrollment No.   11565

Name of mother   Alice Jones   a citizen of   Choctaw   Nation, final enrollment No.   11566

                        Atoka I.T.   Postoffice.

AFFIDAVIT OF MOTHER

UNITED STATES OF AMERICA
    INDIAN TERRITORY
DISTRICT...............

    I   Alice Jones   , on oath state that I am   26   years of age and a citizen by   Blood   of the   Choctaw   Nation, and as such have been placed upon the final roll of the   Choctaw   Nation, by the Honorable Secretary of the Interior my final enrollment number being   11566   ; that I am the lawful wife of   Edmon Jones   , who is a citizen of the   Choctaw   Nation, and as such has been placed upon the final roll of said Nation by the Honorable Secretary of the Interior, his final enrollment number being   11565   and that a   Female   child was born to me on the   4th day of   March   190 4; that said child has been named   Ella Jones   , and is now living.

                                              her
                                     Alice x Jones

WITNESSETH: mark
  Must be two witnesses { Saul Folsom
  who are citizens   { John W. McKinney

Applications for Enrollment of Choctaw Newborn
Act of 1905   Volume XIX

Subscribed and sworn to before me this, the 21ˢᵗ   day of   February   , 190 5

W.S. Farmer
Notary Public.

My Commission Expires:

Affidavit of Attending Physician or Midwife

UNITED STATES OF AMERICA,
   INDIAN TERRITORY,
  Central   DISTRICT

I,   Edman[sic] Jones   *The Husband attended wife*
on oath state that I attended on Mrs. Allice[sic] Jones   wife of   Edman Jones
on the   4ᵗʰ   day of   March   , 190 4, that there was born to her on said date a   Female
child, that said child is now living, and is said to have been named   Ella Jones
his   *of child*
Edman x Jones   *The Father*   ~~M.D.~~
mark

Subscribed and sworn to before me this the   23   day of   February   1905

A.E. Folsom
Notary Public.

WITNESSETH:
Must be two witnesses who are citizens and know the child.
{ G E Folsom
{ C A Betts

We hereby certify that we are well acquainted with   Edman Jones
The Father of child   and know   him   to be reputable and of good standing in the community.

Must be two citizen witnesses.
{ G E Carroll
{ C A Betts

BIRTH AFFIDAVIT.

DEPARTMENT OF THE INTERIOR.
COMMISSION TO THE FIVE CIVILIZED TRIBES.

IN RE APPLICATION FOR ENROLLMENT, as a citizen of the   Choctaw   Nation, of
Ella Jones   , born on the   4ᵗʰ   day of   March   , 1904

Name of Father: Edmond Jones   a citizen of the   Choctaw   Nation.
Name of Mother: Alice   "   a citizen of the   "   Nation.

Applications for Enrollment of Choctaw Newborn
Act of 1905 Volume XIX

Postoffice   Atoka Ind Ter

AFFIDAVIT OF MOTHER.

UNITED STATES OF AMERICA, Indian Territory,
Central   DISTRICT.

I, Alice Jones, on oath state that I am 27 years of age and a citizen by blood, of the Choctaw Nation; that I am the lawful wife of Edmond Jones, who is a citizen, by blood of the Choctaw Nation; that a female child was born to me on 4th day of March, 1904; that said child has been named Ella Jones, and was living March 4, 1905.

           her
         Alice x Jones
Witnesses To Mark: mark
 { WHMartin
  Richard Shanafelt

Subscribed and sworn to before me this 22nd day of April, 1905

        W.H. Angell
        Notary Public.

AFFIDAVIT OF ATTENDING PHYSICIAN OR MID-WIFE.

UNITED STATES OF AMERICA, Indian Territory,
Central   DISTRICT.

I, Edmond Jones, ~~a~~, on oath state that I attended on Mrs. Alice Jones, wife of Myself on the 4th day of March, 1904; that there was born to her on said date a female child; that said child was living March 4, 1905, and is said to have been named Ella Jones, *and that there was no one present at the birth of said child except myself and my said wife.*

          his
        Edmond x Jones
Witnesses To Mark: mark
 { WHMartin
  Richard Shanafelt

Subscribed and sworn to before me this 22nd day of April, 1905

        W.H. Angell
        Notary Public.

Applications for Enrollment of Choctaw Newborn
Act of 1905   Volume XIX

BIRTH AFFIDAVIT.

DEPARTMENT OF THE INTERIOR.
COMMISSION TO THE FIVE CIVILIZED TRIBES.

IN RE APPLICATION FOR ENROLLMENT, as a citizen of the   Choctaw   Nation, of Ella Jones   , born on the 4th day of March , 1904

Name of Father: Edmond Jones   a citizen of the Choctaw   Nation.
Name of Mother: Alice Jones   a citizen of the Choctaw   Nation.

Postoffice   Atoka I T

AFFIDAVIT OF MOTHER.

UNITED STATES OF AMERICA, Indian Territory, }
    Central   DISTRICT.

I,   Cynthia E. Miller   , on oath state that I am 65   years of age and a citizen by ——————, of the   United States   ~~Nation~~; that I am ~~the lawful wife of~~ *personally acquainted with Alice Jones who is the lawful wife of Edmond Jones and* who is a citizen, by blood   of the   Choctaw   Nation; that a   female   child was born to ~~me~~ *her* on *or about the 4th* day of   March   , 1904; that said child has been named Ella Jones   , and was living March 4, 1905.

                                       her
                             Cynthia E. x Miller
Witnesses To Mark: mark
  { Richard Shanafelt
  { WHMartin

Subscribed and sworn to before me this 26th day of   April   , 1905

                        W.H. Angell
                            Notary Public.

AFFIDAVIT OF ATTENDING PHYSICIAN OR MID-WIFE.

UNITED STATES OF AMERICA, Indian Territory, }
    Central   DISTRICT.

                                    am personally acquainted with
I,   Annie M. Rogers[sic]   , a ——————, on oath state that I ~~attended~~ ~~on~~ Mrs. Alice Jones , wife of Edmond Jones *that* on *or about the 4th* day of March , 1904; that there was born to her on said date a   female   child; that said child was living March 4, 1905, and is said to have been named   Ella Jones

Applications for Enrollment of Choctaw Newborn
Act of 1905   Volume XIX

Annie M Rodgers

Witnesses To Mark:
{

Subscribed and sworn to before me this 26th day of   April   , 1905

W.H. Angell
Notary Public.

Choc. New Born 1457
    Martha May Lemon
    (Born March 20, 1905)

(The below typed as given.)

1457

NEW BORN
CHOCTAW
ENROLLMENT

MARTHA MAY LEMON
(BORN MARCH 20, 1905)

As Citizen of the
CHOCTAW NATION
Act of Congress
Approved March 3, 1905

BORN SUBSEQUENT TO MARCH 4, 1905
DECISION RENDERED JUNE 30, 1905
DECLINE TO RECEIVE OR CONSIDER JUNE 30, 1905
COPY OF DECISION FORWARDED ATTORNEYS FOR
CHOCTAW AND CHICKASAW NATIONS. JUNE 30, 1905
COPY OF DECISION FOREARDED APPLICANT'FATHER
                                    JUNE 30, 1905
RECORD FORWARDED DEPARTMENT. JUNE 30, 1905
ACTION APPROVED BY SECRETARY OF INTERIOR.
                                OCTOBER 20, 1905
NOTICE OF DEPARTMENTAL ACTION FORWARDED
ATTORNEYS FOR CHOCTAW AND CHICKASAW NATIONS
                                NOVEMBER 1, 1905

Applications for Enrollment of Choctaw Newborn
Act of 1905   Volume XIX

NOTICE OF DEPARTMENTAL ACTION MAILED APPLI-
CANT'S FATHER NOVEMBER 1, 1905

1457

BIRTH AFFIDAVIT.

DEPARTMENT OF THE INTERIOR.
COMMISSION TO THE FIVE CIVILIZED TRIBES.

IN RE APPLICATION FOR ENROLLMENT, as a citizen of the   Choctaw   Nation, of Martha May Lemon   , born on the   20   day of   March   , 1905

Name of Father: John Lemon   a citizen of the   Choctaw   Nation.
Name of Mother: Ida Lemon   a citizen of the   Choctaw   Nation.

Postoffice   Leon, Ind. Ter.

AFFIDAVIT OF MOTHER.

UNITED STATES OF AMERICA, Indian Territory,
Southern   DISTRICT.

I,   Ida Lemon   , on oath state that I am   26   years of age and a citizen by Blood   , of the   Choctaw   Nation; that I am the lawful wife of   John Lemon   , who is a citizen, by Marriage   of the   Choctaw   Nation; that a   Female child was born to me on   20   day of   March   , 1905; that said child has been named Martha May Lemon   , and was living ~~March 4~~, April 4, 1905.

Ida Lemon

Witnesses To Mark:

Subscribed and sworn to before me this   5   day of   April   , 1905

SEAL.   C. A. Gipson
     Notary Public.

Applications for Enrollment of Choctaw Newborn
Act of 1905   Volume XIX

AFFIDAVIT OF ATTENDING PHYSICIAN OR MID-WIFE.

UNITED STATES OF AMERICA, Indian Territory, }
Southern   DISTRICT.

I,   A. L. Breeding   , a Physician   , on oath state that I attended on Mrs.   Ida Lemon   , wife of   John Lemon   on the   20   day of   March   , 1905; that there was born to her on said date a   Female   child; that said child was living ~~March 4~~, 1905, and is said to have been named   Martha May Lemon
April 4,

A.L. Breeding, M.D.

Witnesses To Mark:
{

Subscribed and sworn to before me this 5 day of   April   , 1905

SEAL.   C. A. Gipson
Notary Public.

W.J.
7-NB-1457.

DEPARTMENT OF THE INTERIOR,
COMMISSION TO THE FIVE CIVILIZED TRIBES.

In the matter of the application for the enrollment of Martha May Lemon as a citizen by blood of the Choctaw Nation.

--: D E C I S I O N :--

It appears from the record herein that on April 7, 1905 there was filed with the Commission application for the enrollment of Martha May Lemon as a citizen by blood of the Choctaw Nation.

It further appears from the record herein and the records of the Commission that the applicant was born March 20, 1905 and is a daughter of Ida Lemon, a recognized and enrolled citizen by blood of the Choctaw Nation whose name appears opposite number 14860 upon the final roll of citizens by blood of the Choctaw Nation, approved by the Secretary of the Interior May 20, 1903, and John Lemon, a noncitizen.

The Act of Congress approved March 3, 1905 (Public No. 212) among other things provides:

> "That the Commission to the Five Civilized Tribes is authorized for sixty days after the date of the approval of this act to receive and consider applications for enrollment of children born subsequent to September twenty-fifth, nineteen hundred and two, <u>and prior to March fourth, nineteen hundred and five,</u> and who were living on said latter date, to citizens by blood of the Choctaw and Chickasaw tribes of Indians whose enrollment has

Applications for Enrollment of Choctaw Newborn
Act of 1905   Volume XIX

been approved by the Secretary of the Interior prior to the date of the approval of this act; and to enroll and make allotments to such children."

It is the opinion of this Commission that, inasmuch as the said Martha May Lemon was not born prior to March 4, 1905, the Commission is without authority to receive or consider the application for her enrollment as a citizen by blood of the Choctaw Nation and that, therefore, the Commission should decline to receive or consider such application under the provision of law above quoted and it is so ordered.

COMMISSION TO THE FIVE CIVILIZED TRIBES,

Tams Bixby
Chairman.

TBNeedles
Commissioner

C. R. Breckinridge
Commissioner.

Muskogee, Indian Territory.
JUN 30 1905

7-NB-1457.

Muskogee, Indian Territory, June 30, 1905.

John Lemon,
Leon, Indian Territory.

COPY

Dear Sir:

Inclosed herewith you will find a copy of the decision of the Commission to the Five Civilized Tribes, rendered June 30, 1905, declining to receive or consider the application for the enrollment of Martha May Lemon as a citizen by blood of the Choctaw Nation.

The decision, with the record of proceedings in the case, is this day transmitted to the Secretary of the Interior for review. The final decision of the Secretary will be made known to you as soon as this office is informed of the same.

Respectfully,
SIGNED

Tams Bixby
Chairman.

Registered.
Incl. 7-NB-1457.

Applications for Enrollment of Choctaw Newborn
Act of 1905 Volume XIX

7-NB-1457.

Muskogee, Indian Territory, June 30, 1905.

Mansfield, McMurray & Cornish, **COPY**
    Attorneys for Choctaw and Chickasaw Nations,
        South McAlester, Indian Territory.

Gentlemen:

    Inclosed herewith you will find a copy of the decision of the Commission to the Five Civilized Tribes, rendered June 30, 1905, declining to receive or consider the application for the enrollment of Martha May Lemon as a citizen by blood of the Choctaw Nation.

    The decision, with the record of proceedings in the case, is this day transmitted to the Secretary of the Interior for review. The final decision of the Secretary will be made known to you as soon as this office is informed of the same.

                      Respectfully,
                      SIGNED *Tams Bixby*
                              Chairman.

Incl. 7-NB-1457.

Muskogee, Indian Territory, June 30, 1905.

The Honorable, **COPY**
    The Secretary of the Interior.

Sir:

    There is herewith transmitted the record of proceedings in the matter of the application for the enrollment of Martha May Lemon as a citizen by blood of the Choctaw Nation, including the decision of the Commission, dated June 30, 1905, declining to receive or consider said application.

                      Respectfully,
                      SIGNED *Tams Bixby*
Through the   Chairman.
    Commissioner of Indian Affairs.

2 Incl. 7-NB-1457.

Applications for Enrollment of Choctaw Newborn
Act of 1905 Volume XIX

DEPARTMENT OF THE INTERIOR,
OFFICE OF INDIAN AFFAIRS,
Land.   WASHINGTON.   July 24, 1905.
50911-1905.

The Honorable,
    The Secretary of the Interior.

Sir:

    I have the honor to enclose a report from the Commission to the Five Civilized Tribes, dated June 30, 1905, transmitting the record of the application made April 7, 1905, for enrollment as a citizen by blood of the Choctaw Nation of Martha May Lemon.

    June 30, 1905, the Commission decided adversely to the applicant.

    The record shows that the applicant was <u>born March 20, 1905,</u> and is a daughter of Ida Lemon whose name appears at No. 14860 upon the final roll of citizens by blood of the Choctaw Nation approved by the Department May 20, 1903, and John Lemon, a non-citizen.

    In view of the record and of the act of March 3, 1903[sic] (33 Stats., 1071) the approval of the Commission's decision adverse to the applicant is recommended.

                          Very respectfully,
                            C. f. Larrabee
M.M.M. (W)   Acting Commissioner.

                DEPARTMENT OF THE INTERIOR,
D C   48812-1905.   WASHINGTON.   GR
                                                      LLB
I T D   9078-1905.   October 20, 1905.

LRS

Commissioner to the Five Civilized Tribes,
    Muskogee, Indian Territory.

Sir:

    June 30, 1905, the Commission to the Five Civilized Tribes transmitted the record of the application made April 7, 1905, under the act of Congress approved March 3, 1905, for the enrollment of Martha May Lemon, an infant, born March 20, 1905, as a citizen by blood of the Choctaw Nation, including the decision of the Commission of same date declining to receive or consider said application, on the ground that said

Applications for Enrollment of Choctaw Newborn
Act of 1905   Volume XIX

Martha May Lemon was not born prior to March 4, 1905, and the Commission is therefore without authority to receive or consider the same.

July 24, 1905, the Acting Commissioner of Indian Affairs. Indian Affairs reporting thereon, recommended that the decision of the Commission, declining to receive or consider said application, be affirmed. A copy of his letter is inclosed.

The Department concurs in the recommendation made an the decision of the Commission to the Five Civilized Tribes dated June 30, 1905, declining to receive or consider the application for the enrollment of Martha May Lemon, an infant as a citizen by blood of the Choctaw Nation is hereby affirmed.

Respectfully,

1 inclosure.   E A Hitchcock
                                                Secretary.

7-NB-1457

Muskogee, Indian Territory, November 1, 1905.

John Lemon,
    Leon, Indian Territory.

Dear Sir:

You are hereby notified that the Secretary of the Interior under date of October 20, 1905, affirmed the decision of the Commission to the Five Civilized Tribes, dated June 20, 1905, declining to receive or consider the application for the enrollment of Martha May Lemon as a citizen by blood of the Choctaw Nation.

Respectfully,

Commissioner.

Applications for Enrollment of Choctaw Newborn
Act of 1905   Volume XIX

7-NB-1457

Muskogee, Indian Territory, November 1, 1905.

Mansfield, McMurray & Cornish,
    Attorneys for Choctaw and Chickasaw Nations,
        South McAlester, Indian Territory.

Gentlemen:

You are hereby notified that the Secretary of the Interior under date of October 20, 1905, affirmed the decision of the Commission to the Five Civilized Tribes, dated June 30, 1905, declining to receive or consider the application for the enrollment of Martha May Lemon as a citizen by blood of the Choctaw Nation.

                Respectfully,

                          Commissioner.

Choc. New Born 1458
    Inez Boswell
    (Born Oct. 10, 1902)

1458

NEW BORN
CHOCTAW
ENROLLMENT

INEZ BOSWELL

(BORN OCTOBER 10, 1902)

As Citizen of the
CHOCTAW NATION
Act of Congress
Approved March 3, 1905

C A C E L L E D[sic]

RECORD TRANSFERRED TO CHOCTAW NEW BORN NO. 452

Applications for Enrollment of Choctaw Newborn
Act of 1905   Volume XIX

ACT OF CONGRESS APPROVED APRIL 26, 1906.
JULY 13, 1906.

1458

CHOCTAW 1458
NEW BORN
ACT OF CONGRESS APPROVED MARCH 30, 1905.

Inez Boswell
(Born Oct. 10, 1902)

CANCELLED

Record transferred to

CHOCTAW   NEW BORN   *No. 452*
ACT OF CONGRESS APPROVED APRIL 26, 1906.

JUL 13 1906

Choc. New Born 1459
    Clara Renee Bell
    (Born March 21, 1905)

Applications for Enrollment of Choctaw Newborn
Act of 1905   Volume XIX

1459

NEW BORN
CHOCTAW ENROLLMENT

CLARA RENA BELL

(BORN MARCH 21, 1905)

As Citizen of the
CHOCTAW NATION
Act of Congress
Approved March 3, 1905

C A N C E L L E D

RECORD TRANSFERRED TO CHOCTAW NEW BORN 785

ACT OF CONGRESS APPROVED APRIL 26, 1906.

JULY 20, 1906

1459

CHOCTAW   1459
NEW BORN
ACT OF CONGRESS APPROVED MARCH 30, 1905.

Clara Rena Bell
(Born March 21, 1905)

CANCELLED

Record transferred to
Choctaw New Born 785
ACT OF CONGRESS APPROVED APRIL 26, 1906.

JUL 20 1906

Applications for Enrollment of Choctaw Newborn
Act of 1905   Volume XIX

Choc. New Born 1460
    Turner Fout
    (Born July 25, 1904)

1460

NEW BORN
CHOCTAW
ENROLLMENT

TURNER FOUT

(BORN JULY 25, 1904)

DIED PRIOR TO MARCH 4, 1905

As Citizen of the
CHOCTAW NATION
Act of Congress
Approved March 3, 1905

NO 1 DISMISSED JUNE 28, 1905

1460

DEPARTMENT OF THE INTERIOR,
COMMISSION TO THE FIVE CIVILIZED TRIBES.

Record in the matter of the application for enrollment as a citizen by blood of the Choctaw Nation of:

    TURNER FOUT   7-NB-1460.

Applications for Enrollment of Choctaw Newborn
Act of 1905   Volume XIX

BIRTH AFFIDAVIT.

DEPARTMENT OF THE INTERIOR.
COMMISSION TO THE FIVE CIVILIZED TRIBES.

IN RE APPLICATION FOR ENROLLMENT, as a citizen of the   Choctaw   Nation, of Turner Fout , born on the 25 day of July , 1904

Name of Father: Sam W. Fout   a citizen ~~of the~~ United States Nation.
Name of Mother: Susie G. Fout   a citizen of the   Choctaw   Nation.

Postoffice   Milton, I.T.

AFFIDAVIT OF MOTHER.

UNITED STATES OF AMERICA, Indian Territory, }
    Central   DISTRICT.

I, Susie G. Fout, on oath state that I am 20 years of age and a citizen by blood, of the Choctaw Nation; that I am the lawful wife of Sam W. Fout, who is a citizen, ~~by~~ *of the United States* Nation; that a boy child was born to me on 25 day of July, 1904; that said child has been named Turner Fout, and ~~was living March 4, 1905~~. *died Sept. 11, 1904*

Susie Fout

Witnesses To Mark:
{

Subscribed and sworn to before me this 17 day of April, 1905

J. L. Lewis
Notary Public.

AFFIDAVIT OF ATTENDING PHYSICIAN OR MID-WIFE.

UNITED STATES OF AMERICA, Indian Territory, }
    Central   DISTRICT.

I, C. C. Fout, a mid wife, on oath state that I attended on Mrs. Susie G. Fout, wife of Sam W. Fout on the 25 day of July, 1904; that there was born to her on said date a boy child; that said child ~~was living March 4, 1905~~ *died on 11 Sept. 1904* and is said to have been named Turner Fout

C.C. Fout

Applications for Enrollment of Choctaw Newborn
Act of 1905   Volume XIX

Witnesses To Mark:
{

Subscribed and sworn to before me this 17 day of   April   , 1905

J. L. Lewis
Notary Public.

W.F.
7-NB-1460.

DEPARTMENT OF THE INTERIOR,
COMMISSION TO THE FIVE CIVILIZED TRIBES.

In the matter of the application for the enrollment of Turner Fout as a citizen by blood of the Choctaw Nation.

---oOo---

It appears from the record herein that on April 19, 1905, there was filed with the Commission application for the enrollment of Turner Fout as a citizen by blood of the Choctaw Nation.

It further appears from the record herein and the records of the Commission that the applicant was born July 25, 1904; that he is a son of Susan Fout, a recognized and enrolled citizen by blood of the Choctaw Nation whose name appears opposite number 7684 upon the final roll of citizens by blood of the Choctaw Nation, approved by the Secretary of the Interior January 17, 1903, and Sam W. Fout, a citizen of the United States; and that said applicant died September 11, 1904.

The Act of Congress approved March 3, 1905 (Public No. 212) among other things provides:

"That the Commission to the Five Civilized Tribes is authorized for sixty days after the date of the approval of this act to receive and consider applications for enrollment of children born subsequent to September twenty-fifth, nineteen hundred and two, and prior to March fourth, nineteen hundred and five, and who were living on said latter date, to citizens by blood of the Choctaw and Chickasaw tribes of Indians whose enrollment has been approved by the Secretary of the Interior prior to the date of the approval of this act; and to enroll and make allotments to such children."

It is, therefore, hereby ordered that the application for the enrollment of Turner Fout as a citizen by blood of the Choctaw Nation be dismissed in accordance with the order of the Commission of March 31, 1905.

COMMISSION TO THE FIVE CIVILIZED TRIBES,

Tams Bixby
Chairman.

Muskogee, Indian Territory.
JUN 28 1905

Applications for Enrollment of Choctaw Newborn
Act of 1905 Volume XIX

7-NB-1460.

Muskogee, Indian Territory, June 28, 1905.

Sam W. Fout   **COPY**
    Milton, Indian Territory.

Dear Sir:

    Inclosed herewith you will find a copy of the order of this Commission, dated June 28, 1905, dismissing the application for the enrollment of Turner Fout as a citizen by blood of the Choctaw Nation.

                          Respectfully,

                    SIGNED

                            Tams Bixby
Registered.   Chairman.
Incl. 7-NB-1460.

7-NB-1460.

Muskogee, Indian Territory, June 28, 1905.

Mansfield, McMurray & Cornish,
    Attorneys for Choctaw and Chickasaw Nations,
        South McAlester, Indian Territory.

Gentlemen:

    Inclosed herewith you will find a copy of the order of this Commission, dated June 28, 1905, dismissin[sic] the application for the enrollment of Turner Fout as a citizen by blood of the Choctaw Nation.

                          Respectfully,
                          SIGNED

                            Tams Bixby
                            Chairman.
Incl. 7-NB-1460.

Applications for Enrollment of Choctaw Newborn
Act of 1905   Volume XIX

7-2646

Muskogee, Indian Territory, April 14, 1905.

Susan Fout,
    Melton[sic], Indian Territory.

Dear Madam:

    Receipt is hereby acknowledged of your letter of April 3, 1905, in which you ask if the application for the enrollment of Turner Fout made sometime in February or march has been filed at this office.

    In reply to your letter you are informed that it does not appear from our records that affidavits have been filed relative to a child born to you since September 25, 1902, and if you desire to make application for the enrollment of a child there is inclosed herewith blank for that purpose which you should have executed and returned to this office within sixty days from March 3, 1905.

    In having the same executed be careful to see that all blanks are properly filled, all names written in full, and that the Notary Public before whom the same are executed affixes his name and seal to each affidavit. Signature by mark must be attested by two disinterested witnesses.

                      Respectfully,

                                Chairman.

Choctaw 2646.

Muskogee, Indian Territory, April 22, 1905.

Sam W. Fout,
    Milton, Indian Territory.

Dear Sir:

    Receipt is hereby acknowledged of the affidavits of Susie Fout and C. C. Fout to the birth of Turner Fout, son of Sam W. and Susie Fout, July 25, 1904.

    It appears from the affidavits that Turner Fout died September 11, 1904, and you are advised that under the provisions of the act of Congress approved July 1, 1902, the provisions of the Act of Congress approved March 3, 1905, the Commission is authorized for a period of sixty days to receive applications for the enrollment of children born to enrolled citizens by blood of the Choctaw and Chickasaw Nations between September 25, 1902, and March 3, 1905, and living on said latter date.

Applications for Enrollment of Choctaw Newborn
Act of 1905   Volume XIX

You will therefore see that the Commission is without authority to enroll your child, Turner Fout, who died September 11, 1904.

Respectfully,

Chairman.

Choc. New Born 1461
    (James Frederic Nale)
    (Born April 10, 1905)

1461

NEW BORN
CHOCTAW
ENROLLMENT

JAMES FREDERIC NALE

(BORN APRIL 10, 1905)

As Citizen of the
CHOCTAW NATION
Act of Congress
Approved March 3, 1905

CANCELLED

RECORD TRANSFERRED TO CHOCTAW NEW BORN NO. 258

ACT OF CONGRESS APPROVED APRIL 26, 1906

JULY 13, 1906

1461

Applications for Enrollment of Choctaw Newborn
Act of 1905   Volume XIX

CHOCTAW   1461
NEW BORN

James Frederic Nale
(Born April 10, 1905)

CANCELLED

Record transferred to
CHOCTAW   NEW BORN   *No 258*

ACT OF CONGRESS APPROVED APRIL 26, 1906.

JUL 13 1906

Choc. New Born 1462
    Roy Vester Impson
    (Born March 6, 1905)

1462

NEW BORN
CHOCTAW
ENROLLMENT

ROY VESTER IMPSON

(BORN MARCH 6, 1905)

As Citizen of the
CHOCTAW NATION
Act of Congress
Approved March 3, 1905

CANCELLED

RECORD TRANSFERRED TO CHOCTAW NEW BORN
NO. 414

Applications for Enrollment of Choctaw Newborn
Act of 1905   Volume XIX

ACT OF CONGRESS APPROVED APRIL 26, 1906

JULY 13, 1906

1462

CHOCTAW   1462
NEW BORN
ACT OF CONGRESS APPROVED MARCH 30, 1905.

Roy Vester Impson
(Born March 6, 1905)

CANCELLED

Record transferred to
CHOCTAW   NEW BORN   *No 414*

ACT OF CONGRESS APPROVED APRIL 26, 1906.

JUL 13 1906

Choc. New Born 1463
    Jolam Ischcomer
    (Born July 4, 1904)

1463

NEW BORN
CHOCTAW
ENROLLMENT

JOLAM ISCHCOMER

(BORN JULY 4, 1904)

DIED PRIOR TO MARCH 4, 1905

Applications for Enrollment of Choctaw Newborn
Act of 1905   Volume XIX

As Citizen of the
CHOCTAW NATION
Act of Congress
Approved March 3, 1905

NO. 1 DISMISSED JUNE 28, 1905

1463

DEPARTMENT OF THE INTERIOR,
COMMISSION TO THE FIVE CIVILIZED TRIBES.

Record in the matter of the application for enrollment as a citizen by blood of the Choctaw Nation of:

JOLAM ISCHCOMER   7-NB-1463.

NEW-BORN AFFIDAVIT.

Number..................

...Choctaw Enrolling Commission...

IN THE MATTER OF THE APPLICATION FOR ENROLLMENT, as a citizen of the Choctaw   Nation, of   Jolam Ischcomer

born on the   4th   day of   July   190 4

Name of father   Lincoln M[sic]. Ischcomer   a citizen of   Choctaw
Nation final enrollment No...........................
Name of mother   Meson Ischcomer   a citizen of   Choctaw
Nation final enrollment No. 2770

Postoffice   Rufe, I.T.

AFFIDAVIT OF MOTHER.

UNITED STATES OF AMERICA
INDIAN TERRITORY
  Central   DISTRICT

          I   Meson Ischcomer   , on oath state that I am
    29   years of age and a citizen by   blood   of the   Choctaw   Nation,
and as such have been placed upon the final roll of the   Choctaw   Nation, by the Honorable

Applications for Enrollment of Choctaw Newborn
Act of 1905   Volume XIX

Secretary of the Interior my final enrollment number being   2770 ; that I am the lawful wife of Lincoln N. Ischcomer   , who is a citizen of the   Choctaw   Nation, and as such has been placed upon the final roll of said Nation by the Honorable Secretary of the Interior, his final enrollment number being .... and that a   Male   child was born to me on the   4th   day of   July   190 4; that said child has been named   Jolam Ischcomer, and is now living.

her
Meson x Ischcomer
mark

Witnesseth.

Must be two Witnesses who are Citizens.   D.E. Baken

H B Jacob

Subscribed and sworn to before me this 22   day of Feb   190 5

W.A. Shoney
Notary Public.

My commission expires: Jan 10th, 1909

AFFIDAVIT OF ATTENDING PHYSICIAN OR MIDWIFE

UNITED STATES OF AMERICA
INDIAN TERRITORY
   Central   DISTRICT

I,   Littie Hakabe   a   midwife on oath state that I attended on Mrs. Meson Ischcomer   wife of   Lincoln N Ischcomer on the 4th day of July , 190 4, that there was born to her on said date a   male   child, that said child is now living, and is said to have been named   Jolam Ischcomer

her
Littie x Hakabe   M.D.
mark

WITNESSETH:

Must be two witnesses who are citizens and know the child.   D.E. Baken

H B Jacob

Subscribed and sworn to before me this, the   22nd   day of Feb   190 5

W.A. Shoney   Notary Public.

We hereby certify that we are well acquainted with   Littie Hakabe a   midwife   and know   her   to be reputable and of good standing in the community.

D.E. Baken

H B Jacob

Applications for Enrollment of Choctaw Newborn
Act of 1905   Volume XIX

DEATH AFFIDAVIT

NO._____

Choctaw Enrolling Commission.

IN THE MATTER OF THE DEATH OF   Jolam Ischcomer   a citizen of the   Choctaw   Nation, who formerly resided at or near   Rufe   Ind. Ter., and died on the   22nd   day of   July   190 4

AFFIDAVIT OF RELATIVE.

UNITED STATES OF AMERICA
INDIAN TERRITORY
Central   DISTRICT.

I,   Lincoln N. Ischcomer   on oath, state that I am   42   years of age, and a citizen of the   Choctaw   Nation, and as such have been finally enrolled by the Honorable Secretary of the Interior, my enrollment number being _____ ; that my postoffice address is   Rufe   , Ind. Ter.; that I am   the father   of   Jolam Ischcomer   who was a citizen, by   blood   , of the   Choctaw   Nation; and that said   Jolam Ischcomer   died on the   22   day of   July   , 190 4

WITNESSETH:

Must be two witnesses who are Citizens.
{ D. E. Baken
  HB Jacob

Lincoln N Ischcomer

Subscribed and sworn to before me this the   22   day of   Feb   190 5

W.A. Shoney   Notary Public.

AFFIDAVIT OF ACQUAINTANCE.

UNITED STATES OF AMERICA
INDIAN TERRITORY
Central   DISTRICT.

I,   Willie Caldwell   on oath, state that I am   31   years of age, and a citizen by   blood   of the   Choctaw   Nation; that my post-office address is   Rufe   Ind. Ter.; that I was personally acquainted with   Jolam Ischcomer   the deceased child above named, who was a citizen of   Choctaw   Nation by blood, and that said   Jolam Ischcomer   died on the   22   day of   July   , 190 4

Willie Caldwell

Applications for Enrollment of Choctaw Newborn
Act of 1905   Volume XIX

Subscribed and sworn to before me this   22   day of   Feb   190 5

W. A. Shoney   Notary Public.

My Commission Expires: Jan 10, 1909

W.J.
7-NB-1463.

DEPARTMENT OF THE INTERIOR,
COMMISSION TO THE FIVE CIVILIZED TRIBES.

In the matter of the application for the enrollment of Jolam Ischcomer as a citizen by blood of the Choctaw Nation

---oOo---

It appears from the record herein that on April 25, 1905 there was filed with the Commission application for the enrollment of Jolam Ischcomer as a citizen by blood of the Choctaw Nation.

It further appears from the record herein and the records of the Commission that the applicant was born July 4, 1904; that he is a son of Lincoln N. Ischcomer and Meson Ischcomer, recognized and enrolled citizens by blood of the Choctaw Nation whose names appear opposite numbers 2769 and 2770, respectively, upon the final roll of citizens by blood of the Choctaw Nation, approved by the Secretary of the Interior December 12, 1902; and that said applicant died July 22, 1904.

The Act of Congress approved March 3, 1905 (Public No. 212) among other things provides:

"That the Commission to the Five Civilized Tribes is authorized for sixty days after the date of the approval of this act to receive and consider applications for enrollment of children born subsequent to September twenty-fifth, nineteen hundred and two, and prior to March fourth, nineteen hundred and five, and who were living on said latter date, to citizens by blood of the Choctaw and Chickasaw tribes of Indians whose enrollment has been approved by the Secretary of the Interior prior to the date of the approval of this act; and to enroll and make allotments to such children."

It is, therefore, hereby ordered that the application for the enrollment of Jolam Ischcomer as a citizen by blood of the Choctaw Nation be dismissed in accordance with the order of the Commission of March 31, 1905.

COMMISSION TO THE FIVE CIVILIZED TRIBES,

Tams Bixby
Chairman.

Muskogee, Indian Territory.
JUN 28 1905

Applications for Enrollment of Choctaw Newborn
Act of 1905   Volume XIX

7-NB-1463

Muskogee, Indian Territory, June 28, 1905.

Lincoln M[sic]. Ischcomer, **COPY**
Rufe, Indian Territory,

Dear Sir:

Inclosed herewith you will find a copy of the order of this Commission, dated June 28, 1905, dismissing the application for the enrollment of Jolam Ischcomer as a citizen by blood of the Choctaw Nation.

Respectfully,
SIGNED
Tams Bixby
Chairman.

Registered.
Incl. 7-NB-1463

7-NB-1463.

Muskogee, Indian Territory, June 28, 1905.

Mansfield, McMurray & Cornish,
Attorneys for Choctae[sic] and Chickasaw Nations, **COPY**
South McAlester, Indian Territory.

Gentlemen:

Inclosed herewith you will find a copy of the order of this Commission, dated June 28, 1905, dismissing the application for the enrollment of Jolam Ischcomer as a citizen by blood of the Choctaw Nation.

Respectfully,
SIGNED
Tams Bixby
Chairman.

Incl. 7-NB-1463.

Applications for Enrollment of Choctaw Newborn
Act of 1905   Volume XIX

Choc. New Born 1464
    Mary James
        (Born June 14, 1903)

1464

NEW BORN
CHOCTAW
ENROLLMENT

MARY JAMES

(BORN JUNE 14, 1903)

DIED PRIOR TO MARCH 4, 1905

As Citizen of the
CHOCTAW NATION
Act of Congress
Approved March 3, 1905

DISMISSED JUNE 28, 1905

1464

DEPARTMENT OF THE INTERIOR,
COMMISSION TO THE FIVE CIVILIZED TRIBES.

Record in the matter of the application for enrollment as a citizen by blood of the Choctaw Nation of:

      MARY JAMES   7-NB-1464.

Applications for Enrollment of Choctaw Newborn
Act of 1905   Volume XIX

NEW-BORN AFFIDAVIT.

Number..............

...Choctaw Enrolling Commission...

IN THE MATTER OF THE APPLICATION FOR ENROLLMENT, as a citizen of the Choctaw Nation, of Mary James born on the 14th day of June 190 3

Name of father   Charley James   a citizen of   Choctaw Nation final enrollment No...............
Name of mother   Selina McAfee   a citizen of   Choctaw Nation final enrollment No.   2887

Postoffice   Garvin IT

AFFIDAVIT OF MOTHER.

UNITED STATES OF AMERICA
INDIAN TERRITORY
   Central   DISTRICT

I   Selina McAfee   , on oath state that I am 24 years of age and a citizen by blood of the Choctaw Nation, and as such have been placed upon the final roll of the Choctaw Nation, by the Honorable Secretary of the Interior my final enrollment number being   2887 ; that I am the lawful wife of   Charley James   , who is a citizen of the   Choctaw   Nation, and as such has been placed upon the final roll of said Nation by the Honorable Secretary of the Interior, his final enrollment number being .... and that a   female   child was born to me on the   14th day of   June   190 3; that said child has been named   Mary James   , and is now ~~living~~.   her
                                                  Selina x McAfee
Witnesseth.   mark
  Must be two ⎫ Allen Watson
  Witnesses who ⎬
  are Citizens. ⎭ Thomas William

Subscribed and sworn to before me this   22   day of   Feb   190 5

W.A. Shoney
Notary Public.

My commission expires: Jan 10 1909

Applications for Enrollment of Choctaw Newborn
Act of 1905   Volume XIX

AFFIDAVIT OF ATTENDING PHYSICIAN OR MIDWIFE

UNITED STATES OF AMERICA
INDIAN TERRITORY
Central   DISTRICT

I, Jency Choate a midwife on oath state that I attended on Mrs. Selina McAfee wife of Charley James on the 14th day of June, 1903, that there was born to her on said date a female child, that said child is now living, and is said to have been named Mary James

her
Jency x Choate   ~~M.D.~~
mark

WITNESSETH:
Must be two witnesses who are citizens and know the child.
{ Allen Watson
  Thomas William

Subscribed and sworn to before me this, the 22 day of Feb 1905

W A Shoney   Notary Public.

We hereby certify that we are well acquainted with Jency Choate a midwife and know her to be reputable and of good standing in the community.

{ Allen Watson
  Thomas William

DEATH AFFIDAVIT

NO._____

Choctaw Enrolling Commission.

IN THE MATTER OF THE DEATH OF   Mary James a citizen of the Choctaw Nation, who formerly resided at or near Garvin Ind. Ter., and died on the 20th day of September 1903

AFFIDAVIT OF RELATIVE.

UNITED STATES OF AMERICA
INDIAN TERRITORY
Central   DISTRICT.

I, Selina McAfee on oath, state that I am 24 years of age, and a citizen of the Choctaw Nation, and as such have been finally enrolled by the

Applications for Enrollment of Choctaw Newborn
Act of 1905   Volume XIX

Honorable Secretary of the Interior, my enrollment number being 2887 ; that my postoffice address is Garvin , Ind. Ter.; that I am the mother of Mary James who was a citizen, by blood , of the Choctaw Nation; and that said Mary James died on the 20th day of September , 190 3

WITNESSETH:

Must be two witnesses who are Citizens.
- Allen Watson
- Thomas William

Selina x McAfee (her mark)

Subscribed and sworn to before me this the 22 day of Feb 190 5

W.A. Shoney   Notary Public.

AFFIDAVIT OF ACQUAINTANCE.

UNITED STATES OF AMERICA
INDIAN TERRITORY
Central DISTRICT.

I, Thomas William on oath, state that I am 22 years of age, and a citizen by blood of the Choctaw Nation; that my post-office address is Garvin Ind. Ter.; that I was personally acquainted with Mary James the deceased child above named, who was a citizen of Choctaw Nation by blood, and that said Mary James died on the 20th day of September , 190 3

Thomas William

Subscribed and sworn to before me this 22 day of Feb 190 5

W.A. Shoney   Notary Public.

My Commission Expires: Jan 10, 1909

W.F.
7-NB-1464.

DEPARTMENT OF THE INTERIOR,
COMMISSION TO THE FIVE CIVILIZED TRIBES.

In the matter of the application for the enrollment of Mary James as a citizen by blood of the Choctaw Nation.

---oOo---

It appears from the record herein that on April 25, 1905 there was filed with the Commission application for the enrollment of Mary James as a citizen by blood of the Choctaw Nation.

Applications for Enrollment of Choctaw Newborn
Act of 1905   Volume XIX

It further appears from the record in this case and the records of the Commission that the applicant was born June 14, 1903; that she is a daughter of Selina McAfee, a recognized and enrolled citizen by blood of the Choctaw Nation whose name appears opposite number 2887 upon the final roll of citizens by blood of the Choctaw Nation, approved by the Secretary of the Interior December 12, 1902, and Charley James, a noncitizen; and that said applicant died September 20, 1903.

The Act of Congress approved March 3, 1905 (Public No. 212) among other things provides:

"That the Commission to the Five Civilized Tribes is authorized for sixty days after the date of the approval of this act to receive and consider applications for enrollment of children born subsequent to September twenty-fifth, nineteen hundred and two, and prior to March fourth, nineteen hundred and five, and who were living on said latter date, to citizens by blood of the Choctaw and Chickasaw tribes of Indians whose enrollment has been approved by the Secretary of the Interior prior to the date of the approval of this act; and to enroll and make allotments to such children."

It is, therefore, hereby ordered that the application for the enrollment of Mary James as a citizen by blood of the Choctaw Nation be dismissed in accordance with the order of the Commission of March 31, 1905.

COMMISSION TO THE FIVE CIVILIZED TRIBES,

Tams Bixby
Chairman.

Muskogee, Indian Territory.
JUN 28 1905

7-NB-1464.

Muskogee, Indian Territory, June 28, 1905.

Charley Jones,   **COPY**
Garvin, Indian Territory.

Dear Sir:

Inclosed herewith you will find a copy of the order of this Commission, dated June 28, 1905, dismissing the application for the enrollment of Mary James as a citizen by blood of the Choctaw Nation.

Respectfully,

SIGNED

Tams Bixby
Registered.   Chairman.
Incl. 7-NB-1464.

Applications for Enrollment of Choctaw Newborn
Act of 1905 Volume XIX

7-NB-1464.

Muskogee, Indian Territory, June 28, 1905.

Mansfield, McMurray & Cornish, **COPY**
    Attorneys for Choctaw and Chickasaw Nations,
        South McAlester, Indian Territory.

Gentlemen:

    Inclosed herewith you will find a copy of the order of this Commission, dated June 28, 1905, dismissing the application for the enrollment of Mary James as a citizen by blood of the Choctaw Nation.

        Respectfully,

SIGNED

Tams Bixby
Chairman.

Incl. 7-NB-1464.

Choc. New Born 1465
    Dan Coxwell
        (Born April 25, 1903)

1465

NEW BORN
CHOCTAW
ENROLLMENT

DAN COXWELL

(BORN APRIL 25 1903)

As Citizen of the
CHOCTAW NATION
Act of Congress
Approved March 3, 1905

NO. 1 DISMISSED JUNE 28, 1905

1465

Applications for Enrollment of Choctaw Newborn
Act of 1905   Volume XIX

DEPARTMENT OF THE INTERIOR,
COMMISSION TO THE FIVE CIVILIZED TRIBES.

Record in the matter of the application for enrollment as a citizen by blood of the Choctaw Nation of:

DAN COXWELL   7-NB-1465.

NEW BORN AFFIDAVIT

No

CHOCTAW ENROLLING COMMISSION

IN THE MATTER OF THE APPLICATION FOR ENROLLMENT as a citizen of the Choctaw Nation, of Dan Coxwell born on the 25th day of April 190 3

Name of father   Johnson Coxwell   a citizen of   Choctaw   Nation,
final enrollment No.
Name of mother   Ida Cogswell   a citizen of   Choctaw   Nation,
final enrollment No...   *deceased*

America IT   Postoffice.

Father
AFFIDAVIT OF ~~MOTHER~~

UNITED STATES OF AMERICA }
INDIAN TERRITORY
DISTRICT   Central

I   Johnson Coxwell   , on oath state that I am   26   years of age and a citizen by   blood   of the   Choctaw   Nation, and as such have been placed upon the final roll of the   Choctaw   Nation, by the Honorable Secretary of the Interior my final enrollment number being   ; that I am the lawful ~~wife~~ *husband* of   Ida Cogswell deceased   , who ~~is was~~ a citizen of the   Choctaw   Nation, and as such has been placed upon the final roll of said Nation by the Honorable Secretary of the Interior, his final enrollment number being   and that a   Male   child was born to ~~me~~ *her* on the   25th day of   April   190 3; that said child has been named   Dan Coxwell   , and is now living.

277

Applications for Enrollment of Choctaw Newborn
Act of 1905 Volume XIX

           Johnson Coxwell

WITNESSETH:
 Must be two witnesses { Stephen McClure
 who are citizens   Reuben Mclure[sic]

  Subscribed and sworn to before me this, the 15 day of Feb , 190 5

          W A Shoney
              Notary Public.

My Commission Expires:
  Jan 10 1909

AFFIDAVIT OF ATTENDING PHYSICIAN OR MIDWIFE

UNITED STATES OF AMERICA
INDIAN TERRITORY
 Central   DISTRICT

  I, Johnson Coxwell   a   Attendant
on oath state that I attended on Mrs. Ida Cogswell wife of Johnson Coxwell
on the 25th day of April , 190 3 , that there was born to her on said date a male
child, that said child is now living, and is said to have been named Dan Cogswell

          Johnson Coxwell
  Subscribed and sworn to before me this, the 15 day of
  Feb 190 5

WITNESSETH: W A Shoney Notary Public.
 Must be two witnesses { Stephen McClure
 who are citizens
        Reuben McClure

  We hereby certify that we are well acquainted with Johnson Cogswell
a attendant and know him to be reputable and of good standing in the community.

   Stephen McClure   _____

   Reuben McClure   _____

Applications for Enrollment of Choctaw Newborn
Act of 1905   Volume XIX

DEATH AFFIDAVIT

No _____

CHOCTAW ENROLLING COMMISSION

IN THE MATTER OF THE DEATH OF   Dan Coxwell a citizen of the   Choctaw   Nation, who formerly resided at or near   America Ind. Ter., and died on the   16th   day of   Jan   190 5

AFFIDAVIT OF RELATIVE.

UNITED STATES OF AMERICA
INDIAN TERRITORY
DISTRICT   Central

I,   Johnson Coxwell   on oath, state that I am   26   years of age, and a citizen of the   blood[sic]   Nation, and as such have been finally enrolled by the Honorable Secretary of the Interior, my enrollment number being _____; that my postoffice address is   America   , Ind. Ter.; that I am   the father   of   Dan Coxwell   who was a citizen, by   blood   , of the   Choctaw   Nation; and that said   Dan Coxwell   died on the   16th   day of   Jan   , 190 5

WITNESSETH: Johnson Coxwell

Must be two witnesses who are Citizens. { Stephen McClure
Reuben Mclure[sic] }

Subscribed and sworn to before me this the   15   day of   Feb   1905

W A Shoney
Notary Public.

AFFIDAVIT OF ACQUAINTANCE.

UNITED STATES OF AMERICA
INDIAN TERRITORY
Central   DISTRICT

I,   John Moore   on oath, state that I am   51   years of age, and a citizen by   blood   of the   Choctaw   Nation; that my post-office address is   America   Ind. Ter.; that I was personally acquainted with   Dan Coxwell   the deceased child above named, who was a citizen of   Choctaw   Nation by blood, and that said   Dan Coxwell   died on the   16th   day of   Jan   , 190 5

John Moore

Applications for Enrollment of Choctaw Newborn
Act of 1905   Volume XIX

Subscribed and sworn to before me this the   15   day of   Feb   1905

W A Shoney
Notary Public.

My Commission Expires: Jan 10 1909

W.F.
7-NB-1465.

DEPARTMENT OF THE INTERIOR,
COMMISSION TO THE FIVE CIVILIZED TRIBES.

In the matter of the application for the enrollment of Dan Coxwell as a citizen by blood of the Choctaw Nation.

---oOo---

It appears from the record herein that on April 25, 1905 there was filed with the Commission application for the enrollment of Dan Coxwell as a citizen by blood of the Choctaw Nation.

It further appears from the record in this case and the records of the Commission that the applicant was born April 25, 1903; that he is a son of Johnson Coxwell and Ida Cogswell, recognized and enrolled citizens by blood of the Choctaw Nation whose names appear opposite numbers 3575 and 2836, respectively, upon the final roll of citizens by blood of the Choctaw Nation, approved by the Secretary of the Interior December 12, 1902; and that said applicant died on January 16, 1905.

The Act of Congress approved March 3, 1905 (Public No. 212) among other things provides:

"That the Commission to the Five Civilized Tribes is authorized for sixty days after the date of the approval of this act to receive and consider applications for enrollment of children born subsequent to September twenty-fifth, nineteen hundred and two, and prior to March fourth, nineteen hundred and five, and who were living on said latter date, to citizens by blood of the Choctaw and Chickasaw tribes of Indians whose enrollment has been approved by the Secretary of the Interior prior to the date of the approval of this act; and to enroll and make allotments to such children."

It is, therefore, hereby ordered that the application for the enrollment of Dan Coxwell as a citizen by blood of the Choctaw Nation be dismissed in accordance with the order of the Commission of March 30, 1905.

COMMISSION TO THE FIVE CIVILIZED TRIBES,

Tams Bixby
Chairman.

Muskogee, Indian Territory.
JUN 28 1905

Applications for Enrollment of Choctaw Newborn
Act of 1905   Volume XIX

7-NB-1465.

Muskogee, Indian Territory, June 28, 1905.

James Coxwell,
    America, Indian Territory. **COPY**

Dear Sir:

    Inclosed herewith you will find a copy of the order of this Commission, dated June 28, 1905, dismissing the application for the enrollment of Dan Coxwell as a citizen by blood of the Choctaw Nation.

Respectfully,
SIGNED

Tams Bixby

Registered.   Chairman.
Incl. 7-NB-1465.

7-NB-1465.

Muskogee, Indian Territory, June 28, 1905.

Mansfield, McMurray & Cornish,
    Attorneys for Choctaw and Chickasaw Nations, **COPY**
        South McAlester, Indian Territory.

Gentlemen:

    Inclosed herewith you will find a copy of the order of this Commission, dated June 28, 1905, dismissing the application for the enrollment of Dan Coxwell as a citizen by blood of the Choctaw Nation.

Respectfully,
SIGNED

Tams Bixby
Chairman.

Incl. 7-NB-1465.

Applications for Enrollment of Choctaw Newborn
Act of 1905   Volume XIX

Choc. New Born 1466
    Isreal Frazier
    (Born Oct. 19, 1902)

1466

NEW BORN
CHOCTAW
ENROLLMENT

ISREAL FRAZIER

(BORN OCTOBER 19, 1902)

As Citizen of the
CHOCTAW NATION
Act of Congress
Approved March 3, 1905

NO. 1 DISMISSED JUNE 28, 1905

1466

DEPARTMENT OF THE INTERIOR,
COMMISSION TO THE FIVE CIVILIZED TRIBES.

Record in the matter of the application for the enrollment as a citizen by blood of the Choctaw Nation of:

ISREAL FRAZIER   7-NB-1466.

NEW BORN AFFIDAVIT

No ....

CHOCTAW ENROLLING COMMISSION

IN THE MATTER OF THE APPLICATION FOR ENROLLMENT as a citizen of the Choctaw Nation, of   Isreal Frazier   born on the 19th day of October   190 2

Applications for Enrollment of Choctaw Newborn
Act of 1905 Volume XIX

Name of father　Wilson E. Frazier　　a citizen of　Choctaw　Nation,
final enrollment No.　2192
Name of mother　Mollie Frazier　　a citizen of　Choctaw　Nation,
final enrollment No.　2193

Norwood, I.T.　　　Postoffice.

AFFIDAVIT OF MOTHER

UNITED STATES OF AMERICA }
　　INDIAN TERRITORY　　　}
DISTRICT　Central　　　　　}

I　Mollie Frazier　, on oath state that I am　33　years of age and a citizen by　blood　of the　Choctaw　Nation, and as such have been placed upon the final roll of the　Choctaw　Nation, by the Honorable Secretary of the Interior my final enrollment number being　2193　; that I am the lawful wife of　Wilson E Frazier　, who is a citizen of the　Choctaw　Nation, and as such has been placed upon the final roll of said Nation by the Honorable Secretary of the Interior, his final enrollment number being　2192　and that a　Male　child was born to me on the　19th　day of　October　190 2; that said child has been named　Isreal Frazier　, and is now ~~living~~.

　　　　　　　　　　　　　　　　　　　her
　　　　　　　　　　　　　　　Mollie x Frazier
WITNESSETH:　　　　　　　　　　mark
Must be two witnesses { Cephus Tohkubbi
who are citizens　　　 { Moody Byington

Subscribed and sworn to before me this, the　14th　day of　March　, 190 5

　　　　　　　　　　　　　W. A. Shoney
　　　　　　　　　　　　　　　　Notary Public.
My Commission Expires:　Jan 10, 1909

Affidavit of Attending Physician or Midwife

UNITED STATES OF AMERICA, }
　　INDIAN TERRITORY,　　　}
　Central　　DISTRICT　　　}

I,　Silvia Thomas　a　midwife on oath state that I attended on Mrs. Mollie Frazier　wife of　Wilson Frazier on the　19th　day of　October　, 190 2, that there was born to her on said date a　male child, that said child is now living, and is said to have been named　Isreal Frazier
　　　　　　　　　　　　　　　her
　　　　　　　　　　　Silvia x Thomas　　~~M.D.~~
　　　　　　　　　　　　　mark

Applications for Enrollment of Choctaw Newborn
Act of 1905   Volume XIX

Subscribed and sworn to before me this the 14th day of March 1905

W.A. Shoney
Notary Public.

WITNESSETH:

Must be two witnesses who are citizens and know the child. { Cephus Tohkubbi
Moody Byington

We hereby certify that we are well acquainted with Silvia Thomas a midwife and know her to be reputable and of good standing in the community.

Must be two citizen witnesses. { Cephus Tohkubbi
Moody Byington

DEATH AFFIDAVIT

NO._____

Choctaw Enrolling Commission.

IN THE MATTER OF THE DEATH OF Isreal Frazier a citizen of the Choctaw Nation, who formerly resided at or near Kullituklo Ind. Ter., and died on the 15th day of January 190 4

AFFIDAVIT OF RELATIVE.

UNITED STATES OF AMERICA
INDIAN TERRITORY
Central DISTRICT.

I, Wilson E Frazier on oath, state that I am 37 years of age, and a citizen of the Choctaw Nation, and as such have been finally enrolled by the Honorable Secretary of the Interior, my enrollment number being 2191 ; that my postoffice address is Norwood , Ind. Ter.; that I am the father of Isreal Frazier who was a citizen, by blood , of the Choctaw Nation; and that said Isreal Frazier died on the 15th day of January , 190 4

WITNESSETH:

Must be two witnesses who are Citizens. { Cephus Tohkubbi
Moody Byington

Wilson E. Frazier

Applications for Enrollment of Choctaw Newborn
Act of 1905   Volume XIX

Subscribed and sworn to before me this the _____ day of _____ 190__

_____ Notary Public.

AFFIDAVIT OF ACQUAINTANCE.

UNITED STATES OF AMERICA
INDIAN TERRITORY
Central   DISTRICT.

I, Philiston Thomas   on oath, state that I am 28   years of age, and a citizen by blood   of the Choctaw   Nation; that my post-office address is Norwood   Ind. Ter.; that I was personally acquainted with Isreal Frazier   the deceased child above named, who was a citizen of Choctaw   Nation by blood, and that said Isreal Frazier   died on the 15th day of January , 190 4

Philiston Thomas

Subscribed and sworn to before me this 14   day of March   190 5

W.A. Shoney   Notary Public.

My Commission Expires: Jan 10, 1909

W.F.
7-NB-1466.

DEPARTMENT OF THE INTERIOR,
COMMISSION TO THE FIVE CIVILIZED TRIBES.

In the matter of the application for the enrollment of Isreal Frazier as a citizen by blood of the Choctaw Nation.

---oOo---

It appears from the record herein that on April 25, 1905 there was filed with the Commission application for the enrollment of Isreal Frazier as a citizen by blood of the Choctaw Nation.

It further appears from the record herein and the records of the Commission that the applicant was born October 19, 1902; that he is the son of Wilson E. Frazier and Mollie Frazier, recognized and enrolled citizens by blood of the Choctaw Nation whose names appear opposite numbers 2191 and 2193, respectively, upon the final roll of citizens by blood of the Choctaw Nation, approved by the Secretary of the Interior December 12, 1902; and that said applicant died January 15, 1904.

The Act of Congress approved March 3, 1905 (Public No. 212) among other things provides:

"That the Commission to the Five Civilized Tribes is authorized for sixty days after the date of the approval of this act to receive and consider

Applications for Enrollment of Choctaw Newborn
Act of 1905 Volume XIX

applications for enrollment of children born subsequent to September twenty-fifth, nineteen hundred and two, and prior to March fourth, nineteen hundred and five, and who were living on said latter date, to citizens by blood of the Choctaw and Chickasaw tribes of Indians whose enrollment has been approved by the Secretary of the Interior prior to the date of the approval of this act; and to enroll and make allotments to such children."

It is, therefore, hereby ordered that the application for the enrollment of Isreal Frazier as a citizen by blood of the Choctaw Nation be dismissed in accordance with the order of the Commission of March 31, 1905.

COMMISSION TO THE FIVE CIVILIZED TRIBES,

Tams Bixby
Chairman.

Muskogee, Indian Territory.
JUN 28 1905

7-NB-1466.

Muskogee, Indian Territory, June 28, 1905.

Wilson E. Frazier,   **COPY**
    Norwood, Indian Territory.

Dear Sir:

Inclosed herewith you will find a copy of the order of this Commission, dated June 28, 1905, dismissing the application for the enrollment of Isreal Frazier as a citizen by blood of the Choctaw Nation.

Respectfully,
SIGNED

Tams Bixby
Chairman.

Registered.
Incl. 7-NB-1466.

Applications for Enrollment of Choctaw Newborn
Act of 1905   Volume XIX

7-NB-1466.

Muskogee, Indian Territory, June 28, 1905.

Mansfield, McMurray & Cornish, **COPY**
    Attorneys for Choctaw and Chickasaw Nations,
        South McAlester, Indian Territory.

Gentlemen:

    Inclosed herewith you will find a copy of the order of this Commission, dated June 28, 1905, dismissing the application for the enrollment of Isreal Frazier as a citizen by blood of the Choctaw Nation.

                Respectfully,
                SIGNED

                Tams Bixby
                Chairman.

Incl. 7-NB-1466.

Choc. New Born 1467
    John Davis
    (Born Jan. 29, 1905)

1467

NEW BORN
CHOCTAW
ENROLLMENT

JOHN DAVIS

(BORN JANUARY 29, 1905)

As Citizen of the
CHOCTAW NATION
Act of Congress
Approved March 3, 1905

NO. 1 DISMISSED JUNE 28, 1905

Applications for Enrollment of Choctaw Newborn
Act of 1905 Volume XIX

DEPARTMENT OF THE INTERIOR,
COMMISSION TO THE FIVE CIVILIZED TRIBES.

Record in the matter of the application for enrollment as a citizen by blood of the Choctaw Nation of:

JOHN DAVIS   7-NB-1467.

NEW-BORN AFFIDAVIT.

Number..............

...Choctaw Enrolling Commission...

IN THE MATTER OF THE APPLICATION FOR ENROLLMENT, as a citizen of the Choctaw Nation, of John Davis

born on the 29 day of January 190 5

Name of father Alekton Davis   a citizen of Choctaw
Nation final enrollment No. 1362
Name of mother Martha Davis   a citizen of Choctaw
Nation final enrollment No. 1363

                                  Postoffice   Valliant, I.T.

AFFIDAVIT OF MOTHER.

UNITED STATES OF AMERICA
INDIAN TERRITORY
  Central   DISTRICT

I Martha Davis , on oath state that I am 23 years of age and a citizen by blood of the Choctaw Nation, and as such have been placed upon the final roll of the Choctaw Nation, by the Honorable Secretary of the Interior my final enrollment number being 1363 ; that I am the lawful wife of Alekton Davis , who is a citizen of the Choctaw Nation, and as such has been placed upon the final roll of said Nation by the Honorable Secretary of the Interior, his final enrollment number being 1362 and that a Male child was born to me on the 29th day of January 190 5; that said child has been named John Davis , and is now living.
                                        her
                          Martha x Davis
                                        mark

Applications for Enrollment of Choctaw Newborn
Act of 1905   Volume XIX

Witnesseth.
  Must be two Witnesses who are Citizens. } Nicholas Jackson
  Lyman Baken

Subscribed and sworn to before me this   24   day of   Feb   190 5

W.A. Shoney
Notary Public.

My commission expires: Jan 10, 1909

AFFIDAVIT OF ATTENDING PHYSICIAN OR MIDWIFE

UNITED STATES OF AMERICA
INDIAN TERRITORY
  Central   DISTRICT

I,   Mollie Baken   a   midwife   on oath state that I attended on Mrs.   Martha Davis   wife of   Alekton Davis   on the   29   day of   January   , 190 5, that there was born to her on said date a   male   child, that said child is now living, and is said to have been named   John Davis

Mollie Baken   ~~M.D.~~

WITNESSETH:
  Must be two witnesses who are citizens and know the child. { Nicholas Jackson
  Lyman Baken

Subscribed and sworn to before me this, the   24th   day of   Feb   190 5

W A Shoney   Notary Public.

We hereby certify that we are well acquainted with   Mollie Baken   a   midwife   and know   her   to be reputable and of good standing in the community.

{ Lyman Baken
  Nicholas Jackson

Applications for Enrollment of Choctaw Newborn
Act of 1905 Volume XIX

DEATH AFFIDAVIT

NO._____

Choctaw Enrolling Commission.

IN THE MATTER OF THE DEATH OF   John Davis
a citizen of the   Choctaw   Nation, who formerly resided at or near   Valliant
Ind. Ter., and died on the   31st day of   January   190 5

AFFIDAVIT OF RELATIVE.

UNITED STATES OF AMERICA
INDIAN TERRITORY
  Central   DISTRICT.

I,   Alekton Davis   on oath, state that I am   32   years of age, and a citizen of the   Choctaw   Nation, and as such have been finally enrolled by the Honorable Secretary of the Interior, my enrollment number being   1362   ; that my postoffice address is   Valliant   , Ind. Ter.; that I am   the father   of   John Davis   who was a citizen, by   blood   , of the   Choctaw   Nation; and that said   John Davis   died on the   31st day of   January   , 190 5

WITNESSETH:

Must be two witnesses who are Citizens.
{ Lyman Baken
{ Nicholas Jackson

                                        Alekton Davis

Subscribed and sworn to before me this the   24th day of   Feb   190 5

                          W A Shoney   Notary Public.

AFFIDAVIT OF ACQUAINTANCE.

UNITED STATES OF AMERICA
INDIAN TERRITORY
  Central   DISTRICT.

I,   Listy Jefferson   on oath, state that I am   20   years of age, and a citizen by   blood   of the   Choctaw   Nation; that my post-office address is   Valliant   Ind. Ter.; that I was personally acquainted with   John Davis   the deceased child above named, who was a citizen of   Choctaw   Nation by blood, and that said   John Davis   died on the   31st day of   January   , 190 5

                                        Listy Jefferson

Applications for Enrollment of Choctaw Newborn
Act of 1905 Volume XIX

Subscribed and sworn to before me this   24   day of   Feb   190 5

W.A. Shoney   Notary Public.

My Commission Expires:

W.F.
7-NB-1467.

DEPARTMENT OF THE INTERIOR,
COMMISSION TO THE FIVE CIVILIZED TRIBES.

In the matter of the application for the enrollment of John Davis as a citizen by blood of the Choctaw Nation.

---oOo---

It appears from the record herein that on April 25, 1905 there was filed with the Commission application for the enrollment of John Davis as a citizen by blood of the Choctaw Nation.

It further appears from the record in this case and the records of the Commission that the applicant was born January 29, 1905; that he is a son of Alekton Davis and Martha Davis, recognized and enrolled citizens by blood of the Choctaw Nation whose names appear opposite numbers 1362 and 1363 upon the final roll of citizens by blood of the Choctaw Nation, approved by the Secretary of the Interior December 12, 1902; and that said applicant died January 31, 1905.

The Act of Congress approved March 3, 1905 (Public No. 212) among other things provides:

"That the Commission to the Five Civilized Tribes is authorized for sixty days after the date of the approval of this act to receive and consider applications for enrollment of children born subsequent to September twenty-fifth, nineteen hundred and two, and prior to March fourth, nineteen hundred and five, and who were living on said latter date, to citizens by blood of the Choctaw and Chickasaw tribes of Indians whose enrollment has been approved by the Secretary of the Interior prior to the date of the approval of this act; and to enroll and make allotments to such children."

It is, therefore, hereby ordered that the application for the enrollment of John Davis as a citizen by blood of the Choctaw Nation be dismissed in accordance with the order of the Commission of March 31, 1905.

COMMISSION TO THE FIVE CIVILIZED TRIBES,

Tams Bixby
Chairman.

Muskogee, Indian Territory.
JUN 28 1905

Applications for Enrollment of Choctaw Newborn
Act of 1905   Volume XIX

7-NB-1467.
COPY

Muskogee, Indian Territory, June 28, 1905.

Alekton Davis,
    Valliant, Indian Territory.

Dear Sir:

    Inclosed herewith you will find a copy of the order of this Commission, dated June 28, 1905, dismissing the application for the enrollment of John Davis as a citizen by blood of the Choctaw Nation.

                  Respectfully,
                    SIGNED
                    Tams Bixby

Registered.   Chairman.
Incl. 7-NB-1467.

7-NB-1467.

Muskogee, Indian Territory, June 28, 1905.
COPY

Mansfield, McMurray & Cornish,
    Attorneys for Choctaw and Chickasaw Nations,
        South McAlester, Indian Territory.

Gentlemen:

    Inclosed herewith you will find a copy of the order of this Commission, dated June 28, 1905, dismissing the application for the enrollment of John Davis as a citizen by blood of the Choctaw Nation.

                    Respectfully,
                    SIGNED
                    Tams Bixby
                    Chairman.

Incl. 7-NB-1467.

Applications for Enrollment of Choctaw Newborn
Act of 1905 Volume XIX

Choc. New Born 1468
    John Thomas Balling
    (Born Jan. 19, 1903)

1468

NEW BORN
CHOCTAW
ENROLLMENT

JOHN THOMAS BALLING

(BORN JANUARY 19, 1903)

DIED PRIOR TO MARCH 4, 1905

As Citizen of the
CHOCTAW NATION
Act of Congress
Approved March 3, 1905

NO. 1 DISMISSED JUNE 28, 1905

1468

DEPARTMENT OF THE INTERIOR,
COMMISSION TO THE FIVE CIVILIZED TRIBES.

    Record in the matter of the application for enrollment as a citizen by blood of the Choctaw Nation of:

JOHN THOMAS BOLLING   7-NB-1468.

Applications for Enrollment of Choctaw Newborn
Act of 1905 Volume XIX

(The affidavit below typed as given.)

United States of America,
    Indian Territory,
Central Judicial District.

    We, Hemp Goins and Eli Crowder, after having been first duly sworn state that we are each of us over 21 years of age and that we were acquainted with Emma Bowlling during her lifetime-That she was a citizen by blood of the Choctaw Nation and that her maiden name was Emma Crowder. That she married W.S.Bolling about March 1902-That they lived together until her death which occurred about the middle of February 1903.and that we know her to be dead-We also are well acquainted with John Thomas Boling the son of the said Emma Bolling and her Husband W.S.Bolling.

    That they resided at the time of her death near Crowder store about 8 miles south of Boswell.in the Choctaw Nation and we know that Dr.James Powell of Garrett's Bluff in the State of Texas waited on said Emma Bolling at the time her said baby was born and at the time of her death.

    We are well acquainted W.S.*Bolling* and know that he was the husband of the said Emma *Bolling*-We are each of citizens of the Choctaw Nation.

                                Hampton Going

                                  Eli Crowder

Subscribed and sworn to before me this the 11th day of March 1905.

                                L.D. Horton
Central District.   Notary Public.
    Indian Territory.

    I.W.S.Bolling after having been duly sworn state that I am the father of John Thomas Bolling for who I am making this application-That the said John Thomas Bolling is now dead-That he was the son of my wife Emma Bolling who died in February 1903-That John Thomas died on the 6th day of August 1903_That Dr.James Powell treated my wife when he was born and treated her when she died-

                                            his
Witness L.D. Horton   W.S. Bolling x
                                          mark

Subscribed and sworn to before me this the 11th day of March 1905.

                                L.D. Horton
                                Notary Public.

Applications for Enrollment of Choctaw Newborn
Act of 1905   Volume XIX

NEW BORN AFFIDAVIT

No ....

CHOCTAW ENROLLING COMMISSION

IN THE MATTER OF THE APPLICATION FOR ENROLLMENT as a citizen of the Choctaw Nation, of   John Thomas Bolling   born on the 19th day of   January   190 3

Name of father   W.S. Boling   a citizen of the United States Nation, final enrollment No.   not enrolled
Name of mother Emma Bowling, ne Crowder   a citizen of   Choctaw   Nation, final enrollment No.   4064 - Enrolled as Emma Crowder

Boswell, Ind. Ter.   Postoffice.

AFFIDAVIT OF MOTHER

UNITED STATES OF AMERICA
   INDIAN TERRITORY
DISTRICT ....

I.., on oath state that I am .... years of age and a citizen by .... of the ....Nation, and as such have been placed upon the final roll of the .... Nation, by the Honorable Secretary of the Interior my final enrollment number being................; that I am the lawful wife of ...., who is a citizen of the .... Nation, and as such has been placed upon the final roll of said Nation by the Honorable Secretary of the Interior, his final enrollment number being .... and that a ....child was born to me on the .... day of .... 190....; that said child has been named ...., and is now living.

WITNESSETH:
   Must be two witnesses { Eli Crowder
   who are citizens   { Hampton Going

Subscribed and sworn to before me this, the 11 day of March , 190 5

L.D. Horton
Notary Public.

My Commission Expires:
   January 12-1905[sic]

Applications for Enrollment of Choctaw Newborn
Act of 1905   Volume XIX

Affidavit of Attending Physician or Midwife

UNITED STATES OF AMERICA,
INDIAN TERRITORY,
Central   DISTRICT

I, James Powell a Practicing Physician on oath state that I attended on Mrs. Emma Bolling wife of W.S. Bolling on the 19 day of January, 190 3, that there was born to her on said date a male child, that said child is now ~~dead~~ ~~living~~, and is said to have been named John Thomas Bolling

JN Powell   M. D.

Subscribed and sworn to before me this the 13 day of March 1905

H.P. Garrett *a Notary Pub in and for Lamar Co* Notary Public. *Texas*

WITNESSETH:
Must be two witnesses who are citizens and know the child.
{ Hampton Going
  Eli Crowder

We hereby certify that we are well acquainted with James Powell a Practicing Physician and know him to be reputable and of good standing in the community.

Must be two citizen witnesses.
{ Hampton Going
  Eli Crowder

DEATH AFFIDAVIT

NO._____

Choctaw Enrolling Commission.

IN THE MATTER OF THE DEATH OF John Thomas Bolling a citizen of the Choctaw Nation, who formerly resided at or near Boswell Ind. Ter., and died on the 6 day of August 190 3

Applications for Enrollment of Choctaw Newborn
Act of 1905 Volume XIX

AFFIDAVIT OF RELATIVE.

UNITED STATES OF AMERICA
INDIAN TERRITORY
   Central   DISTRICT.

I, Green Crowder on oath, state that I am twenty four years of age, and a citizen of the Choctaw Nation, and as such have been finally enrolled by the Honorable Secretary of the Interior, my enrollment number being 4063 ; that my postoffice address is Boswell , Ind. Ter.; that I am an Uncle of John Thomas Bolling who was a citizen, by Blood , of the Choctaw Nation; and that said John Thomas Bolling died on the 6 day of August , 190 3

WITNESSETH:

Must be two witnesses who are Citizens.
{ Thomas C x Crowder (his mark)
  George Crowder

           Green Crowder

My Com Expires 1/24/1907

Subscribed and sworn to before me this the 11th day of February 190 5

        A J Markey   Notary Public.

AFFIDAVIT OF ACQUAINTANCE.

UNITED STATES OF AMERICA
INDIAN TERRITORY
   Central   DISTRICT.

I, *(Illegible)* Crowder on oath, state that I am 34 years of age, and a citizen by Blood of the Choctaw Nation; that my post-office address is Boswell Ind. Ter.; that I was personally acquainted with John Thomas Bolling the deceased child above named, who was a citizen of Choctaw Nation by blood, and that said John Thomas Bolling died on the 6 day of August , 190 3

        (Illegible) Crowder

Subscribed and sworn to before me this 11th day of February 190 5

        AJ Markey   Notary Public.

My Commission Expires: 1/24/1909

Applications for Enrollment of Choctaw Newborn
Act of 1905   Volume XIX

W.F.
7-NB-1468.

DEPARTMENT OF THE INTERIOR,
COMMISSION TO THE FIVE CIVILIZED TRIBES.

In the matter of the application for the enrollment of John Thomas Bolling as a citizen by blood of the Choctaw Nation.

---oOo---

It appears from the record herein that on April 25, 1905 there was filed with the Commission application for the enrollment of John Thomas Bolling as a citizen by blood of the Choctaw Nation.

It further appears from the record herein and the records of the Commission that the applicant was born on January 19, 1903; that he is a son of Emma Bolling, a recognized and enrolled citizen by blood of the Choctaw Nation whose name, as Emma Crowder, appears opposite number 4064 upon the final roll of citizens by blood of the Choctaw Nation approved by the Secretary of the Interior December 12, 1902, and W. S. Bolling, a noncitizen; and that said applicant died August 6, 1903.

The Act of Congress approved March 3, 1905 (Public No. 212) among other things provides:

"That the Commission to the Five Civilized Tribes is authorized for sixty days after the date of the approval of this act to receive and consider applications for enrollment of children born subsequent to September twenty-fifth, nineteen hundred and two, and prior to March fourth, nineteen hundred and five, and who were living on said latter date, to citizens by blood of the Choctaw and Chickasaw tribes of Indians whose enrollment has been approved by the Secretary of the Interior prior to the date of the approval of this act; and to enroll and make allotments to such children."

It is, therefore, hereby ordered that the application for the enrollment of John Thomas Bolling as a citizen by blood of the Choctaw Nation be dismissed in accordance with the order of the Commission of March 31, 1905.

COMMISSION TO THE FIVE CIVILIZED TRIBES,

Tams Bixby
Chairman.

Muskogee, Indian Territory.
JUN 28 1905

Applications for Enrollment of Choctaw Newborn
Act of 1905   Volume XIX

7-NB-1468.

Muskogee, Indian Territory, June 28, 1905.
COPY

W. S. Bolling,
    Boswell, Indian Territory.

Dear Sir:

    Inclosed herewith you will find a copy of the order of this Commission, dated June 28, 1905, dismissing the application for the enrollment of John Thomas Bolling as a citizen by blood of the Choctaw Nation.

                  Respectfully,

                          SIGNED

                         Tams Bixby

Registered.   Chairman.
Incl. 7-NB-1468.

7-NB-1468.

Muskogee, Indian Territory, June 28, 1905.

Mansfield, McMurray & Cornish,   **COPY**
    Attorneys for Choctaw and Chickasaw Nations,
        South McAlester, Indian Territory.

Gentlemen:

    Inclosed herewith you will find a copy of the order of this Commission, dated June 28, 1905, dismissing the application for the enrollment of John Thomas Bolling as a citizen by blood of the Choctaw Nation.

                    Respectfully,

                          SIGNED

                         Tams Bixby
                         Chairman.

Incl. 7-NB-1468.

**Applications for Enrollment of Choctaw Newborn
Act of 1905   Volume XIX**

Choc. New Born 1469
    Helen Bryant
    (Birthdate not given)

1469

NEW BORN
CHOCTAW
ENROLLMENT

HELEN BRYANT

As Citizen of the
CHOCTAW NATION
Act of Congress
Approved March 3, 1905

CANCELLED

RECORD TRANSFERRED TO CHOCTAW NEW BORN NO. 344.

ACT OF CONGRESS APPROVED APRIL 26, 1906.

JULY 13, 1906

1469

CHOCTAW   1469
NEW BORN

ACT OF CONGRESS APPROVED MARCH 30, 1905.

Helen Bryant

CANCELLED

Record Transferred to
    CHOCTAW   NEW BORN   *No* 344
ACT OF CONGRESS APPROVED APRIL 26, 1906.

JUL 13 1906

Applications for Enrollment of Choctaw Newborn
Act of 1905 Volume XIX

Choc. New Born 1470
    Tommie W. Walker
    (Born April 13, 1905)

1470

NEW BORN
CHOCTAW
ENROLLMENT
TOMMIE W. WALKER.

(BORN APRIL 13, 1905)

As Citizen of the
CHOCTAW NATION
Act of Congress
Approved March 3, 1905

CANCELLED

RECORD TRANSFERRED TO CHOCTAW NEW BORN NO. 187.

ACT OF CONGRESS APPROVED APRIL 26, 1906.

JULY 13, 1906

1470

CHOCTAW 1470

NEW BORN
ACT OF CONGRESS APPROVED MARCH 30, 1905.

Tommie W. Walker
(Born April 13, 1905)

CANCELLED

Record transferred to
CHOCTAW   NEW BORN   No 187
ACT OF CONGRESS APPROVED APRIL 26, 1906.

JUL 13 1906

Applications for Enrollment of Choctaw Newborn
Act of 1905 Volume XIX

Choc. New Born 1471
    Frank Allen McCurtain
    (Born April 22, 1905)

1471

NEW BORN
CHOCTAW
ENROLLMENT

FRANK ALLEN McCURTAIN

(BORN APRIL 22, 1905)

As Citizen of the
CHOCTAW NATION
Act of Congress
Approved March 3, 1905

CANCELLED

RECORD TRANSFERRED TO CHOCTAW NEW BORN NO.
NO. 260

ACT OF CONGRESS APPROVED APRIL 26, 1906.

JULY 13, 1906

1471

CHOCTAW 1471
NEW BORN

ACT OF CONGRESS APPROVED MARCH 30, 1905.

Frank Allen McCurtain
(Born April 22, 1905)

CANCELLED

Record transferred to
Choctaw Newborn No 260

ACT OF CONGRESS APPROVED APRIL 26, 1906.

JUL 13 1906

Applications for Enrollment of Choctaw Newborn
Act of 1905   Volume XIX

Choc. New Born 1472
    Bertha May Orndorff
    (Born Dec. 19, 1903)

1472

NEW BORN
CHOCTAW
ENROLLMENT

BERTHA MAY ORNDORFF

(BORN DECEMBER 19, 1903)

As Citizen of the
CHOCTAW NATION
Act of Congress
Approved March 3, 1905

CANCELLED

RECORD TRANSFERRED TO CHOCTAW NEW BORN 786.

ACT OF CONGRESS APPROVED APRIL 26, 1906.

JULY 20, 1906

1472

CHOCTAW   1472
NEW BORN
ACT OF CONGRESS APPROVED MARCH 30, 1905.

Bertha May Orndorff
(Born December 19, 1903)

CANCELLED

Applications for Enrollment of Choctaw Newborn
Act of 1905   Volume XIX

Record transferred to
Choctaw New Born 786

ACT OF CONGRESS APPROVED APRIL 26, 1906.

JUL 20 1906

Choc. New Born 1473
    Willie Charley
    (Born July 7, 1904)

1473

NEW BORN
CHOCTAW
ENROLLMENT

WILLIE CHARLEY

(BORN JULY 7, 1904)

PRIOR TO MARCH 4, 1905

As Citizen of the
CHOCTAW NATION
Act of Congress
Approved March 3, 1905

NO. 1 DISMISSED JUNE 28, 1905

1473

DEPARTMENT OF THE INTERIOR,
COMMISSION TO THE FIVE CIVILIZED TRIBES.

    Record in the matter of the application for enrollment as a citizen by blood of the Choctaw Nation of:

    WILLIE CHARLEY   7-NB-1473.

Applications for Enrollment of Choctaw Newborn
Act of 1905   Volume XIX

BIRTH AFFIDAVIT.

DEPARTMENT OF THE INTERIOR.
COMMISSION TO THE FIVE CIVILIZED TRIBES.

IN RE APPLICATION FOR ENROLLMENT, as a citizen of the Chocktaw[sic] Nation, of Willie Charley, born on the 7th day of July, 1904

Name of Father: David Charley   a citizen of the Chocktaw Nation.
Name of Mother: Mary Charley   a citizen of the Chocktaw Nation.

Postoffice   Corinne

AFFIDAVIT OF MOTHER.

UNITED STATES OF AMERICA, Indian Territory,
Central   DISTRICT.

was

I, Mary Charley, ~~on oath state that I am~~ 22 years of age and a citizen by Blood, of the Chocktaw Nation; that ~~I am the lawful~~ *she was lawful* wife of David Charley, who is a citizen, by Blood of the Chocktaw Nation; that a male child was born to ~~me~~ *her* on seventh day of July, 1904; that said child has been named Willie *Died Sept 23 1904*, ~~and was living March 4, 1905~~.

Mary Charley Deseased[sic]   (*Dead*)

Witnesses To Mark:
{ Gilam x(his) Holman
{ Columbus Tims (mark)

Subscribed and sworn to before me this 26 day of April, 1905

Jno. E. Talbert
Notary Public.

My com expires
Dec 12 1908

AFFIDAVIT OF ATTENDING PHYSICIAN OR MID-WIFE.

UNITED STATES OF AMERICA, Indian Territory,
Central   DISTRICT.

I, Lyman Billy, a midwife, on oath state that I attended on Mrs. Mary Charley, wife of David Charley on the 7 day of July, 1904; that there was born to her on said date a male child; that said child ~~was living~~

Applications for Enrollment of Choctaw Newborn
Act of 1905   Volume XIX

~~March 4, 1905~~ Died on 23 day of September 1904 and is said to have been named
Willie Charley   his
                                                                                          Lyman x Billy
Witnesses To Mark: mark
 { Gilam x Holman
   Columbus Tims

    Subscribed and sworn to before me this 26   day of   April   , 1905

                                              Jno. E. Talbert
                                              Notary Public.
My com expires
   Dec 12 1908

W.F.
7-NB-1473.
DEPARTMENT OF THE INTERIOR,
COMMISSION TO THE FIVE CIVILIZED TRIBES.

    In the matter of the application for the enrollment of Willie Charley as a citizen by blood of the Choctaw Nation.

---oOo---

    It appears from the record herein that on May 1, 1905, there was filed with the Commission application for the enrollment of Willie Charley as a citizen by blood of the Choctaw Nation.
    It further appears from the record herein and the records of the Commission that the applicant was born July 7, 1904; that he is a son of Mary Charley and David Charley, recognized and enrolled citizens by blood of the Choctaw Nation, whose names appear opposite numbers 13437 and 15795, respectively, upon the final roll of citizens by blood of the Choctaw Nation, approved by the Secretary of the Interior March 19, 1903 and March 15, 1905, respectively; and that said applicant died September 23, 1904.
    The Act of Congress approved March 3, 1905 (Public No. 212) among other things provides:
    "That the Commission to the Five Civilized Tribes is authorized for sixty days after the date of the approval of this act to receive and consider applications for enrollment of children born subsequent to September twenty-fifth, nineteen hundred and two, and prior to March fourth, nineteen hundred and five, <u>and who were living on said latter date,</u> to citizens by blood of the Choctaw and Chickasaw tribes of Indians whose enrollment has been approved by the Secretary of the Interior prior to the date of the approval of this act; and to enroll and make allotments to such children."

Applications for Enrollment of Choctaw Newborn
Act of 1905   Volume XIX

It is, therefore, hereby ordered that the application for the enrollment of Willie Charley as a citizen by blood of the Choctaw Nation be dismissed in accordance with the order of the Commission of March 31, 1905.

COMMISSION TO THE FIVE CIVILIZED TRIBES,

Tams Bixby
Chairman.

Muskogee, Indian Territory.
JUN 28 1905

7-NB-1473.

Muskogee, Indian Territory, June 28, 1905.

COPY

David Charley,
   Corinne, Indian Territory.

Dear Sir:

Inclosed herewith you will find a copy of the order of this Commission, dated June 28, 1905, dismissing the application for the enrollment of Willie Charley as a citizen by blood of the Choctaw Nation.

Respectfully,

SIGNED

Tams Bixby
Chairman.

Registered.
Incl. 7-NB-1473.

7-NB-1473.

Muskogee, Indian Territory, June 28, 1905.

COPY

Mansfield, McMurray & Cornish,
   Attorneys for Choctaw and Chickasaw Nations,
      South McAlester, Indian Territory.

Gentlemen:

Inclosed herewith you will find a copy of the order of this Commission, dated June 28, 1905, dismissing the application for the enrollment of Willie Charley as a citizen by blood of the Choctaw Nation.

Applications for Enrollment of Choctaw Newborn
Act of 1905   Volume XIX

Incl. 7-NB-1473.

Respectfully,
SIGNED   *Tams Bixby*
Chairman.

7-4901.

Muskogee, Indian Territory, May 5, 1905.

David Charley,
    Corinne, Indian Territory.

Dear Sir:

    Receipt is hereby acknowledged of the affidavits of Mary Charley and Lymon Billy to the birth of Willie Charley, son of David and Mary Charley, July 7, 1904.

    It appears from these affidavits that Willie Charley died on the 23rd day of September, 1904, and under the provisions of The Act of Congress approved March 3, 1905, the Commission is authorized for a period of sixty days from that date to receive applications for the enrollment of children born to enrolled citizens by blood of the Choctaw and Chickasaw Nations between September 25, 1902 and March 4, 1905 and living on the latter date. You will therefore see that the Commission is without authority to enroll your child who died on the 23rd day of September, 1904.

Respectfully,

Commissioner in Charge.

7-NB-1473

Muskogee, Indian Territory, January 15, 1906.

Mary Charley,
    Glover, Indian Territory.

Dear Madam:

    Receipt is hereby acknowledged of your letter of January 3, 1906, in which you ask if your child now about three years old has been approved; you state that you and your husband are separated and you wish to be informed if he has had this child enrolled and if not you desire blanks for this purpose.

Applications for Enrollment of Choctaw Newborn
Act of 1905 Volume XIX

In reply to your letter you are advised that you do not mention the name of the child referred to, but it appears from the records of this office that application was made for the enrollment of Willie Charley, child of David and Mary Charley born July 7, 1904, but it appearing that he died September 23, 1904, his application for enrollment was dismissed as under the act of Congress approved March 3, 1905, only those children born to citizens by blood of the Choctaw and Chickasaw Nations subsequent to September 25, 1902, who were living March 4, 1905, were entitled to enrollment.

Respectfully,

Commissioner.

Choc. New Born 1474
    Ethel Merree Fox
    (Born April 8, 1905)

1474

NEW BORN
CHOCTAW
ENROLLMENT

ETHEL MERREE FOX

(BORN APRIL 8, 1905)

As Citizen of the
CHOCTAW NATION
Act of Congress
Approved March 3, 1905

C A N C E L L E D

RECORD TRANSFERRED TO CHOCTAW NEW BORN NO. 193.

ACT OF CONGRESS APPROVED APRIL 26, 1906.

1474

**Applications for Enrollment of Choctaw Newborn
Act of 1905   Volume XIX**

CHOCTAW   1474
NEW BORN
ACT OF CONGRESS APPROVED MARCH 30, 1905.

Ethel Merree Fox
(Born April 8, 1905)

CANCELLED
Record transferred to
CHOCTAW   NEW BORN *No 193*
ACT OF CONGRESS APPROVED APRIL 26, 1906.

Choc. New Born 1475
    (Danuel Sanders)
    (Birthdate not given)

1475

NEW BORN
**CHOCTAW
ENROLLMENT**

DANUEL SANDERS

(BORN AUGUST 6, 1900)

As Citizen of the
CHOCTAW NATION
Act of Congress
Approved March 3, 1905

CANCELLED

RECORD TRANSFERRED TO CHOCTAW NEW BORN
NO 787

ACT OF CONGRESS APPROVED APRIL 26, 1906.
                        JULY 20, 1906

1475

Applications for Enrollment of Choctaw Newborn
Act of 1905 Volume XIX

CHOCTAW 1475
NEW BORN
ACT OF CONGRESS APPROVED MARCH 30, 1905.

Danuel Sanders
(Born Aug. 6, 1900)

CANCELLED

Record transferred to
Choctaw New Born No 787
ACT OF CONGRESS APPROVED APRIL 26, 1906.

JUL 20 1906

Choc. New Born 1476
    Georgie B. Welsh
    (Born Nov. 18, 1903)

1476

NEW BORN
CHOCTAW
ENROLLMENT

GEORGIE B. WELSH

(BORN NOVEMBER 18, 1903)

DIED PRIOR TO MARCH 4, 1905

As Citizen of the
CHOCTAW NATION
Act of Congress
Approved March 3, 1905

NO. 1 DISMISSED JUNE 28, 1905

1476

Applications for Enrollment of Choctaw Newborn
Act of 1905   Volume XIX

DEPARTMENT OF THE INTERIOR,
COMMISSION TO THE FIVE CIVILIZED TRIBES.

Record in the matter of the application for enrollment as a citizen by blood of the Choctaw Nation of:

GEORGIE B. WELSH   7-NB-1476.

NEW-BORN AFFIDAVIT.

Number............

...Choctaw Enrolling Commission...

IN THE MATTER OF THE APPLICATION FOR ENROLLMENT, as a citizen of the Choctaw Nation, of Georgie B. Welsh

born on the 18th day of November 1903

Name of father   James Welsh   a citizen of   ~~Choctaw~~
Nation final enrollment No............
Name of mother   Lizzie N Wilburn *now Welsh*   a citizen of   Choctaw
Nation final enrollment No. 6762

Postoffice   Colegate[sic], IT

AFFIDAVIT OF MOTHER.

UNITED STATES OF AMERICA
INDIAN TERRITORY
Central   DISTRICT

now Welsh

I   Lizzie N. Wilburn   , on oath state that I am 26 years of age and a citizen by blood of the Choctaw Nation, and as such have been placed upon the final roll of the Choctaw Nation, by the Honorable Secretary of the Interior my final enrollment number being 6702 ; that I am the lawful wife of James Welsh, who is a citizen of the ~~Choctaw~~ Nation, and as such has been placed upon the final roll of said Nation by the Honorable Secretary of the Interior, his final enrollment number being ——— and that a Female child was born to me on the 18 day of November 1903; that said child has been named Georgie B Welsh, and is now ~~living~~. *Dead*

now Welsh

Lizzie N Wilburn

Applications for Enrollment of Choctaw Newborn
Act of 1905   Volume XIX

Witnesseth.

{ Must be two Witnesses who are Citizens. }   Blanche Brashears

Martha Wilburn

Subscribed and sworn to before me this   12   day of   Jan   190 5

AE Folsom
Notary Public.

My commission expires:
9-Jan 1909

Affidavit of Attending Physician or Midwife.

UNITED STATES OF AMERICA }
INDIAN TERRITORY
................................DISTRICT

I, ... a ....
on oath state that I attended on Mrs. .... wife of
.... on the .... day of ...., 190........,
that there was born to her on said date a .... child, that said child is now living, and is
said to have been named ....

Dr. J Welsh   M.D.

Subscribed and sworn to before me this, the   21st day of   Feb   190 5

(Name Illegible)
Notary Public.

WITNESSETH:

{ Must be two witnesses who are citizens and know the child. }   C N Wilburn

Martha Wilburn

We hereby certify that we are well acquainted with ....
a   Dr   and know   him   to be reputable and of good standing in the community.

{ G.W. Brashears
Blanche Wilburn }
now
Brashears

Applications for Enrollment of Choctaw Newborn
Act of 1905   Volume XIX

DEATH AFFIDAVIT

NO._____

Choctaw Enrolling Commission.

IN THE MATTER OF THE DEATH OF Georgie B. Welsh
a citizen of the Choctaw Nation, who formerly resided at or near Coalgate
Ind. Ter., and died on the 20th day of November 190 3

AFFIDAVIT OF RELATIVE.

UNITED STATES OF AMERICA
INDIAN TERRITORY
  Central   DISTRICT.

now Welsh

I, Lizzie N. Wilburn on oath, state that I am 26 years of age, and a citizen of the Choctaw Nation, and as such have been finally enrolled by the Honorable Secretary of the Interior, my enrollment number being 6702 ; that my postoffice address is Coalgate , Ind. Ter.; that I am Mother of the child who was a citizen, by blood , of the Choctaw Nation; and that said Georgie B. Welsh died on the 20th day of November , 190 3

WITNESSETH:

Must be two witnesses who are Citizens.
{ Blanche Brashears
  Martha Wilburn

Lizzie N Wilburn

Subscribed and sworn to before me this the 13 day of January 190 5

AE Folsom   Notary Public.

AFFIDAVIT OF ACQUAINTANCE.

UNITED STATES OF AMERICA
INDIAN TERRITORY
................................DISTRICT.

I, Georgia Lynch on oath, state that I am 26 years of age, and a citizen by blood of the Choctaw Nation; that my post-office address is Madill Ind. Ter.; that I was personally acquainted with Georgie B Welsh the deceased child above named, who was a citizen of Choctaw Nation by blood, and that said Georgie B Welsh died on the 20th day of November , 190 3

Applications for Enrollment of Choctaw Newborn
Act of 1905   Volume XIX

Subscribed and sworn to before me this .... day of .... 190.....

.... Notary Public.

My Commission Expires:

W.J.
7-NB-1476.

DEPARTMENT OF THE INTERIOR,
COMMISSION TO THE FIVE CIVILIZED TRIBES.

In the matter of the application for the enrollment of Georgie B. Welsh as a citizen by blood of the Choctaw Nation.

---oOo---

It appears from the record herein that on April 25, 1905 there was filed with the Commission application for the enrollment of Georgie B. Welsh as a citizen by blood of the Choctaw Nation.

It further appears from the record herein and the records of the Commission that the applicant was born November 18, 1903; that she is a daughter of Lizzie N. Welsh, who is identified as Lizzie N. Wilburn, number 6702 upon the final roll of citizens by blood of the Choctaw Nation, approved by the Secretary of the Interior January 17, 1903, and James Welsh, a noncitizen; and that said applicant died November 20, 1903.

The Act of Congress approved March 3, 1905 (Public No. 212) among other things provides:

"That the Commission to the Five Civilized Tribes is authorized for sixty days after the date of the approval of this act to receive and consider applications for enrollment of children born subsequent to September twenty-fifth, nineteen hundred and two, and prior to March fourth, nineteen hundred and five, <u>and who were living on said latter date</u>, to citizens by blood of the Choctaw and Chickasaw tribes of Indians whose enrollment has been approved by the Secretary of the Interior prior to the date of the approval of this act; and to enroll and make allotments to such children."

It is, therefore, hereby ordered that the application for the enrollment of Georgie B. Welsh as a citizen by blood of the Choctaw Nation be dismissed in accordance with the order of the Commission of March 31, 1905.

COMMISSION TO THE FIVE CIVILIZED TRIBES,

Tams Bixby
Chairman.

Muskogee, Indian Territory.
JUN 28 1905

Applications for Enrollment of Choctaw Newborn
Act of 1905 Volume XIX

7-NB-1476

Muskogee, Indian Territory, June 28, 1905.

James Welsh, **COPY**
    Coalgate, Indian Territory.

Dear Sir:

Inclosed herewith you will find a copy of the order of this Commission, dated June 28, 1905, dismissing the application for the enrollment of Georgie B. Welsh as a citizen by blood of the Choctaw Nation.

        Respectfully,
        SIGNED

        Tams Bixby
Registered.   Chairman.
Incl. 7-NB-1476

7-NB-1476

Muskogee, Indian Territory, June 28, 1905.

Mansfield, McMurray & Cornish, **COPY**
    Attorneys for Choctaw and Chickasaw Nations,
        South McAlester, Indian Territory.

Gentlemen:

Inclosed herewith you will find a copy of the order of this Commission, dated June 28, 1905, dismissing the application for the enrollment of Georgie B. Welsh as a citizen by blood of the Choctaw Nation.

        Respectfully,
        SIGNED

        Tams Bixby
        Chairman.
Incl. 7-NB-1476

Applications for Enrollment of Choctaw Newborn
Act of 1905   Volume XIX

7-NB-1476

Muskogee, Indian Territory, September 8, 1905.

Harrod & Loden,
    Attorneys at Law,
        Durant, Indian Territory.

Gentlemen:

Receipt is hereby acknowledged of your letter of September 5th in reference to the right to enrollment of George[sic] B. Welsh, as a new-born citizen by blood of the Choctaw Nation.

The record in this case shows that the child was born November 18, 1903 and died November 20, 1903. The child was therefore not entitled to enrollment under the provisions of The Act of Congress approved July 1, 1902, and The Act of Congress approved March 3, 1905, provided for the enrollment of such children as were born subsequent to September 25, 1902 and prior to March 4, 1905, and who were living on the latter date.

Copy of the Commission's order of June 28, 1904, in this case was furnished James Welsh, the father of the deceased child.

Respectfully,

Acting Commissioner.

Choc. New Born 1477
    Nillie[sic] M. Harris
    (Born Feb. 19, 1904)

    Granted June 30, 1905.

Applications for Enrollment of Choctaw Newborn
Act of 1905   Volume XIX

DEPARTMENT OF THE INTERIOR,
COMMISSION TO THE FIVE CIVILIZED TRIBES.

Record in the matter of the application for enrollment as a citizen by blood of the Choctaw Nation of:

NELLIE M. HARRIS   7-NB-1477.

BIRTH AFFIDAVIT.

DEPARTMENT OF THE INTERIOR.
COMMISSION TO THE FIVE CIVILIZED TRIBES.

IN RE APPLICATION FOR ENROLLMENT, as a citizen of the Choctaw Nation, of Nellie M. Harris, born on the 19 day of Feby, 1904

Name of Father: James F. Harris   a citizen of the Choctaw Nation.
Name of Mother: Nellie H Harris   a citizen of the Choctaw Nation.

Postoffice   Leflore I.T.

AFFIDAVIT OF MOTHER.

UNITED STATES OF AMERICA, Indian Territory, }
Central   DISTRICT.

I, Nellie H Harris, on oath state that I am 24 years of age and a citizen by blood, of the Choctaw Nation; that I am the lawful wife of James F Harris, who is a citizen, by Intermarriage of the Choctaw Nation; that a female child was born to me on 19 day of Feby, 1904; that said child has been named Nellie M Harris, and was living March 4, 1905.

Nellie H Harris

Witnesses To Mark:
{

Subscribed and sworn to before me this 3 day of June, 1905

My com exp 7/8/08   W. L. Harris
                                          Notary Public.

Applications for Enrollment of Choctaw Newborn
Act of 1905 Volume XIX

AFFIDAVIT OF ATTENDING PHYSICIAN OR MID-WIFE.

UNITED STATES OF AMERICA, Indian Territory, }
   Central   DISTRICT. }

I, A R Sisk , a Physician , on oath state that I attended on Mrs. Nellie H Harris , wife of James F Harris on the 19 day of Feby , 1904; that there was born to her on said date a female child; that said child was living March 4, 1905, and is said to have been named Nellie M Harris

                                  Dr A R Sisk
Witnesses To Mark:
{

Subscribed and sworn to before me this 3 day of   June   , 1905

My com exp 7/8/08   W. L. Harris
                                        Notary Public.

W.F.
7-NB-1477.

DEPARTMENT OF THE INTERIOR,
COMMISSION TO THE FIVE CIVILIZED TRIBES.

In the matter of the application for the enrollment of Nellie M. Harris as a citizen by blood of the Choctaw Nation.

--: D E C I S I O N :--

It appears from the record herein that on April 17, 1905 there was received by the Commission a letter from James F. Harris, dated April 15, 1905, inquiring relative to the enrollment of his "baby born since September 25, 1902". On April 24, 1905 another letter was received from said James F. Harris, dated April 22, 1905, in which he stated that the name of the mother of said child is Nellie Harris, that the name of said child is Nellie E[sic]. Harris, and that she was born February 19, 1904. He further stated in said letter "if application made is not sufficient, please let me know at once & enclose blank application".

On May 18, 1905 the Commission acknowledged receipt of the letter of said James F. Harris of April 22, 1905 and forwarded him a blank application for the enrollment of an infant child. On June 13, 1905 proper proof of the birth of Nellie M. Harris, daughter of James F. Harris and Nellie H. Harris, born February 19, 1904, was filed with the records of the Commission.

It appears from the records of the Commission that Nellie H. Harris, the mother of said child, is a recognized and enrolled citizen by blood of the Choctaw Nation, that her name appears opposite number 8837 upon the final roll of citizens by blood of the Choctaw Nation, approved by the Secretary of the Interior January 17, 1903 and that

Applications for Enrollment of Choctaw Newborn
Act of 1905   Volume XIX

James F. Harris, the father of said child, is a recognized and enrolled citizen by intermarriage of the Choctaw Nation.

It further appears from the record herein that the applicant was living on March 4, 1905.

It is the opinion of this Commission that application for the enrollment of Nellie M. Harris was made to this Commission within the time prescribed by The Act of Congress approved March 3, 1905 (Public No. 212).

It is further the opinion of this Commission that Nellie M. Harris should be enrolled as a citizen by blood of the Choctaw Nation, in accordance with the provisions of said act of Congress approved March 3, 1905 (Public No. 212), and it is so ordered.

COMMISSION TO THE FIVE CIVILIZED TRIBES,

Tams Bixby
Chairman.
TB Needles
Commissioner.
C. R. Breckinbridge
Commissioner.

Muskogee, Indian Territory.
JUN 30 1905

(The letter below typed as given.)

M. H. Harris   W. L. Harris

HARRIS & SON

GENERAL MERCHANDISE AND LIVE STOCK

Leflore Ind. Ter. 4/15 1905

Commission to the Five Civilized Tribes,
Muskogee I T

Gentlemen:-

Some time ago I made application for the enrollment of my baby borned since Sept 25/02 Since that time I understand all applications have to be made over- If application made is not sufficient please furnish me with blank and let me know and same will be made over

Yours truly

James F. Harris

Applications for Enrollment of Choctaw Newborn
Act of 1905   Volume XIX

INDORSED ON BACK AS FOLLOWS: INDEXED

COMMISSION TO FIVE TRIBES
No. 19141
Received Apr. 17, 1905
1905

Apr. 21, 1904

Harris, James, F.,
    Leflore, I.T.
        Choctaw Nation
            April 15, 1905.

Asks if application heretofore filed is sufficient for enrollment of baby   If not, want B.C.

Choc-Chic enrollment

    7-R-120

7-3016

Leflore, I. T. 4/22/1905.

Commission to the Five Civilized Tribes,
    Muskogee, I. T.

Gentlemen:

    Replying to yours in regard to the enrollment of my child in which you ask for name of mother, name of child and date of birth in order to let me know if application made is sufficient Name of mother Nellie Harris, name of child Nellie E[sic]. Harris borned[sic] Feb'y 19, 1904-   If application made is not sufficient please let me know at once and enclose blank application.

                Yours truly

                      James F. Harris,

                          Leflore,

                              I. T.

Applications for Enrollment of Choctaw Newborn
Act of 1905 Volume XIX

THE MILLER PHARMACY

STATIONERY and
TOILET ARTICLES

DEALER in
DRUGS and
MEDICINES

PAINTS, GLASS
and GENERAL
DRUG SUNDRIES

Leflore
Talihina I.T.   4/22 1905

Commission to the Five Civilized Tribes,
Muskogee, I.T.

Gentlemen:-

Replying to yours in regard to the enrollment of my child in which you ask for name of mother, name of child, and date of birth in order to let me know if application made is sufficient.
Name of mother Nellie   Harris, name of child Nellie E[sic]. Harris borned[sic] Feb'y 19-1904- - If application made is not sufficient, please let me know at once & enclose blank application.

Yours truly

James F. Harris

Leflore

I T

INDEXED

INDORSED ON BACK AS FOLLOWS:

COMMISSION TO FIVE TRIBES
No. 20686   Received Apr. 24, 05   Back   Page
1905

May 18, 1905

Harris, James, F.,
 Leflore I.T.
  Choctaw Nation
   Apr. 22, 1905.

Relative to enrollment
of Nellie Harris.

Choc-Chic enrollment.

7- R120

Applications for Enrollment of Choctaw Newborn
Act of 1905 Volume XIX

7-3016

COPY

Muskogee, Indian Territory, May 18, 1905.

James F. Harris,
    Leflore, Indian Territory.

Dear Sir:

    Receipt is hereby acknowledged of your letter of April 22, 1905, stating that your child is named Nellie E. Harris born February 19, 1904, and that the mother's name is Nellie Harris; you ask if the application heretofore forwarded is not sufficient that you be sent another blank.

    In compliance with your request there is inclosed herewith a blank for the enrollment of an infant child which you are requested to have executed and returned to this office as early as practicable.

                Respectfully,

SIGNED

Tams Bixby
Chairman.

B.C.

Leflore, Ind. Ter. June 5, 1905.

Gentlemen:

    Herewith application for the enrollment of my baby as per your request. Trusting this will be sufficient.

        I am

                Yours truly,
                James F. Harris.

Applications for Enrollment of Choctaw Newborn
Act of 1905 Volume XIX

COPY 7-3016

Muskogee, Indian Territory, June 13, 1905.

James Harris,
    LeFlore, Indian Territory.

Dear Sir:

    Receipt is hereby acknowledged of your letter of June 5, 1905, transmitting affidavits of Nellie H. Harris and A. R. Sisk to the birth of Nellie M. Harris, daughter of James F. and Nellie H. Harris, February 19, 1904, and the same have been filed with our records in the matter of the enrollment of said child.

    Respectfully,

SIGNED *Tams Bixby*
    Chairman.

Choc. New Born 1478
    Roseta Brackeen
    (Born Aug. 16, 1904)

BIRTH AFFIDAVIT.

DEPARTMENT OF THE INTERIOR.
COMMISSION TO THE FIVE CIVILIZED TRIBES.

IN RE APPLICATION FOR ENROLLMENT, as a citizen of the Choctaw Nation, of Roseta Brackeen, born on the 18 day of Aug, 1904

Name of Father: Roy Brackeen   a citizen of the Choctaw Nation.
Name of Mother: Sophia Brackeen   a citizen of the Choctaw Nation.

    Postoffice   Boswell, I.T.

Applications for Enrollment of Choctaw Newborn
Act of 1905 Volume XIX

AFFIDAVIT OF MOTHER.

UNITED STATES OF AMERICA, Indian Territory, }
Central DISTRICT.

I, Sophia Brackeen, on oath state that I am 22 years of age and a citizen by Blood, of the Choctaw Nation; that I am the lawful wife of Roy BRackeen[sic], who is a citizen, by Marriage of the Choctaw Nation; that a Female child was born to me on 18 day of Aug, 1904; that said child has been named Roseta Brackeen, and was living March 4, 1905.

Sophia Brackeen

Witnesses To Mark:
{

Subscribed and sworn to before me this 11th day of May, 1905

Perry M. Clark
Notary Public.

AFFIDAVIT OF ATTENDING PHYSICIAN OR MID-WIFE.

UNITED STATES OF AMERICA, Indian Territory, }
Central DISTRICT.

I, Harriet Voyd, a Midwife, on oath state that I attended on Mrs. Sophia Brackeen, wife of Roy Brackeen on the 18 day of Aug, 1904; that there was born to her on said date a Female child; that said child was living March 4, 1905, and is said to have been named Roseta Brackeen

Harriet Voyd

Witnesses To Mark:
{

Subscribed and sworn to before me this 11th day of May, 1905

Perry M. Clark
Notary Public.

My Commission Expires 2/27/09

Applications for Enrollment of Choctaw Newborn
Act of 1905   Volume XIX

Muskogee, Indian Territory, April 25, 1905.

Roy Brackeen,
    Boswell, Indian Territory.

Dear Sir:

    Receipt is hereby acknowledged of the affidavits of Sophia Brackeen and Harriet Voyd to the birth of Roseta Brackeen daughter of Roy and Sophia Brackeen, August 18, 1904.

    It is stated in the affidavit of the mother that both she and yourself are citizens by blood of the Choctaw Nation. If this is correct you are requested to state the names under which you were enrolled, the names of your parents, and if you have selected an allotment of the lands of the Choctaw or Chickasaw Nation please give your roll numbers as they appear upon your allotment certificate.

                                Respectfully,

                                             Chairman.

Muskogee, Indian Territory, May 31, 1905.

Roy Brackeen,
    Boswell, Indian Territory.

Dear Sir:

    Referring to the application for the enrollment of you[sic] child, Roseta Brackeen, a letter was addressed to you on April 25, 1905, asking information which would enable us to identify the mother of this child upon our records.

    Before further consideration can be given this application, it will be necessary that you give the name under which your wife, Sophia Brackeen, was enrolled, the names of her parents, and if she has selected an allotment of the lands of the Choctaw or Chickasaw Nation, give her roll number as the same appears upon her allotment certificate.

    This matter should receive immediate attention.

                                Respectfully,

                                                  [sic]

Applications for Enrollment of Choctaw Newborn
Act of 1905 Volume XIX

Muskogee, Indian Territory, June 1, 1905.

Perry M. Clark,
    Boswell, Indian Territory.

Dear Sir:

    Referring to the application for the enrollment of Roseta Brackeen as a citizen by blood of the Choctaw Nation, information is requested which will enable the Commission to identify the mother of this child upon its records.

    Before further consideration can be given this application, it will be necessary that you give the name under which Sophia Brackeen was enrolled, her age, the names of her parents and other members of her family, and if she has selected an allotment of the lands of the Choctaw or Chickasaw Nation, give her roll number as the same appears upon her allotment certificate.

    This matter should receive immediate attention.

                            Respectfully,

                                                            [sic]

(The letter below typed as given.)

                          (COPY)

                        Boswell, I. T. June 9th 1905

Commission TO THE FIVE TRIBES
    Muskogee, Indian Territory.

In reply to yours in regard to the enrolement of ROseta Brackeen. you are informed that her Mother was Sophia. James. She being the Daughter of David. James. A Choctaw Freedman. and Mary. McKinney. her Mother a Choctaw by Blood,
Sophia. James. ROLL NO is 4880 and the Land was takened in the Choctaw Nation, I also enclose you Marriage Certificate, of their Marriage.

                    I am sirs Yours Very Respectfully,
                              Perry M. Clark
                                Notary Public.

(Endorsed on back as follows:)

                                                    INDEXED.
    COMMISSION TO FIVE TRIBES.
No.   Received   Answered
28840   Book   Page
1905   JUN 13 1905

Applications for Enrollment of Choctaw Newborn
Act of 1905   Volume XIX

Clark, Perry M.,
    Boswell, I. T.
    June 9, 1905.

In re Enrollment of Roseta Brackeen. Transmits marriage lciense of parents of said child.
CHOC-CHIC ENROLLMENT.

7--1726   7 NB 1478

                                                                                         7-1726

                              Muskogee, Indian Territory, June 17, 1905.

Perry M. Clark,
    Boswell, Indian Territory.

Dear Sir:

    Receipt is hereby acknowledged of your letter of June 9, 1905, in regard to Rosetta[sic] Brackeen in which you state that her mother is Sophia James, Choctaw by Blood, Roll No. 4880 and you inclose marriage license between Roy Brackeen and Sophia James.

    In reply to your letter you are advised that the information contained in your letter has enabled the Commission to identify Sophia James as an enrolled citizen by blood of the Choctaw Nation and the affidavits heretofore forwarded have been filed with our records as an application for the enrollment of said child.

                                        Respectfully,

                                                                   Chairman.

Index

AGEE
  William 1
ALAPASHABBE
  Barnett 8
  Gency 8
ALBERSON
  Ben 102
ALLEN
  D 206
ANDERSON
  Charles E 118
  Georgie Muncrief 118
  Murray Muncrief 117
  Tennessee 175
ANGELL
  W H 160,246,247,248
ARMSTRONG
  J H 66,67
  J H, MD 66,67
BAAWNER
  M E 33,36
BACON
  Daniel 170,171,172,173
  Epsie 170,171,172,173
  Louis 173
  Louisa 170,171,172
  Mattie 170,171,172
BAILEY
  David A 136,137
BAKEN
  D E 267,268
  Lyman 289,290
BAKER
  Hodgen 142,143
BALLING
  John Thomas 293
BATTIEST
  L G 15
BAYLOR
  W O 229
BEAN
  Nicholas 237,238
BEE
  Fannie 105,106,109
  William 106
BELL
  Clara Rena 257
  Clara Renee 256
BEN
  Mollie 289
BENCH
  Sam 18
BETTS
  C A 245
BILLY
  Lyman 305,306
  Lymon 308
BIRDO
  E R 68
  E R, MD 68
BIXBY
  Mr 131
  T 12
  Tams 25,43,77,78,79,83,99,100,
  120,130,207,208,251,252,260,261,269
  ,270,275,276,280,281,286,287,291,
  292,298,299,307,308,315,316,320,323
  ,324
  Tims 128
BLACK
  Fannie ... 105,106,107,108,109,110,111
  Preston Lee 104,105,106,107,108,
  109,110,111
  Thomas . 105,106,107,108,109,110,111
BOATRIGHT
  Bessie 20
BOBB
  Sophie 9,10
BOGEL
  Wm T 56
BOHANAN
  Sim 138
BOHANNON
  Mary 140
BOHANON
  Joe 139,140,141
  Mary 139,140,141
  Sim 139,140,141
BOLING
  Billy 213,214,215,216,217
  Evinie 213,214,215,216,217
  John Thomas 294
  Seanis 213,214,215,216,217
  W S 295

Index

BOLLING
  Emma 294,296,298
  John Thomas 293,294,295,296, 297,298,299
  W S 294,296,298,299
BOOTH
  T S 55,56,58
  T S, MD 56
BOSWELL
  Inez 255,256
BOWER
  James 92,155
BOWLING
  Emma 295
BOWLLING
  Emma 294
BOYD
  Robert 148
BRACKEEN
  Roseta 324,325,326,327,328
  Rosetta 328
  Roy 324,325,326,328
  Sophia 324,325,326,327
BRASHEARS
  Blanche 313,314
  G W 313
BRECKINBRIDGE
  C R 251
BREDKINBRIDGE
  C R 320
BREEDING
  A L 250
  A L, MD 250
BRIGGS
  Jennie 1,2
  Minnie 1,2
  Thomas J 1,2
BROCK
  Henry 175,177
BROWN
  Caroline 242
  Flora 206
  Francis 183,184,186
  John T 179,180,182,183
  Susan 102,103
BRUNSON
  D D 175

BRYAM
  S W 3
BRYANT
  Helen 300
BUNN
  Wm C 70,82
  Wn C 81
BURIS
  Francis 205
BURNS
  A J 68
BURRIS
  Francis 205,207
BURTON
  Sydney W 228
BYFORD
  H M 219,220,221
BYINGTON
  Moody 283,284
BYRAM
  S W 4
CAIN
  P L 22,23
CALDWELL
  Willie 268
CAMEY
  E W 233
CAMPBELL
  Annie 80,81
  Ephraim 71,74,75
  Ephraim F 70,71,77,81,82,83,84
  Ephram 79,81
  Ephriam 72,73,76,85
  Johnie 80,81
  Johnnie 70,71,77,78,79,81,82,83,84
  Johnnie Easter 71,72,74,75,86
  Louisa 8,9,10,12,14
  Luch 81
  Lucy 70,71,74,75,76,77,79,81, 82,83,84,85
  Sillien 7,8,11
CAMPBELLZ
  Johnnie Easter 76
CARR
  Johny 197,198,199
  Osborn 199
  Osborne 197,198

Silen....................197,198,199
Wm C 1
CARROLL
  G E 245
CARTER
  Gertie Allie 241,242,243
  J C......................................242,243
  James C 242
  Jas C 241
  Susie 241,242,243
CASTILOW
  J W 52,214,215,216
CEPHUS
  T J... 9
CHAPMAN
  W R 93,97
CHARLEY
  David 305,306,307,308,309
  Mary 305,306,308,309
  Willie 304,305,306,307,308,309
CHASTAIN
  J D 106
CHOATE
  James 242
  Jency.. 273
CLARK
  Perry M.............. 179,180,181,182,183,
  184,325,327,328
CLAY
  A H 215,217
CLECKLER
  W H 106,109,111
  W H, MD....................................... 106
CLICKLER
  W H 110
CLUCKLER
  Dr.. 105
  W H 106
COCHNAUER
  D W 22,23
COGSWELL
  Dan 278
  Ida 277,278,280
  Johnson.. 278
COKER
  G C 113,114,116
  George C 115,117

Lula............. 112,113,114,115,116,117
  T C 112,116
  T E 113,116
  Willie R E.... 112,113,114,115,116,117
COLBERT
  Charlie 142,143
  Davidson....................46,47,50,51,52
  Davina 52
  Daviney 50
  Davison..................................48,49,50,52
  Julia Ann 46,47,48,49,50,51,52
  Levina................. 46,47,48,49,50,51,52
COLEMAN
  Elie 159,160
  J N 56
  Norman..................................159,160
  Phoebe 159,160
COLLIN
  Jesse.. 163
  Mertha 162,163,164,166
COLLINS
  E L 211,212
  E L, MD.. 212
  Lake.. 102
COLUMBUS
  Celin 40
  Cilin 43
  Tecumseh....................................... 43
COOK
  C F 119
  F C 118
COOPER
  James 154
  Jane 143,144,145
COPELAND
  J J 188,189,190,191
CORNISH
  Martha 218,219
  Rena......................................218,219,220
  Webster 218,219
COSTELOW
  J W 47
COSTILOW
  J W 47
COVINGTON
  W P.. 127
COXWELL

Index

Dan 276,277,279,280,281
James 281
Johnson 277,278,279,280
CRAIG
   J R 189,190,191,192,193,194
   J R, MD 189,190,191,192,193
CROSBY
   Josiah 216
   Seanis 215,216,217
CROWDER
   Eli 178,179,180,181,182,183,
   184,185,186,187,294,295,296
   Elic 177
   Emma 294,295,298
   George 297
   Green 297
   Julia 179,180,181,182,183,
   184,186,187
   Julia A 178
   Lena 178
   Lena Bell 177,182,183,184,185,186
   Maud May ... 177,179,180,181,185,186
   Maude May 185
   Thomas C 297
CULBERSON
   James 160
CULBERTSON
   C E 113
   J 2
   J, MD 2
CUMMING
   J N 108
CUMMINGS
   J N 108,111
CUNNISH
   Martha 220,221
   Rena 218,220,221
   Renner 220,221
   Webster 220
CURRY
   Guy A 19,158
DADEN
   William 64
DAGGS
   Mollie 225,226,227
   Opal 225,226,227
   William W 225,226

DAILEY
   Dr J N 97
   Henry 173
   Martha E 171,172
DAILY
   Dr J N 94
   J N 92,93,94
   J N, MD 92
DALTON
   E M 156
DAVID
   Ruth 229
DAVIS
   Alekton 288,289,290,291,292
   John 287,288,289,290,291,292
   Martha 288,289,291
   Marthey 94
   Marthy 97
DIFENDAFER
   Chas T 104,135,146,170,173,
   174,198,199
DOBLE
   Frank L 10
DONEGAY
   Agnes 205,206
   Annie 205,206
   Cornelius 205,206
DONEGHEY
   Agnas 204,205,207
   Annie 204,205,207,208,209
   Cornelious 204,205
   Cornelius 207,208,209
DRAKE
   Dora 139
   Susan 140
DUNCAN
   G D 179,180,182,183
DYER
   David, Jr 47
   T D 17,18
EASLEY
   John F 56
EBAHATUBBI
   Davis 87,88
   Davis J 88,89
EDWARDS
   Barnabas 234,235

    Betsy 234
    Ebenezer 234
    Isac 234
    Jos A 218
    Louisa 234
    Maneffie 230,231,232,234,235,236
    Moton 234
    Sallie 234,235
    Silway 234
ELAPASHABBE
    Barnett 6,7,10,11,13,14
    Eliza 13
    Gency 6,7,10,11,13,14
    Louisa 6,7,10,11,14
ELAPUSHABBEE
    Barnett 13
    Gency 12,13
EMEYABBI
    Forbis 230,231,232,233,234,
    235,236,237
    Isham 231
    Maneffie 232,233,237
    Maneffie Edwards 236
    Martha 230,231,232,233,234,
    235,236,237
ESAPUSHABBE
    Barnett 13
EVERETT
    Fred 98,99
FARMER
    W S 245
FARRELL
    Emry 1
FARRIS
    W B 76,77,86
FENNELL
    Thoma 124
    Thomas 53,54,121,122,123,239
    Thos 122,123,239
FIKE
    W J 201,202,203
    W J, MD 202
FOLSOM
    A E 66,148,245,313,314
    G E 245
    Saul 244
    Silas 101,102,103

FONDREN
    G B 114,115,116,117
FOOSHEE
    Geo A 175
FOSTER & DALTON 157
FOUT
    C C 259,262
    Sam W 259,261,262
    Susan 260,262
    Susie 262
    Susie G 259
    Turner 258,259,260,261,262,263
FOX
    Ethel Merree 309,310
    John R 96
FOYIL
    A C 167,168,169
    A C, MD 167
FRANKLIN
    Harkin 48,50,52
    Wirt 28,29,30,38
FRAZIER
    Alex 50,52
    Isreal 282,283,284,285,286,287
    Mollie 283,285
    Norwood 236
    Smallwood 232,233,237
    Wilson E 283,284,285,286
FULLER
    F M 64,144
FULTZ
    H F 31,33
    L E 33
GAFFORD
    T F 241,243
    T J 243
GAGE
    Harry 224
    Nancy 223,224
    Sallie 224
GARDNER
    R C 177,178
GARRETT
    H P 296
GIBSON
    Elis 207
    Siliney 207

GIPSON
   Agnes 208
   C A 249,250
GLISSON
   Jane 195
GOFORTH
   R P 48
GOING
   Hampton 294,295,296
   Sophie 16
GOINS
   Hemp 294
GOODNIGHT
   John H 212
GORDON
   Mary Ann 203
GREEN
   Betsey 101,102,103,104
   Ida 101,102,103,104
HAKABE
   Littie 267
HANCOCK
   Albert 20,21
   Kemble 20,21
   A Lee 21
   Viola 20,21
HARDY
   Emily 142,143,144,145
   Josephine 142,143,144,145
   Thomas 142,143,144,145
HARL
   W B 175,176
HARRIS
   Edward A 145,146
   Frances 145,146
   Henry 145,146
   Jame F 320
   James 324
   James F . 318,319,320,321,322,323,324
   Nellie 321,322,323
   Nellie E 319,322,323
   Nellie H 318,319,324
   Nellie M 318,319,320,324
   Nillie M 317
   Nllie E 321
   W H 320
   W L 164,165,318,319,320

HARRISON
   Albert S 196,197
   Matilda A 196,197
HARROD & LODEN 317
HAWKINS
   W H 163
HAYHURST
   J I 176,177
HENSON
   Alice 157,158,159
   Andrew 157,158,159
   Lena 158,159
   Roxy 157,158,159
HERRON
   Lula 112,115,117
HICKMAN
   Lizzie 141
HITCHCOCK
   E A 254
HLICHTAMBI
   Charles 215
   Charlie 215,217
HOCKMAN
   J T 74
HOLLOWAY
   John 161,162,163,164,165,166
   Minnie .. 160,161,162,163,164,165,166
   Sissie 161,162,163,164,166
HOLMAN
   Alfred 6,7
   Gilam 305,306
HOME
   Sophia 239,240
HOMER
   Jacob 125,126
HORTON
   L D 294,295
HOUSE
   Ed 80,81,82
HUBERT
   J C 20
HUDLOW
   G W 204
   W H 205
HUDSON
   P W 143
   Rufus 43

Index

Sallie 43
Sallie Ann 43
HULSEY
  Wm J 106,200
HUNT
  James 222,223
IBAHOTUBBE
  Nancy 87,89,90
IMPSON
  Roy Vester 264,265
INGRAM
  Jas S 200
  John R 210,211,212,213
  Mary A 210,211,212,213
  Milburn Cisney 209,211,212,213
  Nancy J 213
  Nancy Jane 209,210,212,213
ISAAC
  Willie 161,162
ISCHCOMER
  Jolam 265,266,267,268,269,270
  Lincoln M 266,270
  Lincoln N 267,268,269
  Meson 266,267,269
JACKSON
  Ben 154
  Nicholas 289,290
JACOB
  H B 267,268
  Isaac 60,61,63
JAMES
  Charley 272,273,275
  David 327
  Louisa 140
  Mary 271,272,273,274,275,276
  Sophia 327,328
JEFFERSON
  Daniel 15
  Isabelle 91,92
  Israel 92,93
  Listy 290
  A N 24
  Sampson 87,88
  Tennessee 15
JOHN
  Rayson 59
  Sissie 161,162,163,164,166

JOHNSON
  Bettie 86,87,88,89,90,91
  Esias 22,23,24,25,26,27
  Frank 22,23,24,25,26,27
  H C 29
  Henry 41,45
  Lewis 91
  Lila 88,89,90
  Liley 86,87
  Louis 86,87,88,89,90
  O L 102,104,135,146,170,
  171,172,173,174,195,198,199,222,223
  Sallie 22,23,24,26,27
  W J 215
JONES
  Alice 244,245,246,247
  Allice 245
  Ausbon N 177
  Edman 245
  Edmon 244
  Edmond 245,246,247
  Ella 244,245,246,247
  J W 69
  Louisa 160
JULIAN
  W A 214
KANASHAMBE
  Forbis 48,52
KELLEY
  T L 107
KEMALE
  Urban T 21
KEMBLE
  Urban T 21
KEMP
  Richard E 219
KING
  Emma 219
  Lucinda 199,200
  Mitchell 219
KYLE
  S H 23
LAMB
  J J 118
  Mrs J J 118
LARRABEE
  C F 131,253

Index

LAWECHOBE
   Annie 15
LAWECHUBBEE
   Annie 15,16
   Hopel T 15,16
   Tennessee 15,16
LAWRENCE
   Joseph R 68,69
   Raymond Arthur 68,69
   Sudie....................................68,69
   Victoria..................................... 229
LEDBETTER, BLEDSOE &
   THOMPSON 78,85,86
LEE
   L L 201,202,203
   Robert E 161,162,163
LEMON
   Ida 249,250,253
   John 249,250,251,253,254
   Martha May 248,249,250,251,
   252,253,254,255
LENTZ
   John M 18
LEWIS
   Charles S 32,33,34
   J L 259,260
   John 224,225
   Nancy ... 121,122,123,126,127,129,131
   S E 218
   W N 76,77
LILLARD
   Minnie 210,211
LLOYD
   D Conway 73,74,75
LOCKE
   Crystal 37,38
   Susan 37,38
   Wilson 37,38
LOMAN
   Frank L 144
LOVELL
   H C 83
   H P 71,75,81
   H P, MD 75
LYNCH
   Georgia 314
MANNING

A F 68
MANSFIELD, MCMURRAY &
   CORNISH 79,100,252,255,261,270,
276,281,287,292,299,307,316
MARKEY
   A J 297
MARR
   Fred T 80
MARTIN
   Anna 155
   Bertsworth 154,155,156,157
   Charlotte 154,155,156,157
   Lewis T 24
   W H 246,247
   William 155,156,157
   William, Jr 154,155
MASON
   H W 167,168,169
   J P 55
MATTHEWS
   J H 59,61,230,231,232
   Sarah 232
   Tracy 232
MCAFEE
   Selina 272,273,274,275
MCALESTER
   Angline 238,239,240
   James 238,239,240
   Nelson 238,239,240
MCBRIDE
   W A 149,150
MCCARTY
   J E 107,108,111
MCCLELLON
   Kittie 113
MCCLURE
   Reuben 278
   Stephen 278,279
MCCOY
   Elias 43
   Holman 43
   Louisa 43
   Moss 43
MCCRAY
   S B 206
MCCURTAIN
   Frank Allen 302

Green 120,128,129,139,140
MCDANIEL
   J T.. 97
   James T.. 95
MCKINNEY
   Bisey.. 166,167,168
   John W.. 244
   Mary 327
   Swinney..................... 166,167,168,169
   Thompson................. 166,167,168,169
   W H 9,10,233
MCLELLAN
   Kittie... 113
MCLELLON
   Solen...112,113
MCLURE
   Reuben..278,279
MCMARRIET
   L W...112,113
MCMILLAN
   N P... 175
MERRY
   J L...48,49,50
MILLER
   Cynthia E.. 247
   H C...71,81,82,83
   Hattie.......................................27,28,29,30
   James Gordon........................27,29,30
   Myrtle 30
   Myrtle Gladys........................27,28,30
   S G... 30
   Sam... 200
   Samuel G 27,28,29,30
MILTON
   W W 2
MITCHELL
   C T.. 224
MOORE
   E W...93,94,95
   Elie 159,160
   John 279
MORGAN
   John 72,75,76,83,84
   Johnie 80
   Johnnie 82
   Lucy...................... 71,74,75,76,78,85,86
   Mr...73,80,81

   Robert...83,84
MOSES
   Ben 148,149,150
   Sim 150
MURPHY
   Silen..198,199
NAIL
   Eliza...23,24
NALE
   James Frederic 263,264
NANOMANTUBE
   Wilmon...9,10
NEEDLES
   T B...11,251,320
NELSON
   Benjamin 134,135,136,137,138
   Emma C..................... 135,136,137,138
   Jackson F 134,135,136,137,138
NOAH
   Alfered... 174
   Alfred 175,176,177
   John 232,233,236,237
   Johnson... 233
   Sampson 174,175,176,177
   Sibindy 174,175,176,177
NOATABBE
   Antlin... 240
   Lewis 240
   Selin... 240
NOLEN
   W T...226,227
OLIVER
   John H 2
ORNDORFF
   Bertha May 302
ORPHAN
   Levi... 102
PARKER
   Alpho...32,33
   H T 32,33
   Nancey L 32
   Nancy 33,35,36
   Nancy L 34,36
PATTERSON
   E L......................91,92,93,94,95,96,97
   Elic L... 96
   Isabelle 91,92,93,94,95,97

Index

Nancy S 91,92,93,94,95,96,97
PAYTE
  A J 206
PERKINS
  N A 65,66
PERRY
  Charles T 92,93
  Eli 175
PETTEY
  Lizzie 4,5
PFIEFFER
  William 84
PHILLIPS
  A Denton 67,68
  W D 138
  W D, MD 136,137
PICKENS
  Louisa 7,8,10
  Mary 187
PIGG
  W B 28,30
  W B, MD 28
PITCHLYNN
  E P 41,45
POWELL
  Dr James 294
  J N, MD 296
  James 296
PUSH
  Burnett 8,9,10,14
  Burnnett 12
  Jincy 8,9,10,12,14
QUINTON
  Annie 16,17,18,19
  Elizabeth 18,19
  James 18
  Joel 17,18,19
  Katie 17,18,19
REED
  Gladess Lee 65,67
  Inez 67
  Inez Turnbull 67
  M A 67
REID
  Gladys 65
  Glaydis 65,66
  Inez 65,66

Inez Turnbull 67
  M A 65,66
RENNIE
  Albert 80,82,84
REYNOLDS
  D G 229
  David G 228,229
  Elizabeth Eunice 228,229
  Hattie 228,229
RIGGAN
  C E 146
  C E, MD 146
RIGGINS
  C E 146
RISTEEN
  H C 178
  Harry C 70,81,82
ROBERTS
  Sam T 43
  Sam T, Jr 41
ROBERTSON
  George F 153
RODGERS
  Annie M 248
ROGERS
  Annie M 247
ROGUS
  S E 200
ROSE
  Vester W 73,74
ROSENTHAL
  Birdie 98,99
  Floyd 97,98,99,100
  Jacob 98,99,100
ROWLEY
  H G 114,115,116
SAM
  Morris 161,162,165
SAMIS
  Yyman 230,231
SAMPSON
  Marsie 88,89
SANDERS
  Danuel 310,311
SCOTT
  Cephus 222,223
  Emeline 155

SEELY
Bond 198
Silen 198
Susie 198
SHANAFELT
Richard 246,247
SHANNON
Dr T 99
T D 99
T D, MD 99
SHIELD
Anna 147,148
Nancy 148,149,151
Sarah 147,148
SHIELDS
Nancy 151
Sarah 147,149
SHONEY
W A 87,267,268,269,272,273, 274,278,279,280,283,284,285,289,290,291
SIMMONS
Jewel 194,195,196,197
John 194,195,197
Mamie 194,195,197
Mammie 196
Mr & Mrs 196
SISK
Dr A R 319
A R 319,324
SKINNER
W G 28
SMITH
W C 24
SORRELLS
Aney Frances 203
Annie Frances 201,202
Mary Frances 201,202,203
Mary Francis 203
Nancy Elizabeth 201,202,203
Thomas Jefferson 201,202,203
STALEBY
Thos 224
STALLABY
Mary Ann 222,223,224
Sallie 222,223,224
Thomas 222,223,224

STEPHEN
Paul 230
STEPHENS
Paul 59,234
STONE
Agnes 208
STUART
E T 202,203
SULLIVAN
B F 210,212
SUMMER
Amanda L 35
Amanda L M 32,33,34,35,36
Eller 31,32,33,34,35,36,37
James 32,33,34,35,36
SUMMERS
Amanda L M 31,32
Ammanda L M 31
Eller 31,32
James 31,32
SWINK
David R 3,4,5
Lena B 3,4,5
N E 3,4
William 3,4,5
William L 3,4,5
William Lenard 3,4
TAKUBBE
Patsy 141
TALBERT
Jno E 6,305,306
Jno W 8
TAYLOR
Newcomb 57
Newcomb B 54,55,56,57,58
Newcomb Davenport 54,55,56,57,58
Paul B 79,82
Paul E 81
Simon 141
Zuelika Jane 54,55
Zuleika 55,56
Zuleika Jane 54
TERRELL
Houston 140
Jesse James 140
Louisa 140
R F 155,156,157

R F, MD 156
THOMAS
  Charley 98,99
  J R 31
  Jno J 41
  John J 45
  Philiston 285
  Silvia 283,284
  W L 150,151
THOMPSON
  Betsy 53
  Bisey 169
  Isom 167,168
  Jimpson 168,169
  Joseph P 53
  Joseph W 53,54
  Siney 136,137,138
  William 167,168
  Wincey 16
TIDWELL
  ? C 242
TIMMERMAN
  Aug 20
TIMS
  Adeline 126
  Colmbus 6
  Columbus 7,8,305,306
  Emelin 53
  Emeline 54
  J B 14,124,128
  J T 12
  James B 8
  Johnny 121,122
  Mary 121,122,123,124,125,126,
  127,129,131
  Roberson 125
  Robert 121,122
  Willie 119,120,121,122,123,124,
  125,126,127,128,129,134
  Willis 120,131,132
  Wilson 119,120,121,122,123,124,
  125,126,127,128,129,130,131,132,133
  ,134
TOHKUBBI
  Cephus 283,284
TOLBERT
  N J 65,66

TUEY
  L C 242
TURNBULL
  Inez 65,66,67
VOYD
  Harriet 325,326
WADE
  Elsie 234
WALKER
  Tommie W 301
WALLACE
  Fannie 180,181,186
  Virgil M 196
WALLS
  T J 17
WATSON
  Allen 272,273,274
WEIMER
  W G 102
WELCH
  C A 39,40
WELSH
  Dr J 313
  George B 317
  Georgie B 311,312,314,315,316
  J, MD 313
  James 312,316,317
  Lizzie N 312,314,315
WHEAT
  Alice 157,158
  J W 64
  Mary 64
WHITFORD
  J E 33
  S E 31
WILBURN
  Blanche 313
  D N 313
  Lizzie N 312,314,315
  Martha 313,314
WILLIAM
  Benjamin 39
  Thomas 272,273,274
WILLIAMS
  Abel 39,40,41,42,43,44
  Benjaman 45
  Benjamin 39,40,41,42,44,45,46

Benjiman 43,46
Celin 40,41,44,45
Cilin 43
Cillin 46
Della 63,64
J E 192,193,226,227
John 63,64
Minnie 63,64
Morris 61,63
Moses 60
O N 2
Silin 42
Sillin 39,40,42,44
WILLIS
   Allen 58,59,60,61,62,63
   Benjamin 39
   Emerson D 10
   Hickman 58,59,60,61,62,63
   Mose 198
   Silen 198
   Sistie 58,59,60,61,63
WILSON
   Anna 147,148,149,150,151,152,153
   Ed 147,148,149,150,151,152,153
   Jesse E 132
   Sarah 147,148,149,150,151,153
   Sophin 214,216
   W A 229
   W P 88,89
WINANA
   W W 108
WISE
   M J 38
WITT
   Peggy 64
WOODS
   Edgar 229
   Elizabeth Eunice 228
   Hattie 228,229
   Mollie L 229
   Wesley 41
   Willie M 229
WORCESTER
   Alfred 172
WYATT
   Bonnie Pearl 188,192,193,194
   Bunnie Pearl 190,191

Celia 190
Celie 188,189,191,192,193,194
E L 188,189,190,191,192,193,194
Earl Dude 188,189,190,191,192,194
Elijah L 191,192,193
Seely 194

www.ingramcontent.com/pod-product-compliance
Lightning Source LLC
Chambersburg PA
CBHW020241030426
42336CB00010B/574